W9-ABY-352

German writers and the Cold War

German writers and the Cold War
1945–61

edited by
Rhys W. Williams, Stephen Parker and Colin Riordan
with the collaboration of Helmut Peitsch

MANCHESTER UNIVERSITY PRESS Manchester and New York

distributed exclusively in the USA and Canada by St. Martin's Press

published by Manchester University Press
Oxford Road, Manchester M13 9PL, UK
and Room 400, 175 Fifth Avenue,
New York, NY 10010, USA

distributed exclusively in the USA and Canada
by St. Martin's Press, Inc.,
175 Fifth Avenue, New York, NY 10010, USA

British Library Cataloguing-in-Publication Data
A catalogue record for this book is available from the British Library

Library of Congress Cataloging-in-Publication Data applied for

ISBN 0 7190 2662 8 *hardback*

Printed in Great Britain
by Bookcraft (Bath) Ltd

Contents

Contents

Introduction

Officially, the Cold War ended in November 1990. The re-unification of Germany, as swift as it was unexpected, appears to have laid to rest the debate of the last forty years about whether there were two German literatures. Yet four decades of division still cast a long shadow over the political and cultural landscape of the united country; the revelation that a writer and dissident such as Sascha Anderson was a secret informant has shaken even the most cynical of commentators. Yet it is precipitate to judge the aftermath of the way in which Cold War political realities shaped literary relations between the two German states without first assessing the beginning and development of that process. This volume of essays sets out to examine the literature and cultural institutions of Germany, East and West, from the end of the War to the building of the Berlin Wall.

To some extent, literature and cultural policy emerge as a product of political change; but there were counter-pressures, attempts to use literature as a means to shape political attitudes. Soviet policy in the 1950s sought to counter Adenauer's efforts to integrate the new Federal Republic into the West, politically, economically and militarily. Accordingly, the initial emphasis in the German Democratic Republic was on a single German culture, corresponding to the political goal of a united, demilitarised and socialist Germany. In the interests of driving a wedge between West Germany and its Western allies, the East German effort was directed at presenting, through its major literary organs, a notion of German culture as 'gesamtdeutsch'. Adenauer's 'Weststaatlösung' inevitably brought, during the course of the 1950s, a deepening of the split between the two German states. Western critics became increasingly suspicious of the 'one German culture' argument, regarding it as simply a propaganda ploy. Their cynicism played into the hands of the hard-line SED functionaries in the East, who could, with some justification, point to the failure of these over-tures to the West and who hence argued for a separate socialist development. The building of the Wall marked the defeat in the GDR of the 'one German culture' argument. From 1961 onwards it was clear that the GDR would seek to establish its own national identity. The Wall, as well as being an economic necessity for the SED, symbolised the failure of an idea: that of a common German culture. Perversely, the Wall became a depressing monument to the success of Adenauer's policy of Western integration.

It is in an effort to tease out the literary and cultural complexit-ies of the 1950s that this volume has been written. Curiously, the formative period of the two German states has been analysed only peripherally in previous studies of the subject. The sudden West German fascination with East German literature in the late 1960s has tended to divert attention from the period in which Cold War attitudes hardened. What emerges from these essays is that many intellectuals, in both East and West, were more influenced by Cold War attitudes than they realised. The contributions cover the area of what might be termed literary politics from the perspectives of both East and West. It is this bifocal vision which, we believe, offers new insights. There is, perhaps inevitably, some small over-lap. No attempt has been made to excise such references, for it is precisely through approaching the same incidents, institutions or individuals from different perspectives that a more balanced pic-ture emerges. Post-war German literature, far from being, as Günter Grass put it, 'das einzig Gesamtdeutsche, das wir noch haben', was shaped by the conditions under which the two German states were formed. To a hitherto unknown extent both were anchored in their respective power blocs and conditioned by the policies which led to the division of post-war Europe.

The first two essays offer insights into the reception of the literature of one German state by the other. Colin Smith points up the ambivalence displayed by the GDR to the West: pleas for dia-logue and understanding are matched by disparagement of all that is offered in the West. Those journals or critics in the West who opposed what they termed the 'restoration' values of Adenauer were swiftly misunderstood by the East as offering collaboration. The inevitable praise which such values then received in the East attracted unwelcome critical attention at home. Accused of being fellow-travellers, Western critics were swiftly forced to clarify their position, and, not infrequently, to disavow it. After presenting an analysis of this situation, Smith analyses three test cases: those of Brecht, J. R. Becher and Anna Seghers. J. H. Reid offers a valuable corrective to the monolithic view of East German culture. In the 1950s the literary landscape was initially much more complex and varied, with East German publishers anxious to offer readers a wide range of Western texts, and, contrary to expectation, display a predilection for texts by Christian writers of an older generation.

Two further contributions are devoted to East German periodicals. Dennis Tate examines the shifts in editorial policy of *Neue Deutsche Literatur*, while Stephen Parker devotes attention to *Sinn und Form*. *Neue Deutsche Literatur* took up a clearly socialist position only in 1953 and again in 1958–9; for the rest it fostered a German 'Nationalliteratur' and saw its role as helping to create a unified socialist Germany. The pressures on the journal from the SED produced in the late 1950s a narrowing of focus, in keeping with the abandonment of a 'one German culture' position. Peter Huchel, as editor of *Sinn und Form*, was faced with similar problems. Here, the reception in the West is especially illuminating. Huchel's efforts to give the periodical breadth and literary quality exposed him to attack from both sides: in the West for dressing up Soviet ideology in literary garb; in the East for its support of formalism, or its neutrality on political matters.

The Schiller celebrations of 1955 and 1959 offer Maximilian Nutz an opportunity to analyse the way in which contributors to the festivities on both sides of the border shaped this element of the common tradition to reflect their own Cold War prejudices and purposes. In 1955, the celebrations in the GDR were integrated into the co-ordinated presentation of an unquestioned cultural heritage, Schiller being depicted as a revolutionary critic of social and political oppression. In the Federal Republic, by contrast, he appeared as a proclaimer of individual freedom who was suspicious of political activity. Those who, in 1955, had still believed in the binding power of a cultural tradition transcending political barriers were to be disappointed by 1959, for both sides took every opportunity to accuse the other of falsifying the image of the writer and of exploiting the occasion for political purposes. Helmut Peitsch also investigates the way in which the two sides viewed and portrayed each other in his examination of the travelogues written by East and West Germans about the other German state. Here, too, ideological pressures distort both the findings and the mode of presentation. Wolfgang Joho, for example, sets out to discover German unity in his visit to the West, but paradoxically succeeds only in conveying his alienation from what he observes, while Western travellers merely find their bleak expectations confirmed, however 'objective' they may assert themselves to be.

Hans Werner Richter's activity in literary relations between the two German states, contrary perhaps to the expectations raised by his socialist commitment and by his image as a uniter of men, reveals itself to be remarkably insubstantial and, where existent, contradictory. Graeme Cook argues that the 'Gruppe 47' might have been expected to provide the stimulus to overcome political differences, but in the end proved satisfied with its achievements at home, while East Germany remained, for the most part, out of sight and mind. Richter's failure to establish contacts with GDR writers during the Cold War has biographical and emotional, as well as contemporary political origins. The recently-revealed fact that Richter published during the Third Reich and had worked for the Reichsschrifttumskammer helps to explain his anti-communist stance. He was now determined to engage in the sort of oppositional behaviour that he had failed to display ten years earlier. Indeed, Richter publicly drew comparisons between the GDR and Nazi Germany, and fiercely criticised the GDR under a pseudonym in 1953. His preference for a pseudonym is hardly surprising, since his criticism put him in the same camp as those restorative forces to which, in the domestic arena, he was strongly opposed.

If, on the one hand, the volume has been concerned to explore groups of writers or literary institutions, it also seeks to offer case-studies of specific writers or critics. The remaining chapters are all devoted to individual figures. What was touched on in an earlier essay by Colin Smith is developed by Cettina Rapisarda in her study of Seghers. In common with other authors of the time, Anna Seghers's reputation and the reception of her works were shaped by the East–West conflict. Her reputation suffered a blow during the dying months of the SED regime, when Walter Janka in his book *Schwierigkeiten mit der Wahrheit* (Reinbek, 1989) accused her of having been involved in one of the charges brought at his show trial in the 1950s and of having failed to take steps to defend him. More recent evidence shows, however, that behind the scenes Seghers was more critical than anybody in the West could know, and that in fact she was concerned to counteract, rather than encourage, Cold War divisions. During the late 1940s and the 1950s, Seghers was committed to the notion that women's influence in the private sphere could promote the cause of peace and help to bridge the East–West divide. Mothers, in particular, possessed life-giving and life-maintaining qualities which would help to reduce conflict, Seghers believed. Viewed in this light, her fictional works reveal a series of hitherto unsuspected demands for East–West reconciliation which emerge through her portrayal of female characters. These characters become part of an attempt to achieve a synthesis of the personal and the political. Motherhood finds political expression in the cause of peace.

Franziska Meyer's study of Hans Mayer's career in the GDR before his move to the Federal Republic in 1963 offers insights into the pressures which were brought to bear on literary commentators by the East–West conflict. He regarded himself as 'ein erstes Opfer des kommenden kalten Krieges, noch bevor er ausbrach', having broken with his American employers at Radio Frankfurt for expressing unwelcome views on foreign policy in 1947. After moving to Leipzig in 1948, he occupied for more than a decade an exceedingly influential academic post, and moulded generations of GDR Germanists and authors. In the early years of the GDR, Mayer allied himself with the Lukács school. However, the dichotomy between Lukács's classicism and the growing socialist demand for 'Volksverbundenheit' in literature was to lead to conflict later in the 1950s. Mayer's early work in the GDR endeavoured to link the classical tradition with 'Volksverbundenheit'. Yet before 1956, he studiously avoided commenting on contemporary socialist literature, with the exception of his work on Brecht. Mayer's criticism of contemporary socialist literature at the end of 1956 was the turning point. His use of the phrase 'rotangestrichene Gartenlauben' to describe contemporary poetry earned him few friends amongst the cultural establishment. Mayer braved the subsequent furore to remain in the GDR for another six years. Nevertheless, his attempts to alert his audience to the possibility of differing views of literature on the basis of marxist ideology only served to push him further into the role of dissident. Mayer's commitment to the GDR was dissipated, and he saw no alternative but to defend himself from the platform of Western publications.

The publication histories of Uwe Johnson's first two novels exemplify, in Colin Riordan's view, the way in which the Cold War could affect a literary career. Political considerations in both East

and West prevented *Ingrid Babendererde* (written in the GDR between 1953 and 1956) from being published until 1985, after
Johnson's death. *Ingrid Babendererde* thus became a literary victim of the Cold War. The metatextuality of *Mutmaßungen über Jakob*,
on the other hand, meant that the work could be interpreted fa-
vourably in the West (where it was published in 1959) without
sacrificing its highly sophisticated analysis of the personal crises
its characters suffer as a result of the Cold War. After eighteen
months in the West, Johnson suffered a mauling at the hands of
the West German press as a supposed secret communist who
approved of the Berlin Wall. By 1961, the young author had realised the extent to which his literary activity had made him into a
political pawn.

Finally, an examination of Alfred Andersch's political attitudes
reveals that he was much more conditioned by the prevailing
political climate in the Federal Republic than he was prepared, at
the time, to admit. Like Hans Werner Richter, he had supported the
notion of a united, demilitarised, socialist Germany, but with the
increasing virulence of Cold War attitudes he became highly
suspicious of what he saw as the propaganda campaign of the
SED. While he was suspicious of Adenauer's 'restoration' policies,
he became most anxious that his views should not be misconstrued
as in any way supportive of East German views. Retrospectively,
from the vantage-point of the 1970s, he readily confesses to having been more 'Western' than he realised.

This volume was planned to appear before the reunification of
Germany. Difficulties over the availability of potential participants
and with the translation of the German contributions have de-
layed the project. For that delay the editors assume full responsibility. Paradoxically, the events of the intervening period have made
the book perhaps more, rather than less, relevant. The editors
would, however, like to thank the contributors for their patience,
and the Manchester University Press for its forbearance and support. Thanks are also due to David Basker and Helen Jones for
help with the translations.

All quiet on the Eastern front? East German literature and its Western reception (1945–61)

Colin Smith

'Im Osten nichts Neues' was Rudolf Hartung's blunt dismissal of GDR cultural life in a leading critical commentary for *Neue Deutsche Hefte* in 1959.[1] Ostensibly, this was his reaction to Walter Ulbricht's call for closer co-operation between working and writing communities at the Bitterfeld Conference in April 1959. For Hartung, Ulbricht – who had no business interfering in the artistic sphere anyway – was singing a tired tune, and one designed to lull a writer into a position of greater accountability. Much fun is made of the proposed marriage of labour and culture, and, in conclusion, Hartung is unable to resist ridiculing the notion of a budding Thomas Mann or Franz Kafka making his name in an in-house company paper.

Hartung himself was hardly being original. His invective reveals all the signs of an insecurity in Western criticism which was one offshoot of the current political climate. His verdict owes little to literary criteria. Whether consciously admitted or not, the intention is to put the GDR at a further remove from the West, if not by open ridicule then at least by emphasising the evidently foreign element, of which the many conferences and congresses, on the Soviet bureaucratic model, provided ample illustration. Hartung's refusal to await the results of the Bitterfeld initiative is symptomatic of a resistance to any acknowledgement of a creative, artistic life in East Germany.

In their apprehension that the vicinity of a political and social alternative on German soil might lead to encroachments or encourage false loyalties, Western intellectuals fostered the notion that a gulf was emerging between the German states. At its extreme, this even led to an affirmation that two distinct German languages were emerging, an argument born of a fear (however quaint it may now seem) that a Russian influence, or at least an element of SED-jargon, might worm its way into Western currency.[2] At no cost should GDR life – in any sphere – be granted recognition. Literature must be exposed as misjudged in intention, ill-achieved or perfunctory, in line with the provisional nature of the 'soviet zone' itself.

It was through this filter that GDR literary life was received. As the new home for writers of all the various exiled German literatures, East Germany relied on a broad body of realist–critical writing rooted in the traditions and experiences of the Weimar Republic. This may well have contributed in part to its relative neglect in the West; the resistance, both popular and critical, to exiled writers was such that until after 1955 it was virtually impossible to find a market even for Thomas Mann, let alone those authors of more known humanist–socialist persuasion who (as opinion had it) had, by 'choosing' emigration, renounced their right to play a role in the post-war world.[3] Compared to the impact of an anxiety bred by the prejudice of political insecurity, however, this factor is of secondary importance. Indeed, despite the mutual recriminations between writers from exile and those who had remained in Germany, differences in creative intention and practice were not primarily determined by the zonal/state border. East Germany had (to cite merely one example) always possessed strong self-reflective elements and a tradition of poetic–realist prose which were far from alien to the West German writer of the 1950s.[4]

It took a particularly perceptive critic to place the practised indifference towards East German culture firmly in the context of political allegiance. Hans Magnus Enzensberger, writing in 1959, accused the literary world of being hypnotised by political necessity and argued that a new understanding of East German works was needed: 'Der Einwand, "drüben" gebe es nichts Nennenswertes, schlägt nicht zu Buch, da es sich hier um Qualitätsunterschiede nicht handelt; diese lassen sich überhaupt erst treffen, wenn man die Existenz zweier deutscher Literaturen ernstnimmt.'[5] Enzensberger is one of few voices, first raised at the very end of the 1950s, arguing that the recognition of two independent German literatures was an essential prerequisite for any constructive evaluation of cultural production in the East. This argument, which was still controversial enough in 1972 for Fritz J. Raddatz to use it as the provocative opening thesis of his survey of East German literature[6] was based on an understanding of the interdependence of politics and literature, and suggested that only the tolerance of a co-existence policy could release literary criticism from the shackles of Cold War prejudice.

To do justice to the Western critic, however, the cultural politics of East Germany in its early years, alive with blustering initiatives, fervent ideological debate and no small measure of self-congratulation, made for a bewildering spectrum on which to comment. Aesthetic guidelines were adopted, asserted, revised and superseded with an unusual frequency and regularity. The emphasis on Socialist Realism, at times the subject of a keen and open debate on literary innovation, at times the assertion of a single, clearly defined standard, played an important role in shaping East Germany's sense of cultural identity. Periodic attacks on intellectual fashions in the West (existentialism, formalism) served to underline the belief that GDR literature was set on a course both original and quite distinct from that in the West. While this ideological demarcation from the German neighbour state remained crucial, however, there is an equally vocal strain of argument running through the 1950s stressing a common German tradition as the basis for regular incentives towards greater inner-German dialogue and cultural co-operation.

Thus at least two, contradictory, voices went into constituting the public front East Germany presented to the outside world. Nowhere is this more apparent than in the thorny area of cultural heritage. Following Georg Lukács, great importance was attached to cultivating an awareness of a sound classical and realist heritage. Most specifically, this involved the appropriation of a select élite of writers, from Goethe to Gorky and Thomas Mann, as forerunners of a new socialist literature. At the same time, writers of the past, and above all Goethe and Schiller, were regularly cited as proof of traditions uniting all Germans and transcending present differences.[7] The fragile balance between dogmatic assertion and conciliatory gesturing hinged largely on tensions within East German foreign policy, which itself was dependent on Moscow's view of the GDR's political status. The reforming zeal of Ulbricht's political faction, who embarked on widespread socialisation immediately on return from exile, was not always in line with Stalin's political strategy. During the early 1950s, and even in the face of the escalation of the Cold War, Stalin remained publicly in favour of a single Germany, as witnessed by the 1950 'Prague Declaration' of Eastern bloc states in support of establishing an all-German council and Stalin's later initiatives in 1951 and 1952. It seemed evident that Stalin was prepared to sacrifice the communist German state and even jettison the supremacy the SED had achieved, in order to prise West Germany away from the US-dominated alliance. For several years, Russian interest in the possibility of a neutral Germany was certainly strong. Ulbricht's resolute pursuit of one-party socialism and a state with a recognised ideological identity is at striking odds with this policy and may well even have been aimed at forcing Stalin's hand, cementing the divide. There is no clearer sign of this than Ulbricht's announcement of an official programme for the establishment of socialism ('Aufbau des Sozialismus') at the second party conference of the SED in 1952, at a time when Stalin had proposed an 'acceleration' in the negotiation process towards a unified Germany.[8]

The comparative lenience of cultural policy at this stage, and the vigour with which artists and writers – following the lead given by Johannes R. Becher, Stephan Hermlin and Willi Bredel as the first editor of *Neue Deutsche Literatur* – pursued the possibility of communication and co-operation, must be seen in this context. While Becher was capable of assuming the mantle of the anti-capitalist dogmatist as required, there is no doubt that he stood firmly behind the approaches to an increased inner-German dialogue. Nevertheless, the motives for the political toleration of this strategy (which was curtailed severely after 1954) are more ambivalent.[9] At least on the surface, the Western observer was offered the sight of a political élite asserting the state's autonomy in the increasingly aggressive tone of Cold War polemic, while the principal literary and cultural figures presented a concerted front in favour of tolerance, democracy and unity.

One particularly pointed instance of this duplicity is to be found in the pages of *Aufbau*, a periodical which, under Becher's direct patronage, argued vociferously for cultural co-operation until its demise in 1958. Despite its manifestly partisan title, it was always clear that one major priority was the re-establishment of the kind of interzonal understanding which, in a brief early phase, the Kulturbund zur demokratischen Erneuerung Deutschlands had enjoyed. An example from the highly charged atmosphere of 1952 will illustrate this. In May, the journal had re-affirmed its principal goal – 'die Situation zwischen Ost und West klären zu helfen, die drohende Gefahr aufzuzeigen und die Wege, ihr zu begegnen'.[10] This was accompanied by a marked buoyancy in the hope for all-German discussion on culture and democracy, a prospect bolstered by a public exchange between the editor, Bodo Uhse, and Walter Dirks of the *Frankfurter Hefte*.[11] Just three months later, Alexander Abusch could adopt a radically different line in a detailed and argumentative appeal that any new 'national literature' must have a specifically East German character. Having dismissed much of West German war literature as nihilistic, and traced this back to the pessimism and desperation of American literary models, Abusch went on to savage even the newer developments in the West:

> Es entstand eine 'Kahlschlag'-Literatur, die unter Verzicht auf die Schönheit der Sprache, in einem verarmten Reporterstil und ohne menschliche Tiefe in der Gestaltung, den Pseudo-Realismus einer 'neuen Sachlichkeit' schaffen will.[12]

A Western writer or critic had a right to be confused: with the one breath he was being wooed into greater dialogue, while with the next his achievements were disparaged as decadent and destructive.

Always present, a distrust of the motives of East German writers in their drive for cultural discussion often spilled over into rejection and derision. The fate of Becher's first initiative, the Kulturbund, set a pattern which was to become familiar. After a promising start, in which the ageing Gerhart Hauptmann and Ricarda Huch were recruited to honorary positions, and cultural cells founded in all zones, political pressure was soon to stifle its existence in the West. Becher himself made no effort to conceal his inclusion of solid party comrades in the major organisational roles. Indeed, it was a carefully concerted effort, conceived and planned in Moscow exile, to revive the 'Bündnispolitik' of the 1920s, with communists adopting strategic positions in an organisation uniting those of progressive and democratic conviction.[13] Yet this itself hardly accounts for the resolute measures taken against it, culminating in its ban in the American and British zones in November 1947. Rendered impotent as a unifying, anti-fascist force, the organisation in the Eastern zone continued for several years to rely on the force of rhetoric to reproach the Western alliance with destroying the chance of a fruitful dialogue.

Becher, once again, was at the centre of a controversy surrounding the establishment of a German section of the international PEN organisation.[14] Acceptance by PEN was an important stepping-stone to the international recognition of contemporary German culture. Those lobbying for a German PEN section, therefore, had first to convince the rest of the world that German literature, for

all the incriminations and warring factions, had the will and determination to achieve reconciliation and some modest form of unity.
In this process, Becher was a principal driving force and inevitably
emerged as one of the first joint presidents of the new section.
Protests by Western writers, however, followed by a series of
resignations, led rapidly to the founding of a separate West German PEN section in 1951, and writers who objected to Cold-
War-mongering of this sort found themselves cornered. Like the
Kulturbund, the East German PEN association clung to its all-
German pretensions for many years, only abandoning the title
'Deutsches Pen-Zentrum Ost und West' in 1967. In this case the
principal scapegoat was the unfortunate Bavarian writer Johannes
von Tralow, who found himself and his works subject to savage
criticism after his decision to accept the presidency of Becher's
association.

A further victim was the Stuttgart periodical *Die Kultur* (patronised, amongst others by writers of the 'Gruppe 47') which openly
opposed the political restoration of the early 1950s in West Germany. The East German periodical *Neue Deutsche Literatur*, which
since 1952 had provided criticism of and even published extracts
from West German works as a counterpoint to the more direct
appeals for inner-German dialogue in *Aufbau*, responded vigorously to the Western journal's praise for its broad cultural base
and tolerance. The editors of *Die Kultur* – uninterested in getting
entangled in the mesh of inner-German conflict – had used the
open-mindedness of the GDR journal as merely one weapon in
their campaign to expose the prejudices taking root in West Germany. These intentions were overlooked by the editors of *NDL*, who
in 1955 reprinted an entire article from *Die Kultur* in which Western publications were taken to task for showing less initiative and
tolerance than their East German counterparts. The euphoria of
the GDR publication at the first success of its policy betrays a
remarkable naivety. Rather than quietly continuing to allow generous coverage of West German culture, in the hope of awaking
similar sympathies elsewhere, *NDL* went on to single out *Die Kultur*
specifically. Repeated attempts were made to jockey the journal
into some concrete form of collaboration, whether a regular exchange of articles or co-operation in setting up some kind of all-
German literary forum. By the end of 1956, when, for want of a
positive response, *NDL* had even taken to overtly declaring its
support for oppositional articles in the Western publication, *Die*

Kultur, perhaps with some embarrassment, finally felt forced into an isolated position and had to deny publicly any pro-GDR sympathies.[15] Once more the merest hint of readiness for dialogue was immediately misunderstood as a provocatively pro-communist stance, with serious consequences for a public reputation in the West.

It is notable that even the most vehement opponents of the politics of the Adenauer years proved reluctant to be drawn into closer contact with East Germany. The currency reform of 1948 had curtailed many of the early publications and with them the often idiosyncratic and utopian speculations on possible constellations for a future German state.[16] Discursive essays on potential realisations of socialism has lost much of their immediacy, and interest in bridging the information gap on Soviet affairs, a distinctive feature of post-war publications in all zones, had waned.[17] Above all, the force of events in the West had caused intellectuals to turn their attention primarily to applying pressure within the framework of the West German state, and to creating a forum for literary expression which, in undisguised opposition to the restorative forces, could assist in promoting potential alternatives. Given the current tensions, distance from communism in the form rapidly being assumed in the GDR was essential to the credibility of this protest.

One important factor for a number of oppositional writers in West Germany was an entrenched suspicion of party-dictated communism deriving from first-hand encounters during the 1930s. This was certainly the case of Hans Werner Richter and Alfred Andersch, who between them did much to determine the shape of the publishing world during this period.[18] As editors of *Der Ruf* until 1947, both were concerned to distinguish clearly the form of socialist democracy they envisaged from that of official party communism.[19] To take one example: in 1946, *Der Ruf* reported a speech in which the East German writer Eduard Claudius (borrowing his terminology from Otto Grotewohl) confronted a Munich audience bluntly with the choice between the revolutionary tradition of Thomas Münzer (the hammer) or the path of caution and compromise represented by Luther (the anvil). *Der Ruf*'s critic rejected these crude terms and set himself in the tradition of those arguing for a third, alternative way to socialism, the choice, in his words, of 'einfache klar denkende Realisten'.[20] Richter himself has pointed to a widespread disillusionment with the 'Volksfront' policy of the 1930s, which had aimed to create a broad union of communists, socialists and other anti-fascist sympathisers.[21] This helps to explain the cold shoulder Becher's various approaches received from the 'Gruppe 47', despite the fact that the two had many shared targets of criticism.[22]

Such reservations, for the most part implicit, on the political options taken up by East Germany were shared by a broad base of intellectual opposition in the West. More forthright rejection is evident in those publications which saw themselves as heirs to a long standing conservative tradition and sought to emphasise the virtues of historical continuity in the new Western state. This is true particularly of Rudolf Pechel's revived *Deutsche Rundschau*, regularly a severe critic of East German developments, and the *Neue Literarische Welt*, issued by the Deutsche Akademie für Sprache und Dichtung from 1950 to 1953.[23] Both vigorously defended the value of cultural life during the Nazi years (that of the so-called inner emigration) which they saw as providing a link between German classical–realist heritage and the present:

> Auf die zugespitzte, im Grunde törichte und beleidigende Frage, ob es im Augenblick überhaupt eine (nennenswerte) deutsche Literatur gebe, ist zu erwidern: es gab sie auch während der Jahre, in denen nach einem bekannten Wort über Deutschland Finsternis lag, es gibt sie heute, und für die Kontinuität ist gesorgt.[24]

This argumentation was frequently accompanied by open criticism of writers of the exile tradition, in particular if they had expressed doubts about the credentials of those who had continued to publish under Hitler. It is not surprising, therefore, that East German culture, with its strong emigrant basis, met with little sympathy.

The reverberations of the changes in the political climate after 1948 are particularly evident in the review *Welt und Wort*, which set out to offer a comprehensive survey of new publications. The East Berlin Aufbau-Verlag, one of the first and most enterprising of post-war publishers, met with a warm response, as did many of the individual works published, including a large number of emigré writers (Heinrich Mann, Alfred Döblin, Lion Feuchtwanger) alongside the Russian epics and works from the German historical tradition. Initially, East German writers were also granted a comprehensive and often positive reception. Indeed, during the immediate post-war years, the hunger for new reading matter – of any kind – meant that signs of discouragement to the writer, let alone concrete criticism, were barely discernible. Reservations about certain authors on ideological or stylistic grounds were kept muted. It was only at the turn of the 1950s that an occasional comment on the reportage-like nature of GDR publications suggests that there might be a resistance to the kind of realism gradually gaining acceptance in the East.[25]

It is at this point, too, that the unwarranted jibe makes its first appearance, initially as a pendant to an otherwise reasoned review of a collection of poems by Erich Weinert: 'Und bezüglich Ostzone und Gesinnungszwang haben Sie selbstverständlich ein gutes Gewissen, Herr Doktor?'[26] This tone was to become steadily more prominent, reaching a peak during the late 1950s. In separate reviews, the dramatist Friedrich Wolf and Anna Seghers were informed that heroic realism of the kind they practised had no relevance to the modern world. More specifically, both were taken to task for not thematising the workers' revolt of 17 June 1953.[27] Peter Hacks, whose plays otherwise invoke a more sympathetic response, is likewise given recommendations for his next source of material:

> Wie steht's mit der Ausbeutung in Rußland? Vielleicht schreibt der begabte und gescheite Autor einmal ein Stück über einen wirklich gerechten und heldenhaften Krieg, etwa über den ungarischen Aufstand . . .[28]

This line of criticism, indicating sins of omission rather than commission, is not, is it might at first appear, dictated by trivial prejudice alone. At its heart is a fundamental difference in the reading of history. The principal occupation of GDR literature had from the first been a reworking of events during the fascist years. The three major forms which this took – depictions of resistance in the Spanish Civil War, accounts of suffering and survival in concentration camps and examinations of the historical roots of Nazism – shared one thing in common: the enlightened stance of the anti-fascists and their ensuing bravery was always in the foreground.[29] Those who had perceived the true face of fascism and opposed it from the first felt justified in their view of historical development and in holding up the evident alternative of socialism as a model for the future. For the Western writer, in contrast, Stalin's form of communism represented a dictatorship as absolute and as brutal as that of Nazism, and thus those living under (or in the case of many East German writers directly associated with) one authoritarian régime had forfeited the right to comment on or judge the other. Reviews of this kind thus reveal as much about the critic as the author in question. In 1952, for instance, an East German writer's emphasis on the socialist movement's achievements gives rise to accusations of colour-blindness: 'denn der Autor sieht die Braunen nicht braun, sondern pechschwarz und die Roten nicht rot, sondern schneeweiß'. Unwittingly, the critic is exposing the blinkers of his own prejudice: for him, the brown and red dictatorships are both equally, and unequivocally, black.[30]

One regular resort of Western critics who felt obliged to acknowledge the merits of an East German writer was to isolate the writer's achievements from his ideological beliefs. Becher, Seghers, Arnold Zweig, and even the then little-known Stefan Heym, fell victim to this; grudging acceptance of their works was accompanied by expressions of exasperation or regret that misplaced political sympathies had stood in the way of greater achievements.[31] Friedrich Sieburg in *Die Gegenwart* repeatedly pointed to the damaging influence of false political convictions:

> Wir wissen schon, daß Brecht und Anna Seghers, Stephan Hermlin und Peter Huchel durchaus keine literarischen Nullen sind, aber ... kaum einer von ihnen weist nicht Spuren der ständigen politischen Abnützung auf. Ihre Literatur beweist bei aller meisterhaften Widerstandskraft doch allmählich, daß, wie Sartre sagt, 'die Politik des Stalinschen Kommunismus mit der anständigen Ausübung des literarischen Metiers unvereinbar ist.'[32]

Without doubt the most striking instance of this is the reception of Bertolt Brecht. From the first, there were various camps (the Catholic Church included) opposed to staging Brecht's plays at all. When it became apparent that Brecht could not be ignored, a new tactic was needed. Brecht himself, determined to remain awkward, aggravated matters further: constantly frustrating the East German authorities with his assertions of individualism, Brecht at the same time provoked strong reactions in the West due to his apparent willingness to compromise with, or even stress his allegiance to, the GDR. The most spectacular case was the excerpt from a letter published in *Neues Deutschland* immediately after the 1953 workers' rebellion, in which Brecht assured Walter Ulbricht of his solidarity and support. This produced an unprecedented wave of protest in the Western media.[33]

It was soon to become a cliché that Brecht the artist had suffered at the hands of Brecht the marxist, that he was (in the words of one critic) a 'poète malgré lui'.[34] Amongst the few to ground this claim in methodical analysis was Herbert Lüthy in *Der Monat*, whose article did much to disseminate this point of view. Lüthy traced the spontaneity and vitality of Brecht's early phase under expressionist influence before arguing that the onset of theoretical and political interests was to quash this entirely: 'Die Sprache des armen B.B. ist verdorrt und ausgezehrt bis aufs Skelett, erstarrt zum Theorem.'[35] As the key to understanding Brecht's development, Lüthy sees him as having adopted various masks and roles, of which his 'pact with untruth' in the GDR is the latest, if most distasteful. The conclusion – that Brecht was the 'kauzigste, verschmitzteste und versponnenste' poet ever, a kind of calculating chameleon, was to provide the basis for lesser critics to charge Brecht with inconsistency or 'Gesinnungsakrobatik' in years to come. Some critics virtually tied themselves in knots in an effort to make this point. In *Wort und Wahrheit*, Brecht is made out as unpolitical and his plays not communist, but merely based on communist theory, a distinction perhaps too fine for most readers.[36] In *Neue Deutsche Hefte*, Brecht is accused of 'listigen Simplifizierungen' and 'tendenziösen Vereinseitigungen' before a tangled qualifier:

> Es versteht sich, daß alles dies nicht an die dichterische Qualität des Werkes von Brecht rührt. Aber dieses Werk besteht für sich, unabhängig von seinen ideologischen Voraussetzungen, ohne die es freilich nicht zustande gekommen wäre.[37]

Yet even the *Frankfurter Hefte*, otherwise a spirited apologist for staging Brecht's works and a forceful critic of spineless or overlush Western productions, came to a similar conclusion, ostensibly in regard to Brecht's early development, but clearly shot through with disappointment at his conformism in the 1950s. Trapped in a dilemma 'zwischen dem ästhetischen Zwang seiner Parabeln und der moralistischen Menschlichkeit seines politischen Wollens', the critic argues, Brecht the artist is able to break new ground in the drama, while his underlying political convictions remain rigid and conventional.[38] The prime reason for such a heated controversy about Brecht was that he refused to be overlooked; German theatre relied on the new impetus given to it by Brecht in a way unparalleled at the time in poetry or prose. To sweeten this medicine, Western reception persuaded itself that his drama possessed some vital original quality which could be appreciated quite apart from the unfortunate political–historical views which underlay its structure. Even in serious critical commentary, there were few who demurred from this distinction. One voice was that of Walter Mannzen in *Texte und Zeichen*, who was adamant that Brecht 'muß *mit* oder *trotz* seiner politischen Anschauung akzeptiert werden, *ohne* sie aber geht es nicht'.[39]

In the case of Johannes R. Becher, who was to receive almost as much attention as Brecht in Western periodicals, the division between politics and art was not carried out with quite the same ruthless consistency. Among the various volumes published by Becher in the immediate post-war years, some were to meet with a warm and even enthusiastic reception in the West which they have hardly enjoyed since. Hellmut von Cube went as far as to praise not only the humanity and expressive power of Becher's verse but also the poet's understanding of the German national situation.[40] One of the earliest attempts to link a deterioration in aesthetic quality specifically to the writer's full-blooded political commitment is that by Otto Jancke (*Das Literarische Deutschland*, 1951). Jancke adopts a similar line to that taken by Lüthy on Brecht: the quality of the early expressionist poetry is acknowledged, if with some reservation – 'die exhibitionistische Ekstatik fällt zuweilen in einen elegischen Ton, in dem sich ein echter Lyriker nicht eben großer Eigenständigkeit zeigt' – before an alleged demise is associated with his party activities in the late 1920s. By the time Becher emigrated to Moscow in 1933, Jancke claims, he was already a spent force; his works from this time on are not merely sterile and decadent but a retraction of the striking programme he had originally endorsed: 'Da gilt nur linientreu, schlicht um schlicht, da braucht der Dichter strahlende Akkorde nicht zu meiden.'[41]

It was, however, not as a writer that Becher provoked Western journals to reaction, but in his official role, which was to culminate in his appointment as Minister of Culture in 1954. *Der Monat* and *Die Gegenwart*, whose entrenched opposition to stalinist communism led them to monitor closely the repeated calls for East–West consultation from the GDR, frequently singled out Becher as their scapegoat. While their principal concern was to persuade the Western public that the ostensibly attractive approaches from the East were a fraudulent ploy, the critics were not averse to emphasising the worthlessness of Becher's poetry, as if to reinforce their case. In 1951, following a series of articles attacking Becher for his role in the PEN association and condemning the recent meeting at Starnberg between writers from East and West (organised at Becher's instigation), *Der Monat* printed a lengthy review of Becher's *Tagebuch 1950* in which isolated passages of self-criticism from the 700-page volume were cited and endorsed by the critic. At the start the author carefully emphasised that the literary work can only be assessed in the light of its social and political context – a curiously redundant qualifier, since it was unquestionably Becher's political position which had merited paying such attention to the work in the first place.[42]

To fend off the possibility of any serious, long-term collaboration between writers in East and West Germany, two arguments were put forward. The first, presented in the West Berlin *Tagesspiegel* and elsewhere, proposed a kind of legal regulation ('Präventivklausel'), prohibiting a freelance writer from taking part in discussions with state officials – a condition which would immediately exclude talks with all major GDR writers, who were technically classified as civil servants.[43] The second, argued with force by Friedrich Sieburg in *Die Gegenwart*, was that talks at a cultural level between writers made no sense, and could have no impact, if unaccompanied by political negotiation. Only by confronting the political and constitutional differences could the ground be laid for literary dialogue to produce concrete results: 'wir wollen uns nicht mit einem ehemaligen Parteilyriker im Ministerrang auseinandersetzen, sondern mit Herrn Ulbricht. Zwischen hüben und drüben stellen sich keine kulturellen, sondern nur politische Fragen.'[44] Of the two approaches, Sieburg's is the more considered and logical; this cannot, however, disguise the motive for his polemic: if Becher's initiatives were allowed even the smallest leeway, the structure of the capitalist West would have been proved vulnerable. By the mid-1950s Becher is being condemned as a 'Staatssklaven-Bildner' (Stefan Andres) and even 'Teufel' (Sieburg, again): emotive terms which reveal to what extent he had come to embody the West's worst suspicions of a latent threat through the artistic voice of the Soviet system.

The reception of Anna Seghers, a prose writer of recognised stature since the early 1930s, throws an interesting light on the effect of the Cold War on literary attitudes. The publication of her historical epic *Die Toten bleiben jung* in 1949 and that of its sequel, *Die Entscheidung*, exactly a decade later, spans the period

of political tension. Her novel D*as siebte Kreuz*, written during
her emigration, was amongst the first to be issued after the war
and met with immediate popularity in both East and West. In *Welt
und Wort,* Renée Guggisberg admired the depth of characterisation
and the lack of idealization in a work which set out to reveal the
moral resolve of the anti-fascist movement. The vibrant force of
the masses, which can support, absorb or turn against the individual, is successfully evoked in the novel, in striking difference to
the bourgeois realist tradition. This achievement, noted in *Welt und
Wort,* was perhaps captured best by Walter Mannzen in *Der Ruf*:

> Die eigentliche Bedeutung liegt aber in der literarischen Überwindung
> des bürgerlichen Individualismus durch die volle Ausgestaltung
> der Person: sowohl in ihrem eigensten inneren Bezug wie in
> ihrer gesellschaftlichen Verflechtung und ihrer Einbettung in
> die überpersönlich-geistig-seelische Wirklichkeit menschlicher
> Gemeinschaft.[45]

Some of the most critical remarks are to be found, surprisingly
perhaps, in *Aufbau*, where amid sufficient praise of the novel,
reservations as to the portrayal of the marxist cause are expressed.
A second danger of the anti-fascist novel is also pinpointed here:
the difficulty of avoiding the impression that forces of resistance
– active and passive – were located in all sections of the populace
merely waiting to be tapped. Unintentionally, it can be argued,
Georg Heisler's successful escape fosters this impression, hardly
in keeping with the experience of those who (unlike Seghers) had
lived through the fascist years in Germany.

Given the positive response in the West to *Das siebte Kreuz* in
1947, it is at first surprising to find a detailed review of *Transit*, a
mere five years later, intended explicitly as an appeal that Seghers's
works should not fall into neglect. Werner Merklin in the *Frankfurter
Hefte* is not modest in his choice of comparisons. Seghers is set
alongside Brecht as joint initiator of a new literary vision (socialist, or as he terms it 'exemplary' realism) as potent as the major
movements of the past, from the 'Sturm und Drang' through to
expressionism. *Transit*, he argues, with its uncharacteristic use
of the first-person narrative, borrowed some of the subjective involvement and humour of the best French tradition, and provided
Seghers with the release which paved the way for the broad epic
span of *Die Toten bleiben jung.*

Almost in parentheses, Merklin put his finger on the aspect of
Seghers's writing to meet with most frequent resistance in the

West. Seghers's mature prose, he claims, 'vereinigt ohne Bruch die spezielle Realität der Zeitung mit der allgemeinverbindlichen Wirklichkeit, die nur der Dichter gewinnt'.[46] Precisely the documentary element, the wealth of accurate historical detail, was viewed as a limiting, and at worst stultifying, emphasis by Western critics. In the GDR, however, it was this, perhaps above all, which made for the convincing realism of the novel. In his review of *Die Toten bleiben jung* for *Aufbau*, Paul Rilla had objected to certain individual episodes as not sufficiently typical, and in his praise of Seghers's courage ('Gewagtheit') implied some reservation about her final achievement. Yet his primary stress was on Seghers's ability to depict the complex interaction of the various social spheres in their historical context, resulting in a comprehensive vision so powerful that occasional factual inaccuracies are irrelevant: 'Unauflösbar sind nicht die Fakten, unauflösbar ist im Roman die unheimliche Richtigkeit der Gestalten und ihrer Situation, wodurch die Fakten erst Wirklichkeit bekommen.'[47] It was precisely this overall cohesion, however, that Western reviewers found lacking. For *Die Gegenwart*, the development was too predictable, and above all the individual characterisation unconvincing: 'Einem Roman aber muß es notwendig schaden, wenn seine Figuren statt wirklicher Lebewesen ideologische Konstruktionen sind.'[48] This view was seconded by Guido Gaya in *Wort und Wahrheit*, who found the novel sterile and lifeless, amounting to little more than a remarkable and precise collection of facts:

> Ein anatomisches Präparat wird untersucht, kein lebendes Organ. Unzählige Schnitte werden gemacht, Nervenstränge bloßgelegt, Zusammenhänge gezeigt. Der Gesellschaftsprozeß, als reiner Mechanismus erkannt, funktioniert jedoch zu deutlich, um nicht als, zugegeben, großartige Konstruktion zu wirken.[49]

Die Gegenwart could once again not resist concluding its review with a reminder of the parallels between totalitarian socialism and fascism, in the light of which Seghers's protrayal of the survival of the marxist–humanist idea through three generations is rendered meaningless. Having thus used the opportunity to restate its editorial prejudice, the review finishes with a rhetorical question more reminiscent of cultural politics in East Germany: 'Darf man da heute wirklich noch so schreiben?'

Already present in 1950, this principal objection to literature with an ideological framework was to intensify during the decade, as can be seen in the reception of Seghers's *Die Entscheidung*. Helmut Günther's review for *Welt und Wort* is pervaded by an essential rejection on the grounds that history has betrayed socialism and the GDR has failed to live up to its utopian ideal: 'Es gelingt Anna Seghers nicht, es kann ihr gar nicht gelingen, den ostzonalen Alltag mit heroischem Schimmer zu verklären.'[50] In *Der Monat*, Sabine Brandt, who similarly viewed the work less as a novel than an 'ideologische Heilslehre', at least does Seghers the justice of a detailed textual analysis. Here she exposes Seghers's severity, or even pessimism, in letting three principal figures meet their deaths for failing to make the decision of the title – in favour of the GDR – soon enough. This issue had even raised some doubts in the GDR, not least from the young critic Christa Wolf, who, while not shying away from assigning the novel to the ranks of 'Weltliteratur', raised the question of these deaths in interview with the author.[51] For Brandt, they represent one sign of Seghers's championing of an absolute and blind faith in socialism as opposed to reasoned and intelligent choice:

> Unzweifelhaft enthüllt das Buch das Krankheitsbild einer schweren Neurose, hervorgerufen durch ein politisches Hörigkeitsverhältnis, das vor dem wachen Bewußtsein, dem kritischen Verstand nicht bestehen kann.[52]

Once again, the critical bias is blatant: after the rebellion in Hungary and the end of the political experiment in Poland (both mentioned in the review) socialism has lost its last remnants of credibility. A writer of Seghers's stature has no alternative but to resort to a defence of unquestioning loyalty.

Viewed from the present, the literary beginnings of the GDR are unusually lively, the various efforts to forge new expressive possibilities mingling with the firm, and increasingly authoritarian, voice of ideological conviction. By the end of the 1950s, younger writers (the first signs of a specifically GDR literature) were appearing in print, whose initial motivation was derived from the atmosphere of debate during this period. The mature aesthetic understanding of Christa Wolf and Heiner Müller, for instance, which has contributed much to literary developments in both East and West, is rooted in reflections and experiences made at this time. The emphasis on truthful, factual reporting has produced a tradition of journalistic fiction and literary protocol in which the GDR is strong, while also giving rise to questions which in turn made possible the move to lyrical subjectivity in the late 1960s and 1970s.

For several years, however, Western reception was to turn a blind eye on newer developments in the GDR. By 1960, for instance, the GDR had in Erwin Strittmatter a writer who had unpretentiously drawn the life of the rural worker into the novel, and in Franz Fühmann a young writer versed in the German tradition of poetic irony whose short stories of the time remain a powerful examination of the psychological hold of fascism on an individual. These are only two examples (from the field of prose) of achievements almost completely ignored in the West. It was not until the internal controversies of the early 1960s (over Strittmatter's *Ole Bienkopp* and Wolf's *Der geteilte Himmel*) that the younger generation was to arouse at least some kind of attention in the West.

Notes

1 Rudolf Hartung, 'Im Osten nichts Neues', *Neue Deutsche Hefte*, 1959, pp. 546–8.

2 Richard Gaudig, 'Die deutsche Sprachspaltung', *Neue Deutsche Hefte*, 1958–9, pp. 1008–114.

3 The publisher Berthold Spangenberg made this point succinctly. See Peter Merz, *Und das wurde nicht ihr Staat*, Munich, 1985, p. 119.

4 The self-examination in various passages of Becher's *Tagebuch 1950* or the classical poetry of his exile years are by no means remote from contemporary literary taste in the West. The same can be said of some of Seghers's prose as well as the considerable tradition of nature poetry in the GDR dating back to Huchel, Karl Mickel and others in the 1950s. Hans Dieter Schäfer is among those to have noted this point; see Schäfer, *Das gespaltene Bewußtsein*, Munich, 1981, pp. 42, 61.

5 Hans Magnus Enzensberger, 'Die große Ausnahme' (review of Uwe Johnson's *Mutmaßungen über Jakob*), *Frankfurter Hefte*, 12, 1959, pp. 910–12.

6 Fritz J. Raddatz, *Traditionen und Tendenzen*, Frankfurt am Main, 1976, p. 7.

7 The most comprehensive of the many studies on heritage include Wolfram Schlenker, 'Das 'kulturelle Erbe' in der DDR' and Karl Robert Mandelkow, 'Die literarische und kulturpolitische Bedeutung des Erbes', in *Die Literatur der DDR*, edited by Hans-Jürgen Schmitt, Munich, 1983, pp. 78–119.

8 For a perceptive analysis of East Germany's delicate political situation at this time see Dietrich Staritz, *Geschichte der DDR 1945–1985*, Frankfurt am Main, 1985, pp. 66–73.

9 The thaw in cultural policy which had led to Becher's appointment as the GDR's first Minister of Culture in 1954 was to end abruptly soon afterwards. As a result Becher was forced into the final irony of defending the state's

hard-line policy during the last years of his life. See Alexander Stephan, 'J. R. Becher and GDR Cultural Development', *New German Critique*, February 1974, pp. 72–89 (p. 84ff.).

10 *Aufbau*, May 1952, p. 480.

11 See Bodo Uhse, 'Alles spricht für ein Gespräch', *Aufbau*, May 1952, pp. 391–4.

12 Alexander Abusch, 'Nationalliteratur der Gegenwart', *Aufbau*, September 1952, pp. 795–805 (p. 798).

13 On the influence and limitations of Moscow-generated 'Bündnispolitik' see Frithjof Trapp, *Deutsche Literatur in Exil*, Bern, 1983, pp. 201–10. Becher's willingness to put party priorities over his own sympathy for this approach has been traced in detail by Alexander Stephan in *Die deutsche Exilliteratur 1933–1945*, Munich, 1979, pp. 218–40.

14 See Helmut Peitsch, ' "Die Freiheit fordert klare Entscheidungen". Die Spaltung des PEN-Zentrums Deutschland', *Kürbiskern*, 1985, pp. 105–24.

15 *NDL*, January 1955, pp. 5–7; July 1956, pp. 7–8; September 1956, pp. 7–9; October 1956, pp. 7–10; December 1956, pp. 3–4 (in each case in the important editorial commentary 'Unsere Meinung').

16 For further insight into the various short-lived utopias played out in the earliest post-war publications see '*Als der Krieg zu Ende war': Literarische Publizistik 1945–1950*, edited by Bernhard Zeller, Stuttgart, 1973; *Zur literarischen Situation 1945–1949*, edited by Gerhard Hay, Kronberg, 1977.

17 In the British zone, Axel Eggebrecht published a series of detailed articles on various aspects of the Soviet system in practice in the *Nordwestdeutsche Hefte*, as did the French-based *Dokumente* for several years. This informative and critical reporting was to give way to a more polemical form of monitoring after 1948, most evident in the periodical *Der Monat* which was first published that year.

18 However, in *Texte und Zeichen*, the journal he edited between 1955 and 1957, Andersch allows generous coverage of GDR culture, publishing, for instance, a story by the East German writer Karl Mundstock and attempting a survey of GDR publications which comes perhaps as close to an objective analysis as was possible at the time.

19 It is interesting to note, however, that *Der Ruf* was amongst the first to publish prose by the Leipzig writer Erich Loest, an important figure among the younger generation of Socialist Realists until his arrest for alleged dissidence in 1957, and the author of *Es geht seinen Gang*, one of the most discussed GDR works of the 1970s. See *Der Ruf*, 3/1, 1948, p. 11 and 3/16, 1948, p. 10.

20 *Der Ruf*, 1/2, 1946, p. 8.

21 See *Die Gruppe 47: ein kritischer Grundriβ*, edited by Heinz Ludwig Arnold, Munich, 1980, pp. 31–3. In his later function as co-ordinator of the 'Gruppe 47', Richter took a deliberately individualist position, approaching selected writers he considered ripe for serious dialogue, which entailed a certain distance to party officialdom. Richter was, for instance, in occasional correspondence with both Alfred Kantorowicz and Hans Mayer before their respective moves to the West, and succeeded in enticing Johannes Bobrowski to a group conference in 1962, when he was also awarded the group prize.

22 On the tendencies rejected explicitly by both the 'young generation' in which Richter and others placed themselves and (for instance) Hermlin and Becher in the East see Frank Trommler, 'Emigration und Nachkriegsliteratur', in *Exil und innere Emigration*, edited by Reinhold Grimm and Jost Hermand, Frankfurt am Main, 1972, pp. 173–97 (pp. 180–1).

23 For a taste of the exaggerated polemic see Joachim Friese, 'Zur kulturellen Situation im Osten und Westen', *Deutsche Rundschau*, September 1951, pp. 828–36; Wolfgang Schrade, '"Sozialistischer Realismus" realistisch gesehen', *Neue Literarische Welt*, December 1953, pp. 9–11.

24 Otto Flake, 'Am Anfang der Wiederbesinnung', *Das Literarische Deutschland*, January 1951, p. 1.

25 This note can be detected in Helmuth Reitz's review of Anna Seghers, *Welt und Wort*, January 1950, p. 72 and Richard Baring on the poet Kuba's *Gedanken im Fluge*, *Welt und Wort*, July 1950, pp. 310–11.

26 Gotthilf Hafner, review of Erich Weinert, *Das Zwischenspiel*, *Welt und Wort*, October 1950, p. 437.

27 Helmut Günther, *Welt und Wort*, 1957, p. 153 and 1960, p. 55. Wolf, at least, is hardly receiving fair treatment; he died in 1953.

28 Helmut Günther, *Welt und Wort*, 1958, p. 84.

29 Among the principal works of these genres are, respectively, Eduard Claudius, *Grüne Oliven und nackte Berge* (1945); Bruno Apitz, *Nackt unter Wölfen* (1958) and Anna Seghers, *Die Toten bleiben jung* (1949). The continuing reception of the Spanish Civil War met with a particularly harsh response in the West; Claudius's book was attacked in *Der Ruf* and *Welt und Wort*, who also savaged Walter Gorrisch, *Um Spaniens Freiheit*. *Der Monat*, who had given considerable publicity to Ludwig Renn's *Der spanische Krieg* when it ran into censorship problems, felt no scruples about panning it when it finally appeared. See Michael Uhl, 'Ein deutscher Kommunist im Spanienkrieg', *Der Ruf*, January 1946, pp. 14–15; Joseph Bauer, *Welt und Wort*, 1948, p. 265; Joseph Forster, *Welt und Wort*, 1947, p. 87; Jürgen Rühle, 'Mit den Augen des Stabsoffiziers', *Der Monat*, 91, 1956, pp. 73–8.

30 Gotthilf Hafner, review of Adam Scharrer, *Dorfgeschichten einmal anders*, *Welt und Wort*, November 1952, p. 395.

31 See *Welt und Wort*, January 1952, p. 36 (Becher), January 1955, p. 54 (Heym), Jürgen Rühle, 'Arnold Zweig und die Kunst des inneren Vorbehalts', *Der Monat*, 123, 1958–9, pp. 67–74.

32 Friedrich Sieburg, 'Nicht jeder Tor ist rein', *Die Gegenwart*, 215, 1954, pp. 564–5 (p. 565).

33 A useful outline of Brecht's ambivalent role in GDR cultural life is offered by Manfred Jäger, *Kultur und Politik in der DDR*, Cologne, 1982, pp. 48–64. For a retrospective survey of the misunderstandings over the 1953 letter see Wolfgang Paul, 'Aus Bertolt Brechts späten Jahren', *Neue Deutsche Hefte*, 1958–9, pp. 710–23.

34 Albrecht Fabri, 'Notiz über Bertolt Brecht', *Merkur*, 1950, pp. 1214–20 (p. 1218).

35 Herbert Lüthy, 'Vom armen Bert Brecht', *Der Monat*, April 1952, pp. 115–44 (pp. 122–3).

36 Piero Rismondo, 'Wer war Bert Brecht?', *Wort und Wahrheit*, November 1956, pp. 855–68 (p. 860).

37 Günter Blöcker, 'Die Theorie Bertolt Brechts', *Neue Deutsche Hefte*, 1957–8, pp. 746–8 (p. 747).

38 Wilfried Berghahn, 'Bert Brecht und die Konsequenz', *Frankfurter Hefte*, 1954, pp. 383–5 (p. 385).

39 Walter Mannzen, 'Marxistische Werkanalyse', *Texte und Zeichen*, 2, 1956, pp. 649–52 (p. 652).

40 Review of Becher's *Heimkehr*, *Welt und Wort*, 1947, p. 120.

41 Oskar Jancke, 'Die Becher-Probe', *Das literarische Deutschland*, April 1951, p. 1. The allusion is to Becher's aesthetic programme of the 1920s.

42 Ernest J. Salter, 'Die grauen Wände', *Der Monat*, 35, 1951, pp. 543–6.

43 See Wilhelm Girnus, 'Realitäten', *Aufbau*, April 1955, pp. 296–8.

44 Friedrich Sieburg, 'Der kalte Kulturkrieg', *Die Gegenwart*, 225, 1955, pp. 38–40 (p. 39).

45 Walter Mannzen, 'Das Netz und das Gewebe', *Der Ruf*, November 1947, p. 15.

46 Werner Merklin, 'Zwischenspiel im exemplarischen Realismus', *Frankfurter Hefte*, February 1952, pp. 149–51 (p. 150).

47 Paul Rilla, 'Der neue Roman von Anna Seghers', *Aufbau*, March 1950, pp. 216–24 (p. 223).

48 'a.g.', 'Darf man das heute noch?', *Die Gegenwart*, 109, 1950, p. 22.

49 Guido Gaya, 'Niemals vergessen', *Wort und Wahrheit*, June 1950, p. 462.

50 Helmut Günther, review of *Die Entscheidung*, *Welt und Wort*, 1960, p. 55.

51 See 'Fragen an Anna Seghers', in Christa Wolf, *Die Dimension des Autors*, Darmstadt and Neuwied, 1987, pp. 255–62 (pp. 257–9).

52 Sabine Brandt, 'Die Entscheidung der Anna Seghers', *Der Monat*, 139, 1959–60, pp. 77–81 (p. 81).

Christians, pacifists and others: West German literature published in East Germany

J. H. Reid

Der Paß ist der edelste Teil des Menschen
(Brecht, *Flüchtlingsgespräche*)

Any discussion of the reception of West German writers in East Germany at once encounters a problem of definition: what is a West German writer? It is a question which is raised by the authors of neither of the two books which have appeared on the subject, Otto F. Riewoldt and Irene Charlotte Streul.[1]

Wolfgang Borchert, for example, died in 1947 before the two German states came into being. As a citizen of Hamburg, however, he should probably be regarded as a West German *manqué* and he is treated as such in the East German survey of the literary development of the FRG.[2] As it happens, he is the only post-war author apart from Heinrich Böll to have been published more or less in his entirety in both the Federal Republic and the Democratic Republic in the 1950s. As early as 1948 a selection of stories from *An diesem Dienstag, im mai, im mai schrie der kuckuck*, with lithographs by Hans Mayer-Foreyt, appeared in Leipzig, in 1956 Reclam brought out *Die drei dunklen Könige*,[3] while the Rowohlt edition of the *Gesamtwerk* with its biographical postscript by Bernhard Meyer-Marwitz appeared in Halle in 1957, was reprinted in the same year and again in 1961. In 1960 the Insel Verlag in Leipzig published *Draußen vor der Tür*, which had received its first East German productions in 1957 in Weimar and Rostock.

A further problem is illustrated by the reception of Ulrich Becher, who published relatively freely in both East and West and was in the 1950s one of the few contemporary German-language playwrights living outside the GDR to be regularly performed there. His plays are included by Riewoldt as 'westdeutsche Dramatik', but Becher had adopted Austrian nationality in exile, and when he returned to Europe after the War he was quickly disappointed with political developments in West Germany, and settled first in Austria, then in Switzerland. Streul treats Erich Maria Remarque as a West German, but he became an American citizen in 1947 and settled in Ascona when he returned to Europe. Oskar Maria Graf continued to live in New York after the War; his works were published in both West and East.

Then there are the turncoats. Numerous writers left the GDR in the course of the 1950s; these include such characteristic figures of the early years of the Federal Republic as Hermann Kasack and Rudolf Hagelstange; only a few had works published in the GDR thereafter. Hugo Hartung moved from Potsdam to West Berlin in 1950; his stories *Ein Junitag* were published by Reclam, Leipzig in that year and reprinted in 1951. A rather smaller number transferred their allegiance in the opposite direction. Jens Gerlach moved to East Germany in 1953, the year in which two volumes of his poetry, *Der Gang zum Ehrenmal* and *Ich will deine Stimme sein* were published there by Rütten & Loening and Verlag Neues Leben respectively. Peter Hacks's first plays were published in *Sinn und Form* and *Neue Deutsche Literatur* before he moved East in 1955. In the early part of the 1950s especially, before the KPD was proscribed, a number of writers lived in West Germany whose ideological allegiance was to the GDR and the Soviet Union. Werner Ilberg had been a member of the BPRS in the early 1930s, emigrating to England in 1933; in 1947 he returned to his home town of Wolfenbüttel, where he lived until in 1956 he moved to the GDR. During this period Ilberg regularly contributed articles on the West German literary scene to *Sonntag* and *Neue Deutsche Literatur;* his 1948 novel *Die Fahne der Witwe Grasbach* on the 1930 struggle of the KPD against fascism went into a third edition in 1952, but no West German edition appeared. Gotthold Gloger lived in Hessen for a time after the War and contributed reportage on the repression of the West German peace movement to *Aufbau*; his novel *Philomela Kleespieß trug die Fahne* is set in Hessen, although it appeared only in the GDR where he had moved in 1953. The critic and journalist Ernst Schumacher lived throughout the 1950s in Munich, but published exclusively in East Germany; he is best known for his work on Brecht, but he also published a volume of poetry in 1957, *Eurasische Gedichte.* Gerd Semmer remained in West Germany until his death in 1967; at various times he was assistant to Erwin Piscator and a journalist with the *Deutscher Michel* in

Düsseldorf; but his books appeared only in the East, including his verses satirising militarism and the West German Wirtschafts-wunder *Die Engel sind müde*, published by Aufbau-Verlag in 1959; the journals *Aufbau, Neue Deutsche Literatur* and *Sonntag* all published items by him from 1950 onwards. More obscure but possibly similar is the figure of Stefan Scherpner, whose collection of prose and poetry *Weil ich ein Arbeiter bin* appeared in East Berlin in 1959, but was not published in the West.[4] A working definition of a 'West German writer' might be one who both lived and published in West Germany.

Riewoldt is exclusively concerned with the theatre, Streul, in spite of the title of her book, with prose fiction; a number of volumes of poetry by West German writers, however, also appeared in the GDR in the 1950s. Both concentrate on the critical reception of West German literature. I propose to deal rather with what was actually published, which was substantially more than Streul suggests. These two sides of cultural policies had different functions. Publication indicated general approval of the author and work; it was up to the critics to point out the ideological weaknesses, and reviews were frequently unfavourable.

What was published in the GDR does not tell us much about what East Germans actually read, as up to the building of the Berlin Wall in 1961 access to literature published in West Germany was relatively easy. Many West German books which were not officially available in the GDR were reviewed in East German journals. No book by Hans Erich Nossack appeared in the GDR in these years, although Christa Wolf wrote a favourable review of his novels *Spätestens im November* and *Spirale*;[5] Peter Huchel, however, published his two-act burlesque *Die Hauptprobe* in *Sinn und Form* in 1955. The novels of Hans Helmut Kirst were widely covered by the East German media, partly at least as an attempt to ensure that readers of West German copies were not led astray;[6] extracts from his *Null-acht-fünfzehn* novels appeared in *Neue Deutsche Literatur* in 1954 and 1955, but none was printed in its entirety. *Neue Deutsche Literatur*, the official organ of the Writers' Union, published extracts from numerous West German books in the 1950s, some of which were subsequently to appear, others not, as if the journal had been 'testing the water' and finding it 'too cold'; to the latter category belong Gerd Ledig's *Die Stalinorgel* (1955), Hans Werner Richter's *Du sollst nicht töten* (1955), Rüdiger Syberberg's *Daß diese Steine Brot werden* (1956), Hans W. Pump's

Vor dem großen Schnee (1956) and *Die Reise nach Capuascale*
(1957), Wolfgang Ott's *Haie und kleine Fische* (1957) and Martin
Walser's *Halbzeit* (1961). A chronic shortage of paper and of hard
currency with which to pay West German publishers for their
copyright were material constraints. The Amt für Literatur und
Verlagswesen, set up in 1951, and from 1956 its successor body,
the Abteilung Literatur und Buchwesen of the Ministry of Culture,
operated a fairly strict system of censorship according to the SED's
conception of literature as an instrument of political consciousness. In the first ten years of the GDR's existence politicians
stressed the unity of German culture, which was being endan-
gered by American-oriented cosmopolitanism; accordingly the
official policy on publishing works from the West was to propagate authors whose outlook had at least something in common
with the GDR's, not necessarily a wholehearted subscription to
Marxism–leninism – the reviews, as distinct from the publication
itself, could indicate 'deficiencies' in the author's understanding
and values. The dominant question of the 1950s was the peace
issue. There were genuine fears of the American 'rollback' strategy and of a revival of West German militarism as exemplified in
the creation of the Bundeswehr and the joining of Nato; for this
reason one of the major areas of literary interest was the West
German war novel, but it also meant favourable treatment for some
West German writers who came out against rearmament in public
statements. One further point concerning cultural policies must
be made: the emphasis was always on 'realism'; formal experiments, abstraction, avant-garde techniques were rejected. This
principle, however, was subordinate to the others.

   Three main groups of West German writers can be distinguished:
those who had left Germany on the accession of Hitler and returned to settle in the Federal Republic, those who had remained
in Germany during the Third Reich without overtly supporting the
régime (writers of the 'inner emigration'), and the 'new' writers,
those who first established their reputation after the War.

   The returning émigrés are ignored by Streul, but if Anna Seghers
was indisputably an East German author then Alfred Döblin and
Leonhard Frank must equally be reckoned West Germans. It is
well known that those who returned to settle in the East had a
better reception than those who opted for the West.[7] In the case
of the latter, especially those who had been identified with the left
in the Weimar Republic, it was often the GDR which was prepared

to propagate their works rather than the FRG. Peter Martin Lampel had emigrated to Switzerland in 1933, later going on to the United States. He settled in Hamburg in 1949 and died there in 1965, but his reputation was kept alive in the GDR, where his novels for young people *Helgolandfahrer* (1952), *Kampf ohne Ordnung* (1952) and *Wir fanden den Weg* (1955) were published, rather than in West Germany, where in this period only *Kampf ohne Ordnung* appeared, one year later than in the East.[8] His play *Kampf um Helgoland* achieved some notoriety in 1952: it deals with a protest action in 1950 by West German youths against the British occupation of Heligoland, for which the youths were subsequently prosecuted by the West German authorities. The play was boycotted in West Germany but produced in East Berlin.[9] Better known is the fate of Alfred Döblin, who settled in Baden-Baden in 1946. His last novel, *Hamlet oder Die lange Nacht nimmt ein Ende*, was first published in the GDR in 1956 and did not appear in the West until the following year; extracts had previously been printed in *Sinn und Form* in 1954 and 1955. Earlier works by Döblin to appear in the GDR in the 1950s were *Berlin Alexanderplatz* (1955) and *Pardon wird nicht gegeben* (1961). In his preface to his *Bibliographie Alfred Döblin*, Louis Huguet was happy to boast: 'Die "Döblin-Renaissance" ging von der DDR aus...'; and it was 'kein Zufall, daß die erste umfassende Döblin-Bibliographie in der Deutschen Demokratischen Republik erscheint'.[10] What is curious about the GDR's concern for Döblin is that, although in the 1920s he had been associated with the USPD, by the time he returned to Germany he had become a somewhat mystical Catholic. It fits a pattern, however, which is repeated with other writers.

The emigré author who was given most consistent attention by the GDR, however, was the pacifist Leonhard Frank, who settled in Munich on his return from exile in 1950, living there until his death in 1961. Frank received the GDR's Nationalpreis Erster Klasse in 1955. He regarded himself as a West German writer; in 1957 he was quoted as lamenting, 'daß man mich, einen westdeutschen Schriftsteller, in Westdeutschland nicht verlegt... In deutscher Sprache werden meine Bücher nur in der DDR herausgegeben'.[11] This statement is quite untrue – Frank was actually awarded the Bundesverdienstkreuz – but the East Germans did publish more of his works and reprinted them more frequently. Reclam in Leipzig published a selection of novellas, *Absturz* in 1949, the story *Karl und Anna* in 1954, the *Deutsche Novelle* in 1955 and *Michaels*

Rückkehr in 1957. His novels *Die Raüberbande* (1952), *Das Ochsenfurter Männerquartett* (1952), *Der Bürger* (1954), *Links, wo das Herz ist* (1955), *Mathilde* (1955) and *Die Jünger Jesu* (1956), and a collection of stories *Im letzten Wagen* (1954) were all published by Aufbau, which also produced the first collected edition of his works, a six-volume selection, in 1959. Many of these editions were frequently reprinted. In this period *Der Bürger* and *Mathilde* appeared only in the East. *Aufbau*, *Sonntag* and *Neue Deutsche Literatur* all regularly included contributions by Frank.

Günther Weisenborn had published during the Third Reich although his early novel *Barbaren* had been burned in 1933 and his play *Warum lacht Frau Balsam?* proscribed. He emigrated to America in 1936 but returned to Germany the following year, where he was associated with the underground resistance movement Schulze-Boysen Harnack. Arrested in 1942, he was liberated by the Red Army in 1945 and appointed Mayor of Luckau in the Soviet zone of occupation. However, he moved to the West in 1947 and settled in Hamburg in 1951. His 1930s novels *Das Mädchen von Fanö* and *Die Furie* were republished in the GDR in 1955 and 1957 respectively, while Aufbau reprinted his account of his imprisonment by the Gestapo *Memorial* in 1958 and brought out the novel *Der Verfolger* in 1961. Weisenborn was one of the few playwrights living in West Germany to be published and performed in the GDR in the 1950s. Reclam republished *Die Illegalen* in 1955, Aufbau the same play along with *Ulenspiegel* and *Die Neuberin* under the title *Dramatische Balladen* in the same year, and Henschel *Das verlorene Gesicht* in 1956 and *Fünfzehn Schnüre Geld* in 1960. Among other plays to be favoured *Das Spiel vom Thomaskantor* was premiered in Chemnitz in 1950 and *Lofter* in Dresden in 1956. *Die Illegalen* was described by a reviewer in 1956 as 'immer noch das einzige bedeutende Drama des antifaschistischen Widerstandes, das ein Deutscher schrieb'.[12]

Hans José Rehfisch too left Germany in 1936 but he did not return until 1950, when he settled in Munich. He received the Bundesverdienstkreuz in 1956, although he later expressed embarrassment over the award.[13] From the mid-1950s onwards his plays were increasingly adopted by the East German theatre, partly because of their topics, partly because of Rehfisch's expressed sympathies for the GDR. *Bumerang*, on the trial of Bebel and Liebknecht in 1872 for high treason, was premiered in Leipzig in 1960, the year in which Rütten & Loening brought out a selection of seven plays under the title *Nickel und die sechsunddreißig Gerechten*, which was reprinted in 1961. Rehfisch's post-war novels were especially popular: the historical novel *Die Hexen von Paris* had five printings between 1957 and 1960, *Lysistratas Hochzeit* three in 1959 and 1960. By contrast the plays of Carl Zuckmayer were, with the exception of *Der Hauptmann von Köpenick*, largely rejected. *Das kalte Licht*, which attacks as misguided the communist idealism of the 'traitor' Klaus Fuchs, was unperformable, while *Des Teufels General*, the great success of the post-war West German theatre, was seen as a play which, whatever Zuckmayer may have intended, effectively rehabilitated German militarism; surprisingly it was none the less produced in Rostock in 1957.[14]

Ernst Niekisch and Richard Scheringer are two further figures associated with internal resistance in the Third Reich. During the Weimar Republic Niekisch had been a friend of Ernst Toller and a proponent of closer ties with the Soviet Union; arrested in 1937 and sentenced to life imprisonment, he became a member of the Volkskammer after the War and Professor at the Humboldt University, but in 1954 he left for West Berlin. Oddly, his account of the Third Reich, *Das Reich der niederen Dämonen*, appeared in Hamburg in 1953 while he was still in the GDR, but was published by Rütten & Loening in East Berlin in 1957, by which time he was in the West. Scheringer had originally been a National Socialist and was imprisoned in 1930 for conspiracy against the state; in prison, however, he converted to socialism and on his release began working for the KPD. During the Third Reich he had connections to Niekisch and his circle, later to the Scholl circle, and was arrested several times. After the War he remained in the West, presiding over the KPD in Bavaria, where he was again arrested a number of times for subversive activities. During one spell in prison he wrote his autobiography *Das große Los*, which appeared in Hamburg in 1959 and was published by Aufbau in 1961.

Maria Mathi had remained in Germany during the Third Reich, although she had refrained from publishing. Her novel *Wenn nur der Sperber nicht kommt*, on the plight of the Jews in Germany after 1933, was published by Kiepenheuer in Weimar in 1956, one year after its appearance in the West. Other examples were less predictable. Walter von Molo had continued to publish his heroic epics in Nazi Germany, and in a famous post-war controversy had been rebuffed by Thomas Mann, whom he had urged to return to Germany; however, his appeal to President Heuss to help West

German writers, who, he claimed, were being disadvantaged by the flood of American imports, was given widespread publicity in the GDR.[15] In 1957, the year of his death, Ursula Heidow quoted him as having said: 'Es gibt keine westdeutsche und keine ostdeutsche, es gibt nur eine deutsche Sprache.... Was steht also unserer Einheit im Wege, wenn wir alle deutsch sprechen?'[16] On the occasion of his seventy-fifth birthday *Neue Deutsche Literatur* printed an extract from his early *Schiller-Roman*, and in 1956 the Mitteldeutscher Verlag brought out his 1931 historical novel on Friedrich List, *Ein Deutscher ohne Deutschland*. It deals with List's efforts on behalf of the unification of Germany in the nineteenth century, although it received a poor review in *Sonntag*.[17]

Perhaps surprisingly, the Christian writers of the 'inner emigration' are well represented in the lists of East German publishing houses in the 1950s. They are entirely ignored by Streul. Their presence has partly to do with the organisation of the publishing industry in the GDR. The Union Verlag belonged to the East German CDU, the political mouthpiece of the Christian Churches; but in addition there were a few publishing houses which belonged to one or other of the two main Churches, including the Evangelische Verlags-Anstalt in Berlin and the Catholic St Benno-Verlag in Leipzig; although subject to similar conditions of censorship they were partly financed from the West and appear to have had access to supplies of paper from the same source. There were, however, also political issues at stake: many Christian writers were active in the West German peace movement in the 1950s, often contradicting the official line taken by their respective Churches. Reinhold Schneider, who had been arrested in the closing weeks of the Third Reich, actively opposed the rearmament of the Federal Republic in the early 1950s and was vehemently attacked for doing so. His response to the attacks, the essay 'In Freiheit und Verantwortung', was rejected by West German journals, yet appeared in Switzerland in 1951 and in the GDR in December of the same year.[18] His *Las Casas vor Karl V.* appeared in Leipzig in 1955 in the Insel Verlag. In its series Katholische Dichter unserer Zeit the St Benno-Verlag republished Anton Gabele's *Haus zur Sonne* in 1957, nine stories by Schneider under the title *Die dunkle Nacht* in 1958 and Gertrud von Le Fort's *Die Frau des Pilatus, Hymnen an die Kirche* and *Das Schweißtuch der Veronika* in 1959. The same publisher brought out two volumes by Ida Friederike Görres, *Das große Spiel der Maria Ward* in 1957 and *Die Siebenfache Flucht der Radegundis* in 1958, Ruth Schaumann's *Die Messe von Gethsemane* in 1959 and Schneider's *Die himmlischen Wohnungen* in 1960. On the Protestant side, Albrecht Goes was popular with the East as well as the West. Like Schneider he had protested against West German rearmament: as a member of the Paulskirche movement in 1955 he appealed to the West German government not to ratify the Paris Agreements on the creation of the Bundeswehr and West Germany's joining NATO. *Das Brandopfer* was published by Aufbau in 1955, only a year after its first appearance in West Germany, *Unruhige Nacht* by the Union Verlag in the same year, reprinted in 1956 and 1959 and issued together with *Das Brandopfer* in one volume in 1961. The Union Verlag also published *Der Gastfreund* in 1958, while in 1959, under the title *Wagnis der Versöhnung*, Koehler und Amelang in Leipzig, another organ of the CDU, brought out addresses by Goes on Hesse, Buber and Bach. Earlier, two novels by the Swabian writer Georg Schwarz had been republished in the GDR, the historical novel on the liberation of the peasantry from serfdom *Jörg Ratgeb* by Staeckmann in Leipzig in 1952 and *Johann Friedrich Flattich* by the Evangelische Verlags-Anstalt in 1953, both of which had first appeared during the Third Reich. Schwarz had helped to edit the anthology *Wir heißen euch hoffen: Schriftsteller zur deutschen Verständigung* which appeared in Munich in 1951 and included contributions by Johannes Becher, Arnold Zweig, Anna Seghers and Stephan Hermlin as well as by Johannes Tralow, Hanns Henny Jahnn, Walter von Molo, Alfred Döblin and Walter Kolbenhoff. Poems by him appeared regularly in *Aufbau*, *Neue Deutsche Literatur* and *Sinn und Form*. Although Manfred Hausmann was one of the supporters of the Kuratorium Unteilbares Deutschland, which sought German unity on West German, anti-communist terms,[19] he was represented with the two stories 'Die Begegnung' and 'Vor der Weser', published by Reclam in 1954, and with *Das Worpsweder Hirtenspiel*, published by the Evangelische Verlags-Anstalt in 1955 and going into a third printing in 1960. Gertrud von Le Fort, Albrecht Goes and Manfred Hausmann all signed the manifesto protesting against plans to equip the Bundeswehr with atomic weapons in 1958. But the Evangelische Verlags-Anstalt even brought out Ina Seidel's *Das unverwesliche Erbe* in 1956, reprinting it in the same year and again in 1958. This is especially interesting in view of the author's naive support of Hitler in a poem and a declaration of 1939.[20] She too, however, was involved in the West German peace movement when, with Gertrud von Le Fort, she signed the manifesto 'Frauen gegen die Atombewaffnung' in 1957. Josef Winckler had been co-founder of the Werkleute auf Haus Nyland before the First World War, an early group of 'worker writers'. This was not an association which the GDR's cultural functionaries would necessarily wish to cultivate, as it advocated a transcending of class differences rather than the revolutionary aggression of the BPRS, and some of its members were easily assimilated by the National Socialists. Winckler had his difficulties with the Nazis, mainly, it seems, because his wife was not a 'pure Aryan'. After the war he continued to live in the West. His novels *Doktor Eisenbart* and *Der tolle Bomberg*, both of which had appeared during the Third Reich, were republished by the Greifenverlag, Rudolstadt in 1955 and 1956 respectively.

The Christian writer of the older generation who had the highest profile in the GDR in these years was probably Leo Weismantel. Seven titles by him figure in publishers' lists in the 1950s and they were frequently reprinted. The Union Verlag published *Dill Riemenschneider* (1955), *Albrecht Dürers Brautfahrt in die Welt* (1956), *Albrecht Dürer, der junge Meister* (1956) and *Gericht über Veit Stoß* (1958), the St Benno-Verlag *Die guten Werke des Herrn Vinzenz* (1955) and *Elisabeth* (1957), and Reclam *Der Wahn der Marietta di Bernardis* (1957). Although some of his works appeared in the Third Reich, Weismantel had been twice arrested by the Gestapo. After the war he lived in West Germany but was heavily involved in attempts to reconcile East and West, openly resisting the Catholic Church's official policies on relations with the Eastern bloc. His most important and controversial contribution to East–West dialogue was through the Wartburg circle. This was a group of writers from East and West who first met in July 1954 on the initiative of the West German Ludwig Bäte and the East German Otto Riedel, both Protestants, in the historic Wartburg, where in 1817 German students had once before expressed their determination to overcome the division of Germany. More than a hundred writers attended, the motto was 'Vom Brückenschlag des Wortes', and the initial declaration with its appeal for national unity was signed by Ludwig Bäte, Clara Hofer, Otto Riedel, Leo Weismantel, Konrad Beste, Alfred Kurella, Anna Seghers, Kuba, Hans Franck, Arno Poetzsch, Werner Warsinsky, Wieland Herzfelde and Heinz Rusch. In an editorial *Neue Deutsche Literatur* drew attention to the basic Christian message of peace and the important role played by Christian literature in the GDR's publishing output and commented on the pan-German nature of the meeting: 'Nicht nur ein gemeinsames Glaubensbekenntnis führt sie zusammen, auch die gemeinsame Sprache, auch die gemeinsame Zugehörigkeit zum deutschen Volk, zur deutschen Nation.'[21] The West Germans appear to have all been practising Christians, which was evidently not the case with the East Germans, who were concerned to give the event high status. A second meeting took place a year later. As the most prominent West German writer to attend, Weismantel was the subject of a malicious attack in *Die Gegenwart* by Friedrich Sieburg, who accused him of having been manipulated by the East German politicians and demanded that the security services should investigate. Weismantel's reply appeared in *Neue Deutsche Literatur*. Sieburg was using exactly the methods of the Gestapo; in 1933 Weismantel had for reasons of political opportunism been called a Jew, now for similar reasons he was being called a victim of communist manipulation. At the Wartburg meeting he had spoken of the fears some of the West German participants had at attending; these were fears not of the East Germans but of the pressures from the politicians in the so-called 'free West', fears which Sieburg was confirming.[22]

By contrast the 'new' writers of the Federal Republic figure rather more sparsely. The most important of these was Heinrich Böll, but it is important to see him in context. Some of these writers were not strictly 'new' at all. Wolfgang Koeppen had published some works during the Third Reich; *Der Tod in Rom* came out with the Mitteldeutscher Verlag in Halle in 1956 and was reprinted in 1957 (it had to wait until 1963 to be reprinted in the West). This portrait of an unreconstructed German militarist is the most directly polemical of Koeppen's novels. Extracts were published in *Neue Deutsche Literatur* (1955) and *Aufbau* (1956), relating to a debate on the nature of modern music, a further topic of the novel. Wolfgang Weyrauch too was no newcomer. Initially he lived in East Berlin after the War and his first post-war poems were published by Aufbau-Verlag in 1946. Although he had settled in the West and had publicly attacked Brecht in 1952,[23] his poems *Nie trifft die Finsternis* were published by Volk und Welt in 1956 and his surreal dialogues from Hitler's bunker *bericht an die regierung* by the Mitteldeutscher Verlag in 1957. Günter Bruno Fuchs, who had moved from East to West Berlin in 1950, had a collection of poems and woodcuts on the destruction of the gypsy population of Slovakia by the Nazis, *Zigeunertrommel*, published under the same imprint in 1956. A year earlier he had been represented in the collection of poems *Fenster und Weg* along with the Reutlingen poet Richard Salis and the painter Dietrich Kirsch, again with the Mitteldeutscher Verlag. Before the building of the Berlin Wall made such joint East–West enterprises impossible he had collaborated with Johannes Bobrowski, Manfred Bieler and Robert Wolfgang Schnell in a revival of the Friedrichshagener Dichterkreis. The Mitteldeutscher Verlag brought out war novels by Karl Ludwig Opitz, *Der Barras* and *Mein General*, in 1954 and 1955 respectively. Opitz moved to the GDR in 1959, where he published satirical works for the Eulenspiegel Verlag, but he returned to the West in 1965 and became an especially virulent critic of the East. Gerd Ledig's radio play *Das Duell* on the Nitribitt scandal in Frankfurt was published by Aufbau in 1958.[24] *Und keiner weint mir nach*, a novel on petty bourgeois life in the tenements of Munich in the 1920s and 1930s by the columnist Siegfried Sommer, was published by Volk und Welt in 1955.[25] In 1956 the Mitteldeutscher Verlag brought out Ursula Rütt's *In Sachen Mensch*. Rütt, like so many other writers favoured by the GDR, was active in the West German peace movement; her novel satirises militarism and bureaucracy in a small post-war West German town and achieved notoriety when the mayor of Bad Homburg believed himself to be libelled in it and had it temporarily banned.[26] The Stuttgart writer Johannes Weidenheim had the novel *Das türkische Vaterunser* and the stories *Der verlorene Vater* published under the same imprint in 1955 and 1956 respectively; Weidenheim was co-editor of the joint East–West anthology *Deutsche Stimmen*, which is discussed below; *Neue Deutsche Literatur* published stories by him in 1956 and 1957. A contemporary Christian poet, Hedwig Börger, had a collection of poems published by the St Benno-Verlag in 1958, *Wanderer im Wind*. At the very end of our period, Hans Werner Richter's autobiographical novel of 1953 *Spuren im Sand* came out with Rütten & Loening in East Berlin in 1961,[27] while in the same year two stories by Heinz Risse were published by the Evangelische Verlags-Anstalt (*Die letzte Instanz*) and Christian Geißler's novel *Anfrage* on the resurgence of militarism and fascism in the FRG by Aufbau (an extract appeared in *Neue Deutsche Literatur* in 1960). Geißler was a founder member of the Gruppe 61; but he also edited the Catholic journal *Werkhefte*. As already mentioned, however, the major postwar West German writer to figure on the East German publishing scene was Heinrich Böll – another Catholic.

Eight separate volumes of works by Böll appeared in the GDR between 1956 and 1961. The first was the war novel *Wo warst du, Adam?* of 1951, published by Rütten & Loening in 1956 and reprinted by Reclam in 1961. There followed the novel *Haus ohne Hüter* (1954), published by Volk und Welt in 1957, and the long short story *Im Tal der donnernden Hufe*, published simultaneously by the Insel Verlag in Leipzig and Wiesbaden. In 1959 the Union Verlag brought out a selection of short stories written between 1951 and 1957. The following year the same publisher produced an edition of the 1953 novel *Und sagte kein einziges Wort*. In 1961 the Insel Verlag Leipzig brought out Böll's most complex, 'modernist' work to date, *Billard um halbzehn*, only two years after its publication in West Germany, and in the same year Hans Mayer edited a selection of the early works which included the war stories 'Der Zug war pünktlich', 'Wanderer, kommst du nach Spa...', 'Damals in Odessa' and 'Unsere gute, alte Renee', and the post-war stories 'Die schwarzen Schafe', 'Der Mann mit den Messern', 'An der Brücke', 'Die Botschaft', and 'Lohengrins Tod'. Although it falls outside the scope of this study it is also worth noting that when Hans Joachim Bernhard edited a selection of the shorter works in 1966 for the Insel Verlag in Leipzig this 749-page edition was at the time the most complete single-volume collection of Böll's stories available anywhere. By 1961 not all of Böll's works to date had appeared in the GDR. *Das Brot der frühen Jahre* (1955) was not published until 1965, nor *Irisches Tagebuch* (1957) until 1966. Of the satires collected under the title *Doktor Murkes gesammeltes Schweigen* (1958), the most direct polemic against remilitarisation in West Germany, 'Hauptstädtisches Journal', had appeared in *Sonntag* in 1960;[28] the others, the title story, 'Nicht nur zur Weihnachtszeit', 'Es wird etwas geschehen' and 'Der Wegwerfer' had to wait until 1966, as did sixteen of the stories from the collection *Wanderer, kommst du nach Spa...* Nevertheless the essential Böll was available, at least to the extent that the limited print runs enabled potential purchasers to be satisfied.

Why Böll should have been favoured in this way is not entirely clear. He was not especially active in the peace movement, although he did sign the manifesto 'Kampf dem Atomtod' in 1958. Nor did he publicly support recognition of the GDR; indeed his

few allusions to the GDR up to the building of the Wall are entirely
negative, as when in 1953 he described the refugees as fleeing
from the 'Unmenschlichkeit dort' or in 1960 contrasted the GDR as
a 'Gefängnis' with the FRG as a 'Museum'.[29] In *Im Tal der donnernden
Hufe* Frau Mirzow appears as 'eine Nonne, die nicht mehr an ihren
Gott glaubt . . . konserviert in ihrem verlorenen Glauben an etwas,
das Kommunismus hieß . . .'.[30] In the context of the other West
German authors who were published at this time three major factors may have made these aberrations tolerable. The first was
Böll's uncompromising presentation of the crimes committed by
the Nazis, in terms both of militarism (like Opitz and Ledig) and
of racism (like Fuchs). *Wo warst du, Adam?* belongs to a group of
war novels published in the mid-1950s, when the GDR lacked a
war literature of its own.[31] The second was his attack on remilitarisation and the restoration of capitalism in the Federal Republic.
In this respect it is significant that *Haus ohne Hüter* was initially
preferred to *Und sagte kein einziges Wort*; it, like *Billard um
halbzehn*, has much in common with the works published by
Koeppen, Rütt and Geißler. And thirdly Böll's Catholicism was not
only no drawback in the atheist GDR, as witness the many other
Christian writers who were published; it was a positive advantage.
Günther Cwojdrak might criticise Böll for offering his readers no
real hope;[32] none the less the consolation of a better life in the
world to come, the 'Trosteffekt' which made his works palatable
in West Germany, must have had just as much an affirmative and
stabilising effect on East German readers.

As we have seen, many West German writers were officially
introduced to East German readers in the pages of journals such
as *Sinn und Form, Neue Deutsche Literatur, Aufbau* and *Sonntag*. This
was one way in which the unity of German culture could be
stressed. Even more interesting are the anthologies in which writers from East and West were represented side by side. Again the
Christian publishers led the way. Erich Bockholt edited an anthology of contemporary Christian writers for the Union Verlag in
1955, *Vom Licht der Welt*; twenty-one authors were represented,
eleven from the GDR and ten from the FRG (Martin Beheim-
Schwarzbach, Friedrich Ackermann, Ludwig Bäte, Friedl Marggraf,
Elisabeth Lill, Josef Winckler, Friso Melzer, Nikolaus Schwarzkopf,
Gerd Schimansky and Hedwig Börger). In his preface Bockholt
wrote of the Christian writer's task as being

nicht etwa die Menschen vom irdischen Dasein abzulenken auf ein überweltliches Jenseits, sondern sie in ihrem Glauben zu bestärken und hellhörig zu machen für den rätselvollen Zusammenhang von Erdenleben und Himmelreich, für das Geheimnis der Geheimnisse, für Gott.

He also stressed the danger of a further war:

Gerade heute, da Ungerechtigkeit und Unfriede die Welt wieder in Krieg und Vernichtung zu stürzen drohen, haben die christlichen Dichter und Schriftsteller auf die Lichtpfade durch die Finsternisse hinzuweisen, welche uns der Menschensohn geoffenbart hat, auf daß der Friede Gottes mit uns sei und die Menschheit vor einem noch satanischeren Gehenna als der letzte Weltkrieg bewahrt werde. (p. 8)

The third, substantially revised edition of 1958 introduced six Austrian writers, including Heimito von Doderer, beside nine West Germans, seven East Germans and one Dutchman; Stefan Andres, Wilhelm von Scholz and Heinrich Böll ('Wiedersehen mit Drüng') were the West Germans represented for the first time; Friedrich Ackermann, Ludwig Bäte, Friedl Marggraf and Josef Winckler were dropped.

The year 1956 saw the appearance of two secular anthologies which attempted to bridge the gap between East and West. *Deutsche Stimmen 1956: Neue Prosa und Lyrik aus Ost und West* was unique in being a joint venture of the Kreuz-Verlag Stuttgart and Mitteldeutscher Verlag Halle and jointly edited by Marianne Bruns (GDR), Hans Lipinsky-Gottersdorf (FRG), Heinz Rusch (GDR) and Johannes Weidenheim (FRG). In their preface the editors described their venture as 'ein Gespräch' across 'die unsinnigste Grenze Europas'; their aim was to acquaint their readers with writers from the other half of Germany and to remind them 'daß wir trotz aller Differenzen *ein* Volk sind, daß wir *eine* Sprache und *ein* Schicksal haben'; the book had been possible only 'in einer Atmosphäre, die bei aller Abgrenzung der Standpunkte nichts von den Ingredienzen des kalten Krieges enthielt'. Nevertheless the editors did make clear that they did not accept the formalist thesis: 'das künstlerische Wort aus der Zeit und in die Zeit hinein verfolge nur formal-ästhetische oder überhaupt keine Ziele.' Thirty-six authors were represented, twenty from the West, fifteen from the East – the other, Walter Bauer, had emigrated to Canada. Again there was a strong Christian presence. From West Germany short stories by Helmut Harun, Heinz Albers, Johannes Weidenheim, Hans Bender,

Karl Rauch, Georg Schwarz, Otto-Heinrich Kühner, Wolfdietrich Schnurre, Waldemar Augustiny, Rudolf Otto Wiemer, Richard Wolf, Hans Lipinsky-Gottersdorf, Simon Glas and Joseph Christoph Hampe, poems by Tamara Ehlert, Hanna Stephan, Reinhold Schneider, Wolfgang Weyrauch and Manfred Hausmann, and an essay by Albrecht Goes were included. In an editorial *Neue Deutsche Literatur* praised the principle of the enterprise, but felt that it would have been more interesting had contrasting writers been selected; as it was, it would not be easy to detect which were East Germans, which West Germans. Stephan Hermlin and Gerd Gaiser would have made a tantalising couple.[33] In fact Gaiser is completely absent from the GDR's publishing scene. *Anthologie 56: Gedichte aus Ost und West*, published by the Verlag Neues Leben in Berlin in 1956, was an exclusively East German enterprise but was equally conciliatory. In his preface Jens Gerlach characterised the anthology as 'ein Spiegelbild des gespaltenen, ja, des zwiespältigen Deutschlands'. It was to be a contribution to the necessary and unavoidable dialogue between the two sides. Were there two German poetries? Gerlach replied: 'Ja und nein. Gute und schlechte Gedichte werden zu beiden Seiten der Elbe geschrieben.' Differences were due to social developments in the two German states; the West Germans were in danger of succumbing to 'Sprachartistik', to exaggerate the importance of formal experiments; the East Germans tended to overstress content at the expense of form. Thirty poets were represented, eighteen East Germans, ten West Germans and two Austrians. The Austrians were Ingeborg Bachmann and Paul Celan, the West Germans Wolfgang Bächler, Hans Bender, Wolfgang Borchert, Adolf Endler, Helmut Heißenbüttel, Walter Höllerer, Werner Riegel, Peter Rühmkorf, Rolf Seeliger and Albert Thomsen. Endler had in fact turned his back on the West by the time the anthology appeared. Of the East Germans represented Jutta Bartus and Jens Gerlach had previously lived in West Germany; Peter Jokostra was shortly to leave the GDR and become a particularly hostile critic.

The two-volume anthology *Deutsche Erzähler des 20. Jahrhunderts*, edited by Kurt Böttcher and Paul Günter Krohn and also published by Verlag Neues Leben the following year, was less concerned with dialogue. Again the editors stressed the danger which the inner-German frontier posed to the 'Einheit der deutschen Kultur' (I, p. 6). The purpose of the anthology, however, was not to introduce post-war authors but to give a consciously partisan selection of writings from an age of transition, that between capitalism and socialism. Nevertheless the authors included who have connections to West Germany are not altogether predictable: Hans Carossa, Hans Leip, Hans Henny Jahnn, Carl Zuckmayer, Richard Huelsenbeck, Günther Weisenborn, Wolfgang Weyrauch, Wolfgang Borchert and Heinrich Böll. The biographical details on Zuckmayer are unexpectedly conciliatory: the post-war plays, including *Das kalte Licht*, are described as 'Vielumstritten, freilich auch anregend und, wie immer, theaterwirksam' (II, p. 421). But even the anthology *Deutsches Gedichtbuch*, edited by Günther Deicke and Uwe Berger, published by Aufbau in 1959, which surveys the whole of German poetry from the Middle Ages to the generation of poets born before 1916, found room for nine poems by Wilhelm Lehmann, three by Georg von der Vring, four by Günter Eich and three by Karl Krolow.

In 1955 *Neue Deutsche Literatur* commented:

> Gewiß, manche Bücher humanistischer Schriftsteller aus Westdeutschland sind bisher in unseren Verlagen nicht erschienen; es stünde aber bedeutend besser um die Einheit der deutschen Literatur, wenn westdeutsche Verlage erst einmal so viele Bücher unserer Autoren herausbrächten, wie unsere Verlage Bücher westdeutscher Autoren bereits veröffentlicht haben.[34]

By the end of the decade this was certainly the case.

Within the years up to the building of the Wall it is possible to distinguish three stages. An initial period of repressive cultural policies marked by a Zhdanovite insistence on Socialist Realism and a rejection of anything that could be described as 'formalist' lasted until late in 1953. There followed a period of some liberalism until the beginning of 1957, when under the impact of events in Hungary the authorities clamped down on all cultural activities which might remotely lead to similar uprisings in the GDR; from this point on less stress was laid on the unity of German culture. The number of publications, however, does not altogether fit this pattern, as the following table shows; the first figure represents all publications, the second only post-war works; reprints are excluded. Thus little appeared before 1955, and most of that was by the older generation of writers. The striking increase in output in 1955 had clearly to do with new policies: in September 1954 *Sonntag* announced that it was in future to devote greater space to West German literature,[35] and similar developments can be seen in *Neue Deutsche Literatur*. In 1957 the latter journal was accused of going

1950	1951	1952	1953	1954	1955	1956	1957	1958	1959	1960	1961
0	1	6	1	5	19	16	16	7	10	5	9
0	0	2	0	1	13	14	7	4	7	5	6

too far in this direction.[36] The drop in output from 1958 onwards is, however, less dramatic than might have been expected.

Predictably and understandably there was no place on the East German publishing scene for writers such as Ernst Jünger, Gottfried Benn and Hans Grimm, who had identified their interests, however temporarily, with National Socialism. Erich Kästner was too uncomfortable a satirist and is represented only by his children's stories. The 'Gruppe 47', always excepting Böll, does particularly poorly. Alfred Andersch is wholly ignored; as a renegade communist who had publicly made clear his hostility to the post-war role of the Soviet Union he was unpublishable. Richter does not figure until 1961, Paul Schallück's *Engelbert Reineke* was published by Rütten & Loening in 1962, Martin Walser had to wait until 1965. Enzensberger is represented only with three poems in *Sinn und Form*, Schnurre and Rühmkorf only in anthologies. The preference for the older generation over the new had at least partly to do with the GDR's dogmatic insistence on 'realism', which by and large did not much interest West German writers in the 1950s; representative West German writers of the time such as Arno Schmidt are therefore missing and minor figures such as Rütt, Weidenheim and Sommer preferred. But the most unexpected feature of the scene remains the dominance of active Christians. From Döblin and Weismantel to Böll and Börger, religiosity was a characteristic likely to make one respectable in a land dedicated to dialectical materialism.

Notes

1 Otto F. Riewoldt, *Von Zuckmayer bis Kroetz: Die Rezeption westdeutscher Theaterstücke durch Kritik und Wissenschaft in der DDR*, West Berlin, 1978; Irene Charlotte Streul, *Westdeutsche Literatur in der DDR: Böll, Grass, Walser und andere in der offiziellen Rezeption 1949–1985*, Stuttgart, 1988. Streul is particularly vague on nationalities, listing both Doris Lessing (p. 192) and Michael Scharang (p. 193) as West Germans and Wolfgang Hildesheimer as a Swiss (p. 195).

2 *Geschichte der deutschen Literatur von den Anfängen bis zur Gegenwart*, XII (*Literatur der BRD*), edited by Hans Joachim Bernhard, Berlin/GDR, 1983.

3 According to Streul, *Westdeutsche Literatur*, p. 191; neither the Leipzig nor the Frankfurt *Deutsche Bibliographie* mentions it.

4 See *Sonntag*, 21 October 1959, p. 7.

5 ' "Freiheit" oder Auflösung der Persönlichkeit? Uber Hans Erich Nossack "Spätestens im November" und "Spirale: Roman einer schlaflosen Nacht', *Neue Deutsche Literatur*, 5/12, 1957, pp. 119–23.

6 See Streul, *Westdeutsche Literatur*, pp. 38–40.

7 See Peter Mertz, *Und das wurde nicht ihr Staat: Erfahrungen emigrierter Schriftsteller mit Westdeutschland*, Munich, 1985.

8 Under the title of *Macht ohne Ordnung*.

9 See Riewoldt, *Von Zuckmayer bis Kroetz*, p. 89.

10 Berlin/GDR, 1972, p. 10. *Neue Deutsche Literatur* published the story 'Eine Mutter steht am Montmartre' in 1955, and *Sinn und Form* items from the 'Nachlaß' in 1957.

11 Konrad Fedin, 'Leonhard Frank', *Aufbau*, 13, 1957, p. 240.

12 *Aufbau*, 12, 1956, p. 469.

13 Martin Linzer, 'Hans J. Rehfisch oder Die späte Entscheidung: zum 10. Todestag des Dichters', *Neue Deutsche Literatur*, 18/8, 1970, pp. 160–3.

14 See Riewoldt, *Von Zuckmayer bis Kroetz*, pp. 71–4 and p. 84.

15 'Walter von Molo schreibt für die Schublade', *Sonntag*, 22 November 1953, p. 11; 'Unsere Meinung', *Neue Deutsche Literatur*, 2/9, 1954, p. 7.

16 'Begegnungen mit Walter von Molo', *Neue Deutsche Literatur*, 5/1, 1957, pp. 158–9.

17 *Sonntag*, 26 August 1956, p. 5.

18 *Aufbau*, 7, 1951, pp. 1077–9. See *Vaterland, Muttersprache: Deutsche Schriftsteller und ihr Staat seit 1945*, edited by Klaus Wagenbach, West Berlin, 1979, p. 107.

19 See 'Unsere Meinung', *Neue Deutsche Literatur*, 2/9, 1954, pp. 7–8.

20 See Christian Ferber, *Die Seidels: Geschichte einer bürgerlichen Familie*, Stuttgart, 1979, pp. 305–14.

21 'Unsere Meinung', *Neue Deutsche Literatur*, 2/7, 1954, p. 6. Further reports on the Wartburg meetings are to be found in *ibid.*, 2/8, pp. 5–7; *ibid.*, 3/6, 1955, pp. 5–7; Wieland Herzfelde, 'Worte schlagen Brücken: Die Schriftstellertagung auf der Wartburg', *Sonntag*, 18 July 1954, p. 2.

22 'Brief an meine Freunde', *Neue Deutsche Literatur*, 2/11, 1954, pp. 95–9; see also his 'Vom Brückenschlag des Worts', reprinted from *Heute und Morgen* (Düsseldorf), in *Sonntag*, 31 October 1954, p. 3, and 'Jagt ihn – ein freier Schriftsteller', an extract from his letter to the *Deutsche Volkszeitung* (Düsseldorf), *ibid.*, 8 May 1955, p. 5.

23 In *Die Literatur*, 1 November 1952; see *Vaterland, Muttersprache*, pp. 108–10.

24 According to Streul, *Westdeutsche Literatur*, Gerd Ledig's novel *Vergeltung* was published in 1957 by the Mitteldeutscher Verlag (p. 192), but it is listed neither in the Leipzig nor in the Frankfurt *Deutsche Bibliographie*.

25 An extract had appeared in *Sonntag*, 8 August 1954, p. 10. Heinrich Böll wrote a favourable review of the West German edition for *Welt der Arbeit*, 26 March 1954 (in *Essayistische Schriften und Reden I: 1952–1963*, edited by Bernd Balzer, Cologne, 1978, pp. 130–2).

26 See Horst Heitzenröther, 'Tadelswerte Ungenauigkeit', in *Neue Deutsche Literatur*, 4/12, 1956, pp. 163–4, protesting against the publishers' advertising the book as if the ban had been a political one.

27 According to Streul, *Westdeutsche Literatur*, it appeared in 1954 (p. 193), but the catalogues do not bear this out.

28 *Sonntag*, 23 October 1960, p. 9, and 30 October 1960, p. 9. *Neue Deutsche Literatur* published extracts from *Wo warst du, Adam?* in 1955 and *Billard um halbzehn* in 1960, and Böll's review of James Jones's *From Here to Eternity* and Jaroslav Hašek's *Good Soldier Schwejk*, 'Noch Plätze frei im Raritätenkabinett', in 1956.

29 'Offener Brief an den Pfarrer von Meyenn', in *Essayistische Schriften und Reden I: 1952–1963*, p. 77; 'Zwischen Gefängnis und Museum', *ibid.*, pp. 389–94.

30 *Werke: Romane und Erzählungen*, 111, edited by Bernd Balzer, Cologne, 1977, p. 248.

31 See Annemarie Auer, 'Wo steht unsere Kriegsliteratur?', *Sonntag*, 22 July 1956, p. 8; Streul, *Westdeutsche Literatur*, pp. 33–46.

32 'Rückzug vom Realismus: zu einigen Büchern von Nossack, Koeppen und Böll', *Neue Deutsche Literatur*, 7/6, 1959, pp. 113–24. This criticism is repeated in almost all the GDR reviews.

33 'Unsere Meinung', *Neue Deutsche Literatur*, 4/11, 1956, pp. 7–9.

34 'Unsere Meinung', *ibid.*, 3/8, 1955, p. 3.

35 *Sonntag*, 5 September 1954, p. 5.

36 Rudolf Hoffmann, 'Wo steht die "Neue deutsche Literatur"?', *Neues Deutschland*, 18 October 1957 (in *Dokumente zur Kunst-, Literatur- und Kulturpolitik der SED*, edited by Elimar Schubbe, Stuttgart, 1972, pp. 486–9).

Neue Deutsche Literatur:
the forum of the divided nation?
Dennis Tate

The distinctive contribution of *Neue Deutsche Literatur* (*NDL*) to German literature in the 1950s is less easy to define than that of the GDR's other leading periodical, *Sinn und Form*. Whereas the uninterrupted stewardship of Peter Huchel over the period 1949–62 made for an impressive international breadth of reference in *Sinn und Form*, *NDL*'s apparent lack of editorial continuity left it more exposed to the vagaries of SED cultural policy in the years following 1953, when it was launched as the monthly journal of the Writers' Union. Although an initial survey of *NDL* up to the Berlin Wall crisis in the autumn of 1961 reveals its importance as the launching pad for many of today's best-known East German authors, such as Volker Braun (February 1961), Günter de Bruyn (July 1960), Heinz Czechowski (January 1959), Hermann Kant (July 1957), Reiner Kirsch (August 1958), Heiner Müller (December 1955), Erik Neutsch (January 1960) and Klaus Schlesinger (November 1960),[1] it is difficult not to forget the sense of embarrassment with which this generation tends to look back on its literary debuts of these years, as recorded in a volume like Gerhard Schneider's *Eröffnungen: Schriftsteller über ihr Erstlingswerk* (1974). Today's prominent names among the contributors of major articles to *NDL* between 1953 and 1961 have little desire to be reminded of them either. Christa Wolf, for example, the author over this period of more than twenty essays, editorials and reviews, has allowed none of them to be republished in her recent 957-page volume of collected criticism, *Die Dimension des Autors* (1987).[2] Only a brief interview with Anna Seghers from August 1959 has survived from this stage in her career. Similarly, Hermann Kant, a regular contributor of articles and reviews in 1960–1, included none of them in his collection of 1981, *Zu den Unterlagen: Publizistik 1957–1980*.

This may suggest that the *NDL* of the 1950s has little more than curiosity value today. Yet there are other, more compelling, reasons for a fresh look at its early years. It was, for example, also a training-ground for today's best-known West German commentators on the literature of the GDR, Marcel Reich-Ranicki and Fritz Raddatz. (Reich-Ranicki, the up-and-coming Polish critic of contemporary German literature then known as Marceli Ranicki, contributed four pieces to *NDL*, and Raddatz, a reader for the publishing house Volk und Welt, three, between 1954 and 1956.) The discovery of their involvement here has the effect of raising questions about their subsequent portrayals of the GDR in the 1950s, in books which form the basis of the established 'Western' view of the period. Have they done justice to the historical circumstances which encouraged them at that time to contribute to a journal like *NDL*? Reich-Ranicki's first publication after moving to the Federal Republic was the paperback anthology of East German prose *Auch dort erzählt Deutschland: Prosa von 'Drüben'* (1960). Although he introduced it as a first attempt to counteract the 'Zweiteilung der zeitgenössischen deutschen Literatur', his implication that both of the German states had hitherto barred their doors equally firmly to the literature of the other is directly contradicted by the evidence of *NDL*. While mentioning Brecht as the 'Ausnahmeerscheinung' of East German literature in the FRG in the 1950s, he said nothing about the large number of West German authors published and discussed in the GDR during this period, an activity in which *NDL* played the dominant role.[3] Raddatz's *Traditionen und Tendenzen: Materialien zur Literatur der DDR* (1972), the first comprehensive survey to appear in the FRG in the years of détente, reinforced in its lengthy introduction the idea that rigid Party control of literature in the GDR ('Engführung' is his heading) had ensured, apart from a brief 'Thaw' in 1956, the emergence of a distinctive 'second' German literature there by 1961. Why an author like Günter Grass might have been permitted to play the provocative role described by Raddatz at the Writers' Congress of 1961, at the culmination of this relentless 'Engführung', remains a mystery to his reader, while his view that the Writers' Union served only as a 'Forum ideologischer Richtlinien [*sic*] und ästhetischer Konzepte', singlemindedly engaged on 'die politische Programmverkündung der Partei',[4] conflicts with the impression which even a preliminary survey of its official journal *NDL* provides.

It may not, then, prove entirely misguided to look again at a periodical so apparently lacking in editorial independence and dotted with contributions its authors would prefer to forget. Indeed, the evidence shows that *NDL* is of considerable significance for a study of the cultural relations between the two German states in the Cold War. The fact which is obscured behind all this personal reticence is the political sensitivity, from perspectives adopted later in both states, of the role *NDL* attempted to play in the period under review, and with a greater degree of editorial independence than is generally assumed. A re-examination of *NDL* reveals that, in broad chronological terms, it took up an ideologically conformist position as the main outlet for the literature of socialist reconstruction of the GDR only in 1953, its first turbulent year of existence, and in 1958–9, during the campaign for a 'cultural revolution' which would integrate writers into the industrial working class. In contrast, between 1954 and the autumn of 1957, and again in 1960–1, it had a clear editorial policy of encouraging the development of a contemporary 'Nationalliteratur' as a force for the eventual achievement of a re-unified socialist Germany. It is in this latter role, I believe, that the distinctive contribution of *NDL* to the 1950s can be identified. In pursuing this theme it will be necessary to focus attention on the work of certain of its editors during these two periods, Günther Cwojdrak and Günther Deicke in 1954–7, and Wolfgang Joho from 1960, whose names have been largely forgotten in recent years, yet who helped to determine the historical context of the early critical writings of authors as important as Christa Wolf and Hermann Kant.

The origins of NDL were closely linked with those of the Writers' Union in the GDR, which, after emerging in 1950 as a sub-section of the Kulturbund zur demokratischen Erneuerung Deutschlands, was officially granted a degree of autonomy in May 1952, following the Third Writers' Congress.[5] The nomination of Anna Seghers as the new president of the Writers' Union promised some protection against the hard-line imposition of Zhdanovian Socialist Realism, which had virtually snuffed out creative endeavour in the GDR since the state was established in 1949, although its praesidium also included unsubtle exponents of proletarian literature such as Hans Marchwitza and the poet Kuba. NDL was rapidly launched as the organ of the Writers' Union, with a special issue produced in November 1952 to mark the thirty-fifth anniversary of the Soviet revolution. It began to appear monthly in January 1953 and has continued in this form ever since. The original editorial board of three contained only one recognised author, the proletarian novelist Willi Bredel (who had worked with Brecht on the exile journal *Das Wort*), and it soon became clear that he was essentially a figurehead. The main editorial activity was carried out by his two young colleagues Günther Cwojdrak and Günther Deicke, who had come from other sectors of the cultural media. Cwojdrak, an émigré from West Germany, had worked since 1947 for the journal *Die Weltbühne* and the literature section of the Berliner Rundfunk: his unconventionality had evidently appealed to Bredel's 'Lust am Polemischen'. Deicke, formerly a reader with the Aufbau-Verlag, now claims that his selection for this prestigious job was clinched by his willingness to take on the thankless task of writing an afterword to a volume of Kuba's poems for Bredel's *Bibliothek fortschrittlicher deutscher Schriftsteller*.[6]

NDL had an unhappy first year. Its original self-definition as an outlet for young East German talent led to the dominance in its early numbers of lengthy excerpts from would-be socialist epics, such as Fritz Hannemann's *Weißer Rauch am blauen Himmel* (January 1953) and Hans Marchwitza's *Roheisen* (March–April 1953), which soon had Anna Seghers intervening to stop the rot. In an article written just before the political crisis of 17 June 1953 she insisted that *NDL* must set its sights higher, both by publishing more work of quality by established German authors and by placing its thematic emphasis on the overriding goal of German peace and unity: 'Was wir heute von einer Schriftstellerzeitschrift verlangen, muß von dem großen Ziel unserer ganzen Arbeit beherrscht sein: dem Frieden und der Einheit Deutschlands' (August 1953, p. 97). This should also be, she added, the distinctive feature of a broadly defined German Socialist Realism.[7]

This signal to change course accorded with the convictions of *NDL*'s editors. Cwojdrak had set out his own goals for literature in the GDR in an article in the first number of *NDL*, which placed emphasis on quality and accessibility to a West German readership, using Walter Ulbricht's declared aim of 'ein einheitliches demokratisches Deutschland' to support his assertion 'die Thematik unserer Literatur muß gesamtdeutschen Charakter haben' (January 1953, p. 159). He had then echoed Seghers's criticisms in a polemical contribution entitled 'Schreibt die Wahrheit!' to the same issue (August 1953). It was therefore no surprise to find a similar resoluteness in the (unsigned) stocktaking editorial of December 1953, which developed Seghers's phrase about their 'großes Ziel' into a manifesto for *NDL*, boldly exploiting the absence of any comparable journal in the Federal Republic as a justification for claiming a unifying all-German role for itself:

> Die 'Neue Deutsche Literatur' muß ein Forum aller deutschen Schriftsteller in Ost und West sein, die sich zur Idee des Friedens, zur Verteidigung des Friedens bekennen. In Deutschland muß, bei den gegenwärtigen Verhältnissen, ein Bekenntnis zum Frieden zugleich ein Bekenntnis zur demokratischen Einheit Deutschlands sein... Dem großen Ziel, dem Frieden und der Einheit Deutschlands dienen, heißt weiter, alle Möglichkeiten des Bündnisses mit bürgerlich humanistischen und patriotischen Schriftstellern realisieren. Wir müssen darauf hinwirken, daß sich in ganz Deutschland eine nationale Front der Schriftsteller bildet... Unser Hauptaugenmerk wird den besten Schöpfungen der neuen deutschen Literatur gehören. (December 1953 p. 9)

This attempt to revive the spirit of the Popular Front, the broad anti-fascist solidarity of the 1930s, coincided with the creation of the GDR's Ministry of Culture, headed by Johannes R. Becher, who had been articulating similar sentiments since the immediate postwar years. It also followed a political initiative of November 1953 by Ulbricht along the same lines. Yet the evidence of *NDL*'s progress over the next four years suggests that it is misleading to conclude, as Irene Streul does in her informative new study *Westdeutsche Literatur in der DDR*, that this was all simply part of a coherent ideological strategy to undermine the FRG's 'westliche Integrationspolitik'.[8] There are in fact many indications in *NDL* between 1954 and 1957 of open tensions within the SED on issues of cultural policy, and of readiness among the journal's editors to explore the possibilities of unifying German culture without rigid ideological preconceptions.

The new spirit at *NDL* is immediately evident at the level of editorial comment. A section several pages long, entitled 'Unsere Meinung', was established at the front of the journal, in which its editors responded in brief articles to developments in political and cultural life in the two German states and the Soviet Union. Günther Cwojdrak came to the fore here, as a distinctive voice prepared to identify issues and stimulate debate on them. He articulated the frustrations of creative writers at the bureaucratic mishandling of cultural policy, arguing (as in his piece welcoming the abolition of the infamous Amt für Literatur und Verlagswesen) that writers and publishers had to be trusted to make their own decisions (September 1956); he castigated the GDR's failure to persuade potential cultural allies like Fritz von Unruh that it could lay the foundations for Hölderlin's 'anderes Deutschland' (July 1955); he advocated a new course for German cultural development between the extremes of 'Provinzialismus' (his code for slavish imitiations of Soviet models) and 'Amerikanismus' (June 1954). Where, on the other hand, Khrushchev's Soviet Union could be seen as setting an example in the vigour of its attacks on bureaucratic dogmatism, Cwojdrak supplied summaries and key quotations from official journals and Central Committee resolutions (March, August 1956). At the same time he was constantly on the lookout for encouraging developments in West German cultural life, supporting the political breadth of Ernst Rowohlt's publishing policy (February 1954), noting the sudden appearance of an editorial on 'Europas unteilbares Erbe' in the *Süddeutsche Zeitung* (June 1954), or praising the initiative of Hans Werner Richter in setting up his Grünwalder Kreis to combat manifestations of neo-Nazism in the Federal Republic (June 1956). This valuable chronicle contains many bleaker moments too: the record of the banning of *NDL* (like all other East German publications) from the FRG from July 1954 onwards, following a decision ostensibly by the Bonn Ministry of Posts and Telegraphs, serves as a reminder of the lengths to which Adenauer's policy of non-recognition of the existence of the GDR went at this time (September 1954).

A second indication of change at *NDL* was the considerable scope given from 1954 onwards to the work of the exile generation. This included those living in the GDR who had held out against the imposition of Soviet literary models, such as Bertolt Brecht and Arnold Zweig, but also led to a new prominence being given to authors who had not identified themselves with either German state (Thomas Mann, Alfred Döblin, Lion Feuchtwanger, E. M. Remarque) and the relatively few living in the Federal Republic who were sympathetic to the GDR (Leonhard Frank, Hans Henny Jahnn). This focus took the form of lengthy extracts from the creative work of these authors (the original publication of Brecht's *Tage der Kommune* as the main feature of January 1954 signalled in itself this change of emphasis), as well as articles about them (there were pieces on Feuchtwanger, for example, by Alfred Kantorowicz (April 1954), Zweig (July 1954) and Reich-Ranicki (March 1956), while Feuchtwanger himself reviewed Mann's *Felix Krull* (February 1955). A notable scandal surrounding the bowdlerised West German edition of Remarque's *Zeit zu leben und Zeit zu sterben* (Witsch Verlag) was unearthed (February 1955); when, in a Cold War irony, the necessities of copyright obliged the Aufbau-Verlag to take over the same text for its edition of 1957, *NDL* was able, working from the English version of the novel, to provide a list of the cuts for the benefit of its readers (April 1957).

The third aspect of *NDL*'s endeavour to turn itself into the forum for contemporary German culture was its search for radical social analysis in the creative work of the new generation of West German authors. This led, as Irene Streul has shown, to a number of bizarre misjudgements – notably the identification of Hans Hellmut Kirst as the standard-bearer of a new critical literature – which had to be rapidly revised as authors failed to fulfil the political expectations they had aroused in the GDR.[9] Nevertheless, *NDL* occupies a unique position amongst German periodicals of the 1950s through the range of its coverage of the literature of the 'other' state. In the period 1954–7 alone it published extracts from new novels by Wolfgang Koeppen (February 1954, August 1955), H. E. Nossack (February 1954), Siegfried Sommer (May 1954), Kirst (July, December 1954, June 1955), Heinrich Böll (March 1955), Gerd Ledig (June 1955, March 1957), K. L. Opitz (June 1955), H. W. Richter (December 1955), Hans Pump (June 1956, October 1957), Günther Weisenborn (June 1956) and Wolfgang Ott (March 1957). Furthermore it carried articles or reviews on all of these authors and many others besides – including Hermann Kasack, Ernst Kreuder, Peter Bamm, Carl Amery, Albrecht Goes, Willy Heinrich and Walter Jens – whom it was prepared to take seriously as potential cultural allies.[10] Its mediating role also involved encouraging the publication in book form in the GDR of West German authors featured on its pages (see Cwojdrak's editorials of February and May 1954, or his review of Weisenborn's *Der dritte Blick*, June 1956), and acknowledging the injustice of some of its own earlier attacks on Western authors (e.g. Cwojdrak's rehabilitation of Richter in a review of December 1955 after an ideological assault on him in February 1954); Deicke's revision (September 1956) of the dismissal of Gottfried Benn as a decadent nihilist in October 1954). This contrasts dramatically with the almost total exclusion (Brecht being the obvious exception) of East German literature from the FRG in the same period.

There was, of course, a highly problematic assumption behind *NDL*'s Popular Front programme: that there could be agreement on the acceptable limits of 'humanistic' literature, and that the already deeply rooted Western suspicions of ideological motives behind such conciliatory overtures could be assuaged. Its attacks on the publication in the West of unrepentant ex-Nazi authors such as Grimm, Blunck and Dwinger (February 1954) and on the flourishing market for cheap 'Landserromane' (August 1957) would presumably have met with widespread support, but the status of an Ernst Jünger or a communist renegade like Theodor Plievier could not have been resolved in a situation where *NDL* was attempting to equate anti-communism with all forms of militarism and neo-fascism (May 1954). Its response to the outbursts of established West German authors such as Hermann Kesten and Hermann Kasack against East Germany's cultural institutions and leading authors was to assume that they were part of a campaign orchestrated by the Bonn government (August and September 1954), while it regularly identified *Der Monat* as little more than an organ of the CIA.

There was some evidence, however, that *NDL*'s initiative to re-establish a sense of cultural unity was making an impact in the FRG, despite the blanket ban on East German publications. The Stuttgart journal *Die Kultur* (1953–62) aroused hopes for a time that it might become a partner in this bridge-building activity. Early in 1955 it expressed considerable admiration for what *NDL* was doing (as the nationally orientated counterpart to the cosmopolitan *Sinn und Form*):

> [es] muß zu dieser Zeitschrift [*NDL*] gesagt werden, daß man als westdeutscher Schriftsteller schon bei ihrem Anblick neidisch werden möchte: denn ein ähnliches Organ, das sich auch nur annähernd auf solcher Basis mit unserem Leben und Wirken, unseren Nöten und Wünschen als Schriftsteller befaßt, besitzen wir nicht. (as reported in February 1955, p. 13)

NDL's success was viewed by *Die Kultur* as exposing the bankruptcy of the 'Taktik des Totschweigens' in the FRG. This provided *NDL* with a welcome opportunity to modify its unilateral approach to its all-German objectives, by suggesting the creation of a 'Deutsches Literaturforum', in which each journal would regularly publish and discuss examples of the work of authors from the other state. After a delay which appeared to derive from internal political pressure on *Die Kultur* (editorial of November 1955), a breakthrough was achieved in 1956. (The successful Fourth Writers' Congress, which had been fully supported by *NDL* in its efforts to promote a 'Nationalliteratur' freed from stalinist constraints, helped to pave the way.) The launching of the Literaturforum was announced by *NDL* as a 'realer Schritt' towards mutual understanding, and *Die Kultur* was praised as 'eine in der Bundesrepublik tapfer gegen Remilitarisierung und Refaschisierung auftretende unabhängige Publikation' (July 1956, pp. 7–8). But it all came to nothing. If *NDL* is to be believed, the editor of *Die Kultur* was again pressurised into denying all knowledge of their agreement before this forum became a reality (editorial of October 1956); in any case, the political aftermath of the Hungarian popular uprising in the autumn of 1956 presumably ensured that there was no possibility of reviving the idea thereafter.[11]

NDL's efforts to broaden the base of literature available in the GDR were clearly also intended to stimulate the creative originality of younger East German authors. The great shortfall in this aspect of its endeavours was, however, its editorial blindness, amidst its general promotion of the exile generation as models to be emulated, to the radical aesthetic represented by the work of Bertolt Brecht. Despite the fact that *Tage der Kommune* launched the revitalised *NDL* in January 1954 and was rapidly followed by the first publication of Brecht's crucial contribution to the realism debate of the 1930s, 'Weite und Vielfalt der realistischen Schreibweise' (May 1954), the dominant source of the conception of realism on which the journal sought to build a new German literature was Georg Lukács. Brecht's essay has subsequently been recognised as a seminal text in the development of a non-prescriptive Socialist Realism.[12] In *NDL*'s early years, however, the number of texts it published which significantly extend realism in the way Brecht has urged could be counted on the fingers of one hand: Erwin Strittmatter's *Tinko* (October 1953) and *Der Wundertäter* (January 1956), Stephan Hermlin's anti-heroic perspective on 17 June 1953, *Die Kommandeuse* (October 1954), and the 'hard realism' of Karl Mundstock's war story *Bis zum letzten Mann* (March 1956) are amongst the rare exceptions.

Instead, we have *NDL*'s young literary theoretician, Christa Wolf, embarking, also in January 1954, on the quest for a new German epic able to meet the criteria established by Lukács. Her articles and reviews of the period 1954–7 find a remarkable range of texts variously lacking the totality which, in her view, ought to be within their reach. The specifically national subject matter for a revival of the 'Tradition des großen Gesellschaftsromans' (the opening phrase of her first contribution) clearly exists: the abortive German revolution of 1918, treated in Ehm Welk's 938-page novel *Im Morgennebel*, but with a 'spätbürgerliche Furcht vor dem großen Pathos' (January 1954); the Second World War ('der große Roman über diesen Krieg, von Deutschland aus geschrieben'), to which the West German author Peter Bamm's bestseller *Die unsichtbare Flagge* fails to do justice (March 1955); and the post-war process of personal as well as social reconstruction amidst the complexities of the division of Germany ('wie der Mensch in dieser Welt zu sich selbst finden kann'), of which ideologically opposed authors like Rudolf Fischer and Hans Erich Nossack provide perceptive, yet unsatisfactory, accounts (November 1955, April 1957). There was, however, an early sign of conflict between these theoretical preconceptions and Wolf's sensitivity to creative originality, in her review of Strittmatter's *Tinko*. Despite Strittmatter's use of the limited first-person perspective of his youthful protagonist, and the unaccustomed 'Verfremdungseffekt' (Brecht's name is not mentioned!) this produces in the portrayal of post-war Germany, Wolf has to acknowledge that 'selbst in einem begrenzten Stoff' she has detected 'die Totalität eines Weltbildes' and 'die innere Einheit eines wirklichen Kunstwerkes' (July 1955, pp. 139–44).[13] This is, significantly, a level of praise which no work conforming to Lukács's criteria of realism achieves from Wolf in the *NDL* of the middle 1950s.

While *NDL* failed markedly to fulfil its hopes of revitalising German literature in both states virtually overnight, it had nevertheless established by 1956 an editorial identity and self-confidence which helped it to withstand for a good year the repressive measures which followed the crushing of the Hungarian uprising. 1957 saw the publication of important creative works such as Heinar Kipphardt's *Der Hund des Generals* (January 1957), Franz Fühmann's *Das Gottesgericht* (March, 1957) and Heiner Müller's *Der Lohndrücker* (May 1957), without any marked reduction of its efforts to promote West German authors, while, in the area of literary criticism, it published the GDR's first assessment of Walter Benjamin (January 1957) and 'Weiskopf der Mittler', the essay by the officially maligned Hans Mayer, which provided a coded endorsement of its open-minded policies (October 1957).[14] It was only after the SED's infamous Kulturkonferenz of October 1957 that *NDL* was forced to jettison its all-German cultural aspirations, following the dismissal of its entire original editorial board of Bredel, Cwojdrak and Deicke.

The main source of Christa Wolf's embarrassment about her association with *NDL* was probably her period on its editorial board in 1958–9. The first editorial of the interregnum from January to April 1958, when *NDL*'s rubric stated simply 'Herausgegeben vom deutschen Schriftstellerverband', included a contribution by her; she was named on the new editorial board in May 1958, and was promoted to chief editor between June and November 1959, until the demands of the 'cultural revolution' took her away from Berlin to the industrial front line in Halle. There was little room for editorial manoeuvre during this period of ideological retrenchment: the forthright 'Unsere Meinung' section was dropped after March 1958, and cultural contact of any kind with the Federal Republic would have aroused suspicions of the now unacceptable search for a 'Third Way' between communism and capitalism. The supply of work by the exile generation seemed to be rapidly drying up: Brecht, Becher, Feuchtwanger and Döblin all died between 1956 and 1958, without satisfying the GDR's cultural–political hunger for progressive masterpieces. All of this threatened to reduce *NDL* to its status of 1953 as an outlet for mediocre Socialist Realism.

The only significant new Western author to be reviewed in 1958–9 was a Swiss, Max Frisch, who was adjudged, in his *Homo Faber*, to be politically at the same 'kritische Grenze' which many of his West German counterparts were felt to have reached in the middle 1950s (July 1950) – and even this interest was short-lived, once Frisch's Büchner Prize speech, which emphasised his equal lack of commitment to both ideological systems, had been denounced as 'die große Kapitulation' (March 1959). The keynote was now the failure of Western authors generally to sustain the political impetus of their earlier work. It fell to Günther Cwojdrak (determined now, it seems, to demonstrate that his earlier editorial role had not been a subversive one), to show that H. H. Kirst's 'Third World War' novel *Keiner kommt davon* was no better than the mass of West German 'Landserromane' in its anti-communist prejudice (February 1958), and to accuse Nossack, Koeppen and Böll of a 'Rückzug vom Realismus' on the flimsy basis of interim works such as Böll's *Irisches Tagebuch* (April 1959).[15]

This was only one side of a curiously contradictory attitude to West German authors. Such dismissals of their creative progress were accompanied by attempts to use the emerging nuclear weapons debate in the Federal Republic as a way of soliciting their political support. Following the federal election of September 1957, when Adenauer's CDU won an absolute majority for a manifesto advocating the arming of the Bundeswehr with nuclear weapons, *NDL*'s coverage of the FRG was focused on this prime source of moral and political dissent. Anti-nuclear writing, notably Ingeborg Bachmann's poem 'Freies Geleit' (October 1957) and Günther Weisenborn's *Göttinger Kantate* (January 1959), was featured periodically, as were lists of signatories to protest documents, in the illusory expectation (after the events of 1956 in Hungary) that they would accept the East's propaganda view that only Western weapons escalation represented a threat to world peace. The official Soviet view of its overwhelming interest in the peaceful use of nuclear energy was put in the poem 'Das Atom' by *NDL*'s other ex-editor, Günther Deicke (May 1958).[16]

Christa Wolf's editorial contributions reveal the strains of a sincere personal endeavour to justify *NDL*'s sudden narrowing of focus to essentially parochial concerns. The contradictions in her programmatic articles, 'Kann man eigentlich über alles schreiben?' (June 1958) and 'Eine Lektion über Wahrheit und Objektivität' (July 1958), have been recognised, since Manfred Jäger's pioneering analysis of 1973, as exposing the self-doubts of an author with 'überhaupt kein Talent zum Zynismus' who did not allow herself to become simply the 'Sprachrohr einer kulturpolitischen Zielsetzung'.[17] Although Wolf clearly endorsed *NDL*'s editorial willingness to give itself a new identity as the sponsor of a new industrial literature, the 'Bitterfelder Weg' (June 1959), it was to be a short-lived personal commitment. It led her, however, to attempt to eliminate the wider German dimension of her earlier literary analyses. Otto Gotsche's *Die Fahne von Kriwoj Rog*, for all its historical German context (the miners' uprising of 1921 in Mansfeld), is now presented by Wolf in terms of Soviet solidarity, with the emphasis on the symbolism of the flag, presented to the strikers by their Ukrainian comrades: this is simply '*sozialistische* Literatur der Gegenwart' (my emphasis), marked by 'das saubere Klassenbewußtsein, die durch bittere Erfahrung erworbene Härte' of Gotsche's characters, while its stylistic weaknesses are of secondary importance (May 1959, pp. 3–7). More surprisingly, in her interview with Anna Seghers on the publication of *Die Entscheidung* – the beginning of Wolf's long involvement with Seghers's work – she suggests that the focus of the novel, 'Treffpunkt der wichtigsten Fäden, das Entwicklungszentrum für die bedeutendsten Gestalten', is 'die sowjetische Besatzungszone und später unsere Republik'; the fact that the action covers 'andere Länder und Kontinente' is simply mentioned in passing (August 1959, pp. 52–7).

Since this attempt on the part of *NDL* to insulate itself culturally from the Federal Republic was largely a response to ideological pressure, it is not surprising that the SED's reversion to a more conciliatory approach to German–German relations early in 1960 found the journal eager to re-establish its credentials as an informed commentator on West German literature. Developments on the international stage – the hopes of a summit meeting between Khrushchev and Eisenhower to end years of Cold War hostility – coincided neatly with an upsurge of socially critical writing in the FRG in encouraging *NDL* to extend its horizons again. The tone of its commentaries was now, however, markedly aggressive: nowhere is this more obvious than in the first contributions of its new critic of West German culture, Hermann Kant. The Hamburg-born author, who had made a modest creative debt on the pages of *NDL* with three stories in 1957–8, began by tackling Günter Grass's *Die Blechtrommel*, which he acknowledged as having some political substance, given its author's obvious opposition to 'Faschisten, Revanchisten, Ostlandreiter und heuchelnde Kleriker'. But this guarded respect is virtually swamped by his outpourings on *Die Blechtrommel* as a cynical attempt to provoke a cultural scandal and make a fortune by indulging the West German public's taste for 'Kot-, Eiter- und Spermaphantasien'. Kant's concluding suggestion that Goethe would have provided better models for a literary protagonist than the 'physisches und psychisches Monstrum' Oskar Mazerath of Grass's imagination underlined the gulf which had opened up between the two cultures since the middle 1950s (May 1960, pp. 151–5).[18] It also looked as if Kant was ready to turn his polemical attentions to the otherwise unmentionable GDR exile Uwe Johnson, whom he referred to in his next contribution as the 'Mutmaßer Johnson', the 'Dumm-Dünn-Aufgießer' of William Faulkner...' (August 1960).

But by then the impact of the SED's Kulturkonferenz of April 1960, at which the spirit of the Popular Front had again been revived, was being felt. The official mood changed to one of respect for West German authors resisting the 'Kriegspolitik von Bonn'.[19] *NDL* was given a new chief editor, Wolfgang Joho, an established author, born in Karlsruhe, who had contributed regularly to the journal's coverage of culture in the FRG in the 1954–7 period, and whose creative interests were centred on identity conflicts arising from the division of Germany.[20] Joho's first editorial – a report on the Kulturkonferenz – revealed his intention to use the general dissatisfaction expressed there at the poor quality of recent East German writing as a justification for reviving the notion of a 'sozialistische Nationalliteratur', now rooted in the GDR alone, but 'über die Grenzen unserer Republik wirkend' and 'vorbildlich ... für ganz Deutschland' (August 1960, pp. 3–5). This paved the way to a return to a more positive reception of 'humanistic' West German literature and an increase in coverage to something resembling the levels of 1954–7. Excerpts began to appear again (accompanied by detailed reviews) of important novels – Christian Geißler's *Anfrage* (October 1960), Heinrich Böll's *Billard um halbzehn* (November 1960) and Martin Walser's *Halbzeit* (March–April 1961) – while other Western authors – Hans Werner Richter (December 1960), Hans Magnus Enzensberger (June 1961) and Ingeborg Bachmann (December 1961) – were the subject of relatively balanced articles (the latter two by the young Dieter Schlenstedt, the GDR's most respected Germanist of today). There was a new openness to the modernist tradition in twentieth-century poetry: Gerhard Wolf boldly suggested that poets such as Enzensberger, Bachmann, Günter Eich and Paul Celan had absorbed the innovations of Mayakovsky and Brecht rather better than most of their East German counterparts (February 1961). The tone of Hermann Kant's contributions moderated accordingly: his article on the volume of essays *Ich lebe in der Bundesrepublik*, took seriously the statement of its editor, Wolfgang Weyrauch, that he and his fellow-authors were intent on transforming the FRG into 'ein Modell des Maßes, der Vernunft und einer friedlichen Ordnung', although Kant still criticised them for their negativity towards the GDR (March 1961). There were, of course, limits to this *rapprochement*: Günther Cwojdrak, for example, provided a cautionary reminder that the 'flagranter Antihumanismus' of the militaristic *Trivialliteratur* of a J. M. Bauer or a H. G. Konsalik had a much more profound social impact in the Federal Republic than the critically respectable work of a Böll or a Koeppen (May 1961). But overall this represented a striking attempt by *NDL* to re-establish its 'Literaturforum' role, in the face of continuing West German indifference to literary life in the GDR.[21]

This change of policy also allowed Christa Wolf to restore the national dimension which she had loyally attempted to eliminate from her writing during her period of editorship.[22] Her conception of the literary realism required to come to grips with the issue of divided Germany had still not changed, however, as her review of a West German anthology of prose indicated:

> Die subtile Wahrheit dieser Literatur, leidenschaftslos, wohltemperiert, vorgetragen, regt nicht auf, weil sie Randwahrheit, Teilwahrheit bleibt. Ins Zentrum sozialer und nationaler Fragen stößt keine dieser Geschichten vor. (June 1960, pp. 126–9)

In a speech of March 1961 Wolf showed herself entirely in tune with Joho's editorial policy for *NDL*, in rejecting the 'Provinzialismus' of an industrial literature which left West German readers cold, as a distraction from the ultimate goal of a 'sozialistische deutsche Nationalliteratur'.[23] She now felt free to discuss Anna Seghers's *Die Entscheidung* in the terms she had manifestly avoided in her interview of 1959: as the first great epic of post-war German literature, on the strength of its broad portrayal of the effects of national division: here 'die Probleme unserer Nation' are integrated into

> die große Weltproblematik . . . *ein* Land ist der Schauplatz des Buches, was einem seiner Teile geschieht, geschieht ihm als Ganzem, geschieht jedem seiner Bewohner. Einheit wird nicht proklamiert, sie ist vorhanden, widersprüchlich, unterbrochen, aber nicht zerstört und nicht zerstörbar. (May 1961, pp. 49–65)

NDL had thus placed itself, as in 1956, in the vanguard of preparations for a Writers' Congress intended to demonstrate, against all the counter-pressures of Cold War politics, that authors in both German states still had substantial shared concerns. The East German Writers' Union invited a delegation of its West German counterparts to attend the Fifth Congress, held in May 1961, and so became host to the previously much maligned Günter Grass. It also arranged that Anna Seghers's wide-ranging presidential speech would be accompanied by another by Hermann Kant taking stock of recent West German literature. Reading Wolfgang Joho's report on the Congress, it would appear that this East–West dialogue had been a pronounced success, fulfilling the hope which *NDL* itself had originally nurtured: 'Zum erstenmal wurde auf einem so großen und repräsentativen Forum eine echte Zwiesprache mit westdeutschen Schriftstellern geführt.' This was the proof that 'die Auseinandersetzung mit Westdeutschland und das Ringen um eine neue deutsche Nationalliteratur nicht voneinander zu trennen sind'

(August 1961, p. 11). The reality appears less euphoric, however, when Günter Grass's response to Hermann Kant (not published in *NDL* alongside the main speeches) is examined: he spoke out angrily against Kant's distorted presentation of West German literature, at the GDR's blindness to the work of its own émigrés, such as Uwe Johnson, and at the hollowness of the rhetoric which had reduced its cultural spokesmen to 'Geranien am Podium'.[24] For all *NDL's* efforts to demonstrate that there still was only one German literature (a point reiterated by Alfred Kurella at the Congress), Grass's criticisms were a reminder that, from the Western perspective, the split had long since occurred and the way back to mutual understanding would be a long and difficult one.

Whether Grass made any direct impact on his East German audience is impossible to assess, but this period generally was a watershed in the creative development of *NDL's* yonger generation of critics, bringing home to them the obsolescence of their Lukácsian ideas of epic totality as a basis for a new German literature. Ironically, the shock of the final physical separation of the two German states in August 1961 seemed to impel authors like Wolf and Kant to liberate themselves from the stylistic norms which had hitherto made the work of their Western counterparts so inaccessible intellectually. *Der geteilte Himmel* (1963) and *Die Aula* (1965) – with a Western dimension but no aspiration to 'balanced' portrayal of the two states, and personalised narrators making no claim to didactic omniscience – were to become the GDR's first enduring contributions to what might today be regarded as post-war 'Nationalliteratur'. Wolf's radical development is just becoming evident in her review of Karl-Heinz Jakobs's *Beschreibung eines Sommers*. Here she detects a new quality of authenticity ('Lebenswirklichkeit') arising from the unconventional first-person narrative of a problematic hero, in a work describing the conflict of 'das Leben, eine große Leidenschaft' with 'Normen der Gesellschaft' in the GDR (October 1961, p. 131).

NDL itself provided a surprising continuity of focus on the issue of national cultural identity throughout Wolfgang Joho's period as chief editor, in the face of the SED's reversion to the politics of 'Abgrenzung' following the crisis of 1961. It was probably his robust criticism in 1965 of the 'provinzielle Enge und mangelnde Modernität' of the bulk of East German literature (March 1965, pp. 88–97) which finally cost him his job: he was ousted following the repressive Central Committee plenum of December 1965. Only then is there a significant break in the editorial policy to which *NDL* owes its early claim to distinctiveness. Although the journal made little real progress in its first decade towards becoming a literary forum, in the sense of initiating a genuine dialogue between authors in the two German states, it at least succeeded in keeping the channels of cultural communication open through the bleakest period of the Cold War.

Notes

1 All references to issues of *Neue Deutsche Literatur* are included in the body of the text in this abbreviated form, with page numbers added only in the case of quotations.

2 Wolf has adhered since the early 1970s to a dismissive view of her early criticism as 'unschöpferische, rein ideologisierende Germanistik': see her interview with Joachim Walther in the latter's *Meinetwegen Schmetterlinge: Gespräche mit Schriftstellern*, Berlin, 1973, p. 129.

3 M. Reich-Ranicki, *Auch dort erzählt Deutschland*, Munich, 1960, pp. 7–9.

4 F. J. Raddatz, *Traditionen und Tendenzen*, Frankfurt am Main, 1972, pp. 7–69 (esp. 57–61).

5 See M. Jäger, *Kultur und Politik in der DDR: Ein historischer Abriß*, Cologne, 1982, pp. 29–33.

6 See G. Deicke, 'Über meine Jahre als NDL-Redakteur', in *Sinn und Form*, 2, 1988, pp. 330–41.

7 For the wider context of this debate see my chapter ' "Breadth and Diversity": Socialist Realism in the GDR', in *European Socialist Realism*, edited by M. Scriven and D. Tate, Oxford and New York, 1988, pp. 60–78.

8 I. C. Streul, *Westdeutsche Literatur in der DDR*, Stuttgart, 1988, pp. 9–12.

9 *Ibid.*, pp. 33–47.

10 Streul's numerical summary of the West German material in *Sinn und Form* and *NDL* in the 1950s suggests virtual parity of importance (*ibid.*, pp. 23–6), whereas the predominance of her footnote references to *NDL* gives a truer indication of the two journals' difference in emphasis.

11 There is, significantly, no mention of this in Hermann Kant's *Neues Deutschland* article of 1962 on the demise of *Die Kultur*, which saw it as a victim of 'Third Way' delusions: see his *Zu den Unterlagen*, Berlin and Weimar, 1981, pp. 32–6.

12 See above, note 7.

13 See the analysis of this review in Stephan Bock, *Literatur – Gesellschaft – Nation: Materielle und ideelle Rahmenbedingungen der frühen DDR-Literatur*, Stuttgart, 1980, pp. 253–6.

14 The exiled author F. C. Weiskopf had become a member of *NDL*'s editorial board in 1954. Although he died the following year, he had rapidly become associated with the journal's new identity.

15 Cwojdrak's attack on Koeppen in particular seems implausible, since he had gone to some lengths in his final editorial for *NDL* to defend Koeppen against 'massive Diskriminierungen, die jede Diskussion ausschließen' in the GDR (October 1957, pp. 6–7).

16 The main documents on which this campaign was based are now usefully collected in Klaus Wagenbach's anthology *Vaterland, Muttersprache: Deutsche Schriftsteller und ihr Staat von 1945 bis heute*, Berlin, 1979, pp. 139–58.

17 See M. Jäger, *Sozialliteraten: Funktion und Selbstverständnis der Schriftsteller in der DDR*, Düsseldorf, 1973, pp. 15–20.

18 Grass's poems *Die Vorzüge der Windhühner* had earlier been treated dismissively by Heiner Müller (January 1957).

19 See Streul, *Westdeutsche Literatur*, pp. 15–16.

20 Joho's best-known creative work is his subsequent novel *Das Klassentreffen* (1968).

21 Reich-Ranicki's pioneering series of articles for *Die Welt* in 1959 grew into the East German half of his *Deutsche Literatur in West und Ost* of 1963. An unsigned article in *NDL* accused him of blatant opportunism for the way he had altered opinions expressed in work previously published in the GDR (March 1960).

22 Wolf's review of Rudolf Bartsch's *Geliebt bis ans bittere Ende* (November 1958) was a curious exception amongst her editorial contributions. In it she proposed a debate (which never materialised) on Bartsch's portrayal of divided Germany.

23 C. Wolf, *Die Dimension des Autors*, Darmstadt and Neuwied, 1987, pp. 381–3.

24 See *V Deutscher Schriftstellerkongreß: Referate und Beiträge*, edited by Deutscher Schriftstellerverband, Berlin, 1961, pp. 178–80.

The obstructed dialogue: a discourse analysis of the Schiller celebrations in 1955 and 1959

Maximilian Nutz

In his acceptance speech at the Schillerpreis ceremony held in Mannheim on 9 November 1959, Friedrich Dürrenmatt expressly departed from the traditional pattern of literary hagiography by rejecting the cult of classicism:

> Es geschieht nicht aus Respektlosigkeit, wenn ich es unterlasse, Schiller ins Absolute, Endgültige, Vorbildliche aufzublähen, überhaupt mich so aufzuführen, als wären die Klassiker die heiligsten Güter der Nation, nicht weil ich die Klassiker für kein Gut halte, sondern weil ich den Nationen in dieser Sache mißtraue.[1]

Dürrenmatt's mistrust is understandable, for the history of Schiller's reception, more than that of any other writer, shows him to have been exploited for political and cultural advantage.[2] Schiller became the 'Zeitgenosse aller Epochen'[3] not only because the ideas in his work were made topical but because he has been turned into a monument, a national hero; the 'Kampfgenosse' as a paragon of human proportions. After 1945 West German academics sought by means of objective analysis (as they saw it) to free the portrayal of Schiller from the 'Klischeevorstellungen und Etiketten'[4] typical of Schillerian reception history. But in the GDR, so the West German argument went, efforts continued to be made (at the commemorations in 1955 and 1959) to contemporise Schiller in another political light. West Germans saw the guidelines laid down in the cultural policy of the SED as an attempt to misuse Schiller as an intellectual forebear of the communist state, and to proclaim the GDR the 'einzige und wahre Erbin von Schillers Ideengut'.[5] Meanwhile, in the GDR, the analyses of West German Schiller research were seen as no more than subtle propaganda for the capitalist system. The Schiller committee of the GDR drew a sharp distinction between their celebration of the bicentenary of Schiller's birth and 'die verfälschenden "Schiller-Ehrungen" der Machthaber von Bonn, die im Zeichen der antinationalen, für unser Volk verhängnisvollen NATO-Politik stehen'.[6]

At first sight it may seem as though the speeches of the two commemorative years in East and West were merely an expression of the wholly different discourses which resulted from political and social developments in the divided Germany. Contemporaries had the impression 'daß man hüben und drüben eine andere Sprache spricht, auch wenn man Schiller sagt'.[7] There were more than enough reproaches and accusations from both sides to prevent any possibility of a dialogue on the common cultural tradition. Such abuse mostly took the form of Cold War rhetoric, used by commemorative speakers in the GDR, and to some extent by the West German press. Many West German academics tried to distance themselves from the popular pastime of deepening the German divide by justifying the integration of each state into its respective power bloc.[8] Yet their success was limited.

All the polemics and ideological distortions in the GDR celebrations point to a political and social context which speakers in the Federal Republic preferred to omit from their analyses of Schiller in favour of 'reinere Motive'.[9] This is the framework in which the commemorative celebrations take on their communicative functions. An historical examination of the changes in the portrayal of Schiller does not take these functions into account.[10] An examination of the socio-political situation seems to reveal two separate languages. But a discourse analysis of texts taken from the celebrations shows what connects these apparently discrete languages, and demonstrates how the different strategies and functions of the speeches prevented the emergence of the kind of dialogue expected by those who still believed in the binding power of a cultural tradition which transcends political barriers.

Let us first of all look at how the differences in the Schiller addresses during the two commemorative years manifested themselves, how contemporaries saw these differences and how they appear today. In the resolution of the SED's Politbüro on 25 January 1955, essential features concerning the portrayal of Schiller were established,[11] which, in the nature of 'ideological guidance', shaped the commemorations on various levels.[12] The GDR's monolithic picture of Schiller was 'academically' substantiated in essays and lectures and then further developed in the commemorative speeches under different aspects. In contrast to this there seemed to be a 'Vielfalt der Methoden und Ergebnisse'[13] in the Federal Republic which appeared 'außerordentlich inkohärent'.[14] The Schiller celebrations in the GDR were integrated into the co-ordinated presentation of an unquestioned 'cultural heritage', and thus were being used not only for purposes of domestic policy – to help construct a socialist national consciousness – but also to present the GDR abroad as a practitioner of humanist ideals.[15] Meanwhile, in the Federal Republic, commemorative speakers voiced a certain embarrassment with respect to Schiller,[16] as he seemed to some 'heute auch geistig endgültig begraben zu sein'.[17] The picture of Schiller in the East, as a revolutionary critic of social and political oppression, a patriotic fighter for national unity and a poet whose pathos was an expression of the 'reine Gefühle und schöne Hoffnungen des Volkes',[18] seemed to have little in common with the new contours drawn by the Federal Republic commemorative speakers, who were depicting an artist with the 'Neigung zum l'art pour l'art im Spätwerk',[19] a proclaimer of personal freedom for the individual which could only be realised in the 'Reinheit des Untergangs',[20] but not in systems of social order, a dramatic portrayer of 'Fragwürdigkeiten und Zwielichtigkeiten des menschlichen Daseins und besonders des politischen Handelns',[21] and a sceptical analyst of the 'Antinomien der menschlichen Gesellschaft'[22] which could only be resolved by means of a contemporary 'ästhetische Erziehung'.

By no means did the celebrations give credence to the hope that Schiller's 'geistiges Vermächtnis' was 'nicht teilbar'.[23] A bilateral Schiller committee was set up during the preparations for the celebrations in 1955, and further contacts were made both through arrangements for guests of honour at Weimar and Marbach and through guest performances on stages in both parts of Germany. These were 'Kontakte, . . . an deren Möglichkeit man vielfach kaum noch glauben wollte'.[24] And yet the contrasts in the aims of the celebrations were obvious.

Moreover, the barrier which separated those who advocated political contemporisation of the national hero and poet of freedom in the divided Germany, and those who claimed that Schiller's 'true' message could be discovered precisely by relinquishing such 'zeitentsprungene Wünsche und Ziele',[25] was not located solely along the border between the East and West zones. To some extent it also existed within the Western commemorations. The

Kuratorium Unteilbares Deutschland staged an all-German Schiller celebration in West Berlin, where the audience used Carlo Schmid's exposition on Schiller's concept of freedom as an opportunity to stage a political demonstration which stopped the speech.[26] A speech which Fritz von Unruh was meant to deliver to young people in Düsseldorf, in which he was to denounce the misuse of Schiller's conception of freedom by American imperialism and Bonn's policies of remilitarisation, was cancelled for political reasons.[27] In accordance with the resolution of the SED's Politbüro, the KPD used a brochure entitled 'Zum Schillerjahr' to place the commemorations in the context of the contemporary present, 'da das deutsche Volk um seine nationale Existenz gegen den amerikanischen Imperialismus kämpft'.[28] In contrast, an article in the *Frankfurter Allgemeine Zeitung* praised the Stuttgart commemorations for not dragging expressions such as 'Freiheit, Menschheit, Nation, Einheit ... in den gefährlichen Gebrauch der Tagespolitik'.[29]

A typical feature of the addresses is that each side accused the other of falsifying the image of the writer and of political exploitation. In the resolution proclaimed by the SED's Politbüro, Schiller's reception in West Germany is presented as the continuation of a 'Verfälschung durch die Ideologen des preußisch–deutschen Militarismus, des wilhelmischen Imperialismus und des Faschismus', which reinterprets Schiller's great notion of the free development of the personality as 'die kapitalistische "Freiheit" der Unterdrückung der menschlichen Persönlichkeit durch Ausbeutung und Krieg'.[30] The 'objective' historical causes of such a reinterpretation are considered to be that the ruling 'imperialistic bourgeoisie' in West Germany have long relinquished the progressive spirit of the bourgeois age as embodied in Schiller, and so deny their own past.[31] In his speech at the Weimar National Theatre, the Minister of Culture, Johannes R. Becher, caricatured West German politicians and commemorative speakers as modern embodiments of the 'Finsterlinge und Bösewichte' in Schiller's dramas, who 'Herrn Hofrat von Schiller ihre Reverenz erweisen, um ihrer Schäbigkeit und Niedertracht eine Art von klassischer Legitimät zu verleihen'.[32]

But criticism of the political integration of Schiller into the GDR made by commemorative speakers in the Federal Republic was rarely so direct as the attack launched by Theodor Heuss, who, in his speech at the celebrations of the German Schiller Society in

Stuttgart, spoke of an 'arges Unterfangen . . . den völlig wehrlosen Schiller posthum zum unbefragten Ehrenmitglied einer Partei zu machen', and distanced himself from the embarrassing 'Formen und Formeln politischer Aktualisierung'.[33] But, in a more restrained manner, Germanists in the Federal Republic did implicitly pass judgement on the Schiller celebrations in the GDR, by explicitly distancing themselves from any attempts to make Schiller's reception history relevant to topical issues, attempts which, in their view, showed a confusion of 'dichterische Gestalt mit ideologischer Kundgabe'.[34] By placing their image of Schiller 'oberhalb der Tageskonflikte',[35] in a timeless realm of existentialist, philosophical and aesthetic dicta, they tacitly dissociated themselves from the GDR's contemporisation of Schiller in commemorative speeches. In such speeches he was interpreted purely in the context of the historical conditions needed for emancipating the bourgeoisie, and celebrated as a model for the modern struggle over national unity.

If it is a part of the Cold War 'die andere Seite jeweils zu verkennen',[36] then it is possible to consider the attacks and dissociations, claims to truth and ideological reproaches in the context of the political and cultural climate of the 1950s.[37] But in the Schiller commemorations these mutual misunderstandings did not directly follow the strategies of the ideological debate between East and West, despite both sides' claims with respect to the other. Instead they were determined by the development of different discourses on both sides of the border, discourses in which the Schiller debate is embedded.

When talking about Schiller, speechmakers in both parts of Germany were also talking about problems which had arisen from divergent political, social and cultural developments, whereby one part was 'stets im andern als täglich neu gestelltes Problem mitenthalten'.[38] In the GDR celebrations, this asymmetrical structure gave rise to aggressive rhetoric of accusation, exclusion and self-aggrandisement, whilst political abstinence characterised the celebrations in the Federal Republic. So, in each case, references to the other part of Germany must be viewed in the light of the discourses which laid down the pattern of thought for the speeches.

One common heritage from the history of Schiller reception belongs to both East and West Germany; the way Schiller was exploited and falsified by fascism.[39] After 1945 the SED was able to take up the fight to save Germany's 'cultural heritage' from the 'fascist barbarians' by means of an 'antifascist and democratic' plan of renewal. This struggle had been an important element of the KPD's policy of the Popular Front in the 1930s, and by continuing it the SED saw a political role for classical humanism.[40] Just as the Goethe celebrations of 1949 were used to emphasise that the heritage left by Goethe now lay in the 'starke Hände der Arbeiterklasse',[41] the 150th anniversary of Schiller's death was used to depict the working classes as the 'wahre Erbin der edelsten Ideen'.[42] Becher announced that for the first time in the history of the German people there was a state which would do justice to Schiller's legacy, which would end the 'Tragik Schillers'; that is, both his personal tragedy of having to wait in vain for a political movement which would realise his ideas, and the tragedy of the subsequent falsification of those ideas.[43] In this way the GDR assigned to itself an almost Messianic role as the fulfilment of progressive and cultural developments in the history of Germany, a role which can barely hide its function to legitimise the GDR as a state.

The history of Schiller reception was an onerous legacy for West German literary criticism after 1945, evoking as it did memories of the ideological function of German studies in the Third Reich. In his report on 'Schiller-Deutung von 1937 bis 1953', Benno von Wiese palliatively discovered an 'Ermüdung des Interesses an Schiller', which he explained as a result of the 'anarchischen Eindruck' left behind by the 'Schiller Renaissance' of the Third Reich which was based on intellectual history and ideology.[44] By excluding examples of the ideological exploitation of Schiller from the review, von Wiese's report suppressed the socio-political determinants of Schiller research and reduced the confrontation with the past to matters of methodological change. In the shift from idealistic and existentialist interpretation to formal analysis,[45] a new picture of Schiller's 'artistic greatness' developed which threatened to diminish the historical dimension of his work. Where research still questioned the meaning of the works' 'Ideengehalt', as did von Wiese and May,[46] sceptics and realists were discovered, finding the tragic inability of human beings to achieve self-fulfilment embedded in the fundamental contradiction between ideal and reality.

Avoidance of concrete historical reality by means of formal analysis or by using an updated existentialist and anthropological approach determined the portrayal of Schiller at the commemorations

of 1955 in the Federal Republic. Despite some attempts to avoid
presenting a falsified history of Schiller reception, it was precisely
the chapter on fascist interpretation that was omitted, so as not
to insult Schiller 'mit unseren schlimmen Erinnerungen'.[47] In Fritz
Martini's work the world of history and politics appeared as 'Leiden
und Schicksal', as the 'Dunkel des Daseins' which confronted the
individual in his or her autonomous moral decision.[48] The reliance
on attitudes of mind and on philosophical positions typical of the
'Restauration' in the Federal Republic[49] was clear from the terms
in which the image of modernity was described, in which the
individual was meant to regain the transcendental meaning of his
or her existence in accordance with Schiller's ideal. Where the
'Despotie des Kollektiven' reigned, 'Verzweiflung am Menschen'
spread as a result of the 'Aufstand der Massen und Dämonen', and
where the individual was threatened by the 'Sog des Allgemeinen'
people could only preserve their freedom if they tragically suffered the 'antinomies' of the 'terrestrial' and turned towards the
'divine' in the 'Übergang zum Erhabenen'.[50] Through the portrayal
of Schiller in the GDR, literary research in the Federal Republic
was confronted with the parts of its own history which it had
relinquished or suppressed. Such loaded terms as 'Nation', 'Volk'
and 'deutsch', which in the GDR served to build up a socialist
national identity, had been replaced in the West by patterns of
thinking and values that could be harmonised with the restorative
development in politics and society.[51] By contrast, the West German discovery of the sceptical realist, the problematisation of
'das Pathetische', the discovery of contradictions in Schiller's view
on political emancipation, would, had they been voiced in the
GDR, certainly have led to criticism of the monumentalisation and
heroic stylisation of Schiller. In the absence of a differentiated
marxist approach to Schiller's work, such a process might have
been wholly salutary. Instead of examining new aspects that had
come to light, these aspects were represented as an element of a
Cold War strategy against the GDR: 'Unsere Gegner in Westdeutschland', ran Günther Dahlke's Cold War rhetoric, had attempted
'Schiller in einen volksfremden, antidemokratischen und antinationalen Geisteshelden umzufälschen, um mit ihm "eins" zu
werden.'[52]

In addition to the discourse on cultural heritage, which shifted
away from an anti-fascist, democratic renewal and co-operation
with the intelligentsia, moving more towards the presentation of

national identity, the commemorations in the GDR in 1955 were characterised by the debate over the division and reunification of Germany.[53] The split was deepened when the Federal Republic joined NATO on 5 May 1955, a few days before the 150th anniversary of Schiller's death, and when the GDR was accepted into the Warsaw Pact on 14 May 1955. These developments took place even though the political discussions of previous years had centred on suggestions on how to solve the 'German question'. In order to counter the integration of the Federal Republic into a Western military alliance, the Soviet government and the government of the GDR had continued to propose possible solutions for the German question since 19 September 1950, when a resolution was passed by the European Defence Community at a conference in New York of Foreign Ministers from the three Western powers plus a West German representative. Adenauer and the Western powers saw these suggestions, however, as a strategy to widen the communist sphere of influence through a neutralised Germany. Meanwhile, the East considered the Western suggestion to reunite Germany through 'free elections' as merely a strategy to extend American imperialism.

Policy with regard to reunification in both German states reveals, nevertheless, a distinct symmetry when it comes to ideological strategies; on each side the cause of the division was seen to be the endeavour of the opposite system to expand, doing so by economically, politically, and militarily integrating the part of Germany it had occupied and then aiming for reunification to extend its sphere of power. Both states claimed that they alone represented the true interests of the German people; each accused the other of blocking any productive dialogue that could lead to reunification. As had happened during the celebrations of the Bach year in 1950 and the Beethoven year in 1952, the SED used the Schiller celebrations of 1955 to launch massive attacks on Cold War policies in the Federal Republic. In a speech to mark a tribute to Schiller by German youth in Weimar, Grotewohl portrayed the 'Pariser Todesverträge' as an enslavement of the West German people and as preparation for war-serving monopoly capitalism:

> Machen Adenauer und seine Helfer . . . mit Westdeutschlands Jugend nicht das gleiche wie die Landesfürsten zu Schillers Zeiten? Wollen sie nicht Millionen junge Deutsche an . . . die amerikanischen Milliardäre verschachern . . .?[54]

Against the background of such 'betrayal' of national interests and national culture in the West, young people were called upon to realise Schiller's national longings in a struggle for 'unsere freie, wiedervereinigte Nation'.[55] This, they were told, was a fight with Schiller in the forefront and on their side.[56]

In this way the Schiller celebrations in the GDR became a forceful attempt to present an identity in which important discourses for self-image and self-portrayal were integrated: a claim to be the sole representative of the classicial humanist heritage, the struggle for the national interest of the whole people and therefore for German unity and the historical optimism of the working class 'daß der Sieg unser ist – wo ein Genius wie Schiller unser ist'.[57] Anyone who interpreted these efforts by the GDR as merely a means of compensating for its 'asymmetric' position with respect to the Federal Republic – for the GDR was deficit in economic power and political legitimacy when compared with the Federal Republic[58] – would underestimate the importance of continuity and links with tradition for the development and support of a collective identity, on which importance had also been placed in the Federal Republic for some time.[59] By rediscovering the 'cultural nation', the Federal Republic began to compete with the GDR in its presentation of identity and its adoption of historical heritage, whereas during the Schiller celebrations of 1955 the appropriation of tradition had been reduced to the process of individual analysis. Wherever cultural identity for all the German people was postulated in the interpretation of Schiller's 'German greatness', as in the speech by Carlo Schmid, it came embarrassingly close to being a compensation for the injury to national ego dealt by the defeat in 1945.[60] For Schmid, cultural identity materialised as an intellectual power that was less teleological than devoted to working on the 'ewigen Bau der Menschenbildung' and might therefore also perhaps be able to unite a politically divided world 'unter der Fahne der Freiheit und Schönheit'.[61] If that did not exclude even for Schmid the concrete political struggle for the 'Freiheit . . . eines Volkes, sich in *einem* Hause einzurichten', then the struggle received its higher legitimation through the humanising process in the history of mankind.

Because the celebrations in both parts of Germany were bound into the context of competing or opposing discourses, they failed to fulfil the hopes for a dialogue which some had pinned on the occasion. Even the speech by Thomas Mann, which he gave at the commemorations in Stuttgart and repeated in Weimar, and in which he clearly alluded to the state of the Cold War, became integrated into the rituals and discourses of the time. If, for the SED, the speech was proof of their 'Übereinstimmung mit den friedliebenden demokratischen Kräften in ganz Deutschland',[62] then Theodor Heuss, in his Schiller speech, recalled the 'gift' of this 'Stunde, da das geistreiche Finden von konstitutiven Kräften in des Dichters Werk durchwärmt war vom liebenden Dank an den großgearteten Menschen'.[63] Two languages were used to talk not only about Schiller but also about Thomas Mann. In order for both parts of Germany to be able to regard Mann's speech as a 'highlight', his critical thrust and his appeal for dialogue had naturally to be overlooked. Thomas Mann had called for the healing insight 'daß unter verschiedenen historischen Voraussetzungen, einem anderen sozialen Regime Lebende, auch Menschen sind',[64] and appealed to all to think of the humanising potential of Schiller's work and person in a world which was threatened by atomic destruction. He fully agreed that the divided nation needed political unity and yet his was also an appeal to 'universal' thinking over and above all national interest.

A West German commentator, on looking back at the Schiller celebrations of 1955, saw how Thomas Mann's speeches had hardly shown 'daß in dem gespaltenen Deutschland noch so etwas wie eine gesamtdeutsche Schiller-Ehrung möglich war'.[65] Mann's speech showed instead how the heritage of bourgeois humanism, which he embodied, was either integrated or stripped of its socio-political importance in the discourses of the divided Germany. The SED built this tradition into its classicist cult as an instrument of cultural and political self-portrayal, while in West Germany the tradition's vital impetus was lost in aesthetic and abstractly intellectual questions.

The celebrations of Schiller's 200th birthday in 1959 were used even less as opportunities for a dialogue and even more for political ends, building up socialist 'achievements' on the one hand and demonstrating a supposedly non-ideological approach to literature on the other. Where there were still any attempts in the West to understand Schiller in the light of present-day problems, he appeared as a 'guter Geist jenseits aller politischen Triumphe und Katastrophen', who had seen in freedom 'kein politisches, sondern ein geistiges Problem'.[66] In contrast to such celebrations, which released Schiller 'vom Kampf unseres Zeitalters und unserer Tage',[67] tributes were staged in the GDR as manifestations of the fight of the working classes for the 'Verteidigung der humanistischen deutschen Kultur gegen die kulturzerstörenden, tagtäglich die geistige Freiheit knebelnden, zutiefst antihumanistischen Mächte des westdeutschen Militarismus und Imperialismus'.[68]

The SED's self-image led it to consider the use of aggressive rhetoric at the commemorations to be merely a result of the 'Zuspitzung der Politik des Kalten Krieges'[69] undertaken by the Federal Republic since the Paris treaties had come into force. The rejection of the 'confederacy plans' proposed by the GDR as a way of uniting the country through the Bundestag, the stationing of American medium-range missiles with atomic warheads in the Federal Republic, and the debate on nuclear weapons for the Bundeswehr were all taken by the SED as proof that the government of the Federal Republic had given up national unity in favour of policies of armament and concentration of capital, policies which they termed 'volksfremd'. Because, according to the SED, 'die kapitalistischen Geldfürsten der Konzerne und Banken' were deeply alienated from and inimical to the true 'Geist Schillers',[70] West German academics were deliberately depoliticising Schiller's work in favour of formal analysis. To Abusch this was no more than a

> raffiniert verhülltes Engagement, ein Liebesdienst für die derzeitigen Regenten in Bonn, die in ihrem Kalten Krieg auch an einer anti-kommunistischen und antiwissenschaftlichen Verfälschung von Schillers Erbe interessiert sind.[71]

The Wissenschaftliche Konferenz über das Schaffen Friedrich Schillers which took place on 6–9 November 1959 not only served to legitimate the GDR's outward claim that it was the only representative of Germany's classical heritage, but it was also used to overcome 'revisionist' and 'liberal' standpoints among GDR Germanists.[72] Whereas the humanistic discourse in the Schiller celebrations of 1955 still followed a policy of co-operation with the intelligentsia, in 1959 the emphasis was on developing the capacity of a historical–materialistic method which has since been developed in works by Hans Günther Thalheim, Hans Jürgen Geerdts, Ursula Wertheim and others. In his concluding appraisal of the conference, Helmut Holtzhauer took the comment made by a 'young West German friend' that many aspects of the depiction of Schiller were foreign to him as an opportunity to criticise the blocking of a possible dialogue; the fact that the results of marxist research had been ignored by 'die offizielle Schillerforschung in Westdeutschland' showed that 'der vielberufene "eiserne Vorhang" gar nicht von hier aus, sondern von anderer Seite herabgelassen worden ist'.[73]

During the 1959 celebrations, Schiller's legacy was exploited as a means of demonstrating not only the 'Überlegenheit der historisch-materialistischen Methode gegenüber der westdeutschen Schillerforschung',[74] but also the concept of the 'sozialistische Kulturrevolution'. With the publication of the 'Dokumente zum Schillerbild der deutschen Arbeiterklasse', the academic appropriation of the writer was linked with a tradition in which the 'Aneignung des nationalen Kulturerbes' was to appear as 'Ausdruck einer objektiven Gesetzmäßigkeit'.[75] If this documentation relied primarily on Mehring's book on Schiller (published 1905), along with the views of Marx and Engels, then it is clearly related to the criticism of the 'revisionist' position adopted by Lukács, who had been accused of not fundamentally representing the 'revolutionary standpoint of the working classes'. At the same time the aim was to show that the appropriation of the tradition by the working classes itself represented a form of class struggle, and that the critical comments by Marx and Engels on 'idealism' as a flight from the 'deutsche Misere' as well as their observations on the petty bourgeois and liberal 'forgeries' of Schiller were both to be understood from the perspective of the 'Klassenkämpfe des 19. Jahrhunderts'.[76] Just as the history of Schiller's reception seemed in the past to be a reflection of ideological forms in which the historical process was expressed, criticism of the West German portrayal of Schiller became an objective necessity resulting from the responsibility of the workers' movement in its capacity as the 'Erbin aller großen Menschheitsleistungen'.[77]

The shift in the image of Schiller in the service of the workers' movement is closely linked with the cultural–political programme of overcoming the bourgeois 'Trennung von Kunst und Leben', the 'Entfremdung von Künstler und Volk', a course of action which was resolved at the Fifth Party Conference of the SED in July 1958.[78] After Ulbricht, at the Party conference, had reduced the second cultural revolution to the formula that the workers must now storm 'die Höhen der Kultur',[79] the organisational efforts of 1959 served to direct a spotlight on to the successes that supposedly had already been attained. It was the reports in *Neues Deutschland* above all which depicted the celebrations as 'wahrhaft nationale Ehrung', through which the poet's words had reached 'bis in die Betriebe und selbst in kleinste Dörfer'.[80] In contrast to the celebrations in West Germany, where evidence of the 'Auseinanderklaffen von Wissenschaft, Kunst und Volk' was apparently to be found, in the GDR idyllic pictures were painted of a people's tribute to Schiller. The new quality of the 'Arbeiter- und Bauernstaat', according to the official view, could be seen by the fact 'daß sich Arbeiter eines volkseigenen Betriebes zwei Tage Urlaub nehmen, mit ihren Frauen einen Omnibus mieten und viele Kilometer fahren, um Schiller zu ehren'.[81]

Whereas the Schiller commemorations of 1959 in the GDR were characterised by discourses which reflected the social and political changes since 1955, the commemorations in the Federal Republic essentially followed the same pattern of interpretation that had emerged four years previously. The characteristic feature of most of the Germanists among the speakers was the unwillingness to refer to the concrete social and political situation. Hagelstange, the writer, was one of the few to mention recent events, but when he did the intellectual arsenal of the Cold War came to the fore. For him, the contemporary experience that made Schiller's concept of freedom meaningful was the contrast between 'serfdom' under communism and the opportunities for self-development in the West; 'denjenigen, denen das Menschsein streitig gemacht wird, leuchtet dieses Ideal, diese Freiheit wie ein nächtliches Sternbild weiter; der freien Welt ist sie das unentbehrliche Tagesgestirn, unter dem die Dinge und Menschen wachsen und atmen'.[82] The only thing that could work against the 'gewaltsam fortgesetzte Teilung und Entzweiung' for which the 'unaesthetic' and 'unartistic' powers on the other side of the Elbe were responsible, was the education of people in 'jene innerere heitere, gleichsam metaphysische Freiheit, die unser Glück und unsere Würde ausmacht'.[83] It becomes clear from such formulations how easily a concept of freedom that belongs, in its non-political, abstract state, to the German tradition of 'introversion' was capable of being integrated into the intellectual climate of the Cold War.

In the few cases where the social dimension of freedom was taken into account, for example in that of Muschg, the individual appears purely and simply as a victim of totalitarian structures of the modern state: freedom has

nicht nur in den Diktaturstaaten geschwunden, sondern auch in den
sogenannten freien Ländern. Es haben sich überall neue Machtfaktoren
gebildet, die das Dasein des Menschen beherrschen und undurchsichtige
neue Formen der Sklaverei erzeugen.[84]

However, the message that Schiller's concept of freedom held for
Muschg in this situation was only directed towards the individual.
In the full sense of existentialist philosophy people were urged
to overcome their 'Sehnsucht nach Unfreiheit, nach Erlösung von
der Last der Selbstbestimmung' and thereby gain both moral and
spiritual independence.

West German Germanists agreed that Schiller's greatness lay
in the way he served as a model of personal autonomy. Schiller's
development from a young revolutionary and moralist to a rigor-
ous aestheticist was for Storz the consequence of recognising that
freedom was only attainable in an 'inner' form: 'ein Dichter, der
ausgezogen war, die Welt zu verändern, – wie seitdem und in letzter
Zeit so viele –, erkannte, daß es heilsamer sei, sich und die
Menschen zu sich selbst zu führen'.[85] For Staiger the 'Not der Welt'
could gradually be overcome by means of the aesthetic experience to be gleaned from an autonomous work of art, and Schiller
constantly succeeded in doing so throughout his struggle for existence against the adverse reality of his time; being fully absorbed
in artistic work led to release from 'die Welt im Ganzen'.[86] Only when
the classical inheritance was understood in this way did it gain
that affirmative character which Marcuse diagnosed; bourgeois
culture answered 'auf das leibliche Elend mit der Schönheit der
Seele, auf die äußere Knechtschaft mit der inneren Freiheit'.[87] Dolf
Sternberger explicitly formulated what is only to be found between the lines in Staiger and Storz; the political writer Brecht is
the negative, opposite pole to Schiller and is a contemporary
example of how commitment to a 'doctrine' or 'ideology' is detri-
mental to the aesthetic success of a work.[88]

West German Germanists evaded making what would have been
a salutary study of the relationship between literature and politics,
by attempting 'den Dichter Schiller als Formkünstler gegen seine
eigenen Stoffe und Gehalte auszuspielen', while placing him in
a theological context and turning his theatre (as Hans Mayer
pointedly formulated it)[89] from one bringing 'der Menschheit große
Gegenstände' on to the stage into 'eine Dramatik der häuslichen
vier Wände'.

The provocative elements in Dürrenmatt's speech lay, therefore, not so much in his having pointed out that Brecht was 'in vielem mit Schiller zu vergleichen' but rather in his call for a 'dialogue' with the 'communist' answer which Brecht's work supplies 'auf unsere Welt'.[90] Although Dürrenmatt also criticised the segregation of fiction and politics which used Schiller's conception of freedom as an excuse 'das Notwendige zu unterlassen' and which treated Brecht's communism as 'eine bloße Verirrung, als eine Neben-sache', his view of the present world nevertheless fitted into the pattern of thought typical of the time, which was to be critical of the tendencies towards totalitarianism in modern society. The answer which Dürrenmatt hinted at also remains abstract; he in-dicated that one should keep trying to find 'new models' in art to shape the world.[91]

Dürrenmatt reflected as little on how to transfer such models into society as the Germanist speakers did on their own interests and methods. The undialectic opposition set up between 'Aktualisierung' and interpretation of the works, between con-temporary needs and concentration on the 'Dichter schlechthin',[92] had become the legitimation for research into Schiller in the Federal Republic, academics not feeling it necessary to devote any attention to the results of research from 'Mitteldeutschland', to use their term for the GDR.[93] Nevertheless, the themes and the questions raised both by the commemorative speakers and by academic research in the Federal Republic showed that the 'new' depiction of Schiller was also determined by the 'Blick über die Elbe',[94] in the light of which the forms of political preoccupation were no more than the fatal consequences of any social analysis. No matter whether Kohlschmidt understood Schiller's *Wilhelm Tell* as an 'allgemein menschlich gemeintes Drama sittlicher Entscheidung'[95] or Martini stressed the interest of Schiller as narrator in the 'innere Struktur des individuellen Menschen',[96] whether Muschg saw the 'Kampf zwischen Gut und Böse' in the classical dramas as a ques-tion of human nature[97] or Benno von Wiese regarded the 'schwäbische Theologie der Eschatologie'[98] as central to the young Schiller's criticism of society; these interpretations implicitly claimed to correct the consequences of making Schiller politically topical, a process which GDR German studies carried right through into analyses of individual works.

The Schiller celebrations of 1955 and 1959 show how West Ger-man academics were integrated in discourses which determined the intellectual and cultural climate of the 1950s, even if they believed themselves to be serving the word of the writer free of topical interests. The portrayal of Schiller was determined by contemporary patterns of thinking and by values that are associated with repression, exclusion, even taboos; that is, with escapism into a world of the intellect, by utter suspicion of ideology, by rejection of politics and history, by elevating works of art to the absolute, and not least by anti-materialism and anti-communism.[99]

But the portrayal of the writer in West German *Germanistik* was not the result of attempts 'sich mit peinlicher Beflissenheit . . . der weltanschaulichen Position der Bonner Politik anzupassen'[100] as the GDR commemorative speakers claimed in their polemical strategy. Instead, it was the product of discourses which determined the self-image of *Germanistik* as the Federal Republic established itself. Because functionaries and literary critics in the GDR were so fixed on their own political utilisation of Germany's cultural heritage to increase the political legitimacy of their 'socialist nation state' and to present its identity, they overlooked the fact that 'Bonner Politik' hardly needed such cultural values for purposes of stabilisation and justification. The insistence on the humane message of Schiller's 'Freiheitsidee' and the declaration of his greatness of personality paled into insignificance before the real possibilities of developing an identity through achievements in manufacture and ownership of consumer goods. This, of course, did not exclude the possibility of the 'Verbrauchergesinnung' drawing Schiller's idea 'in den abendländischen Supermarkt',[101] or harmonising it with the fight for the 'freie Welt'.[102] What emerges is not so much the functionalisation of a subject but a subject in crisis over its function, a crisis which arose from the dwindling significance of cultural tradition.

Although the Schiller celebrations were only partly integrated into the strategies of the Cold War, they were nevertheless governed by Cold War communication structures. Whatever happened on one side of the Elbe was used by the other to enhance its own status and legitimacy. Just as the GDR was used in the economic field by the Federal Republic as a 'negative Vergleichsgesellschaft',[103] the 'ideological' image of Schiller portrayed by the GDR helped to confirm anti-marxist and anti-communist prejudices. The same Cold War rhetoric that was deftly employed by the GDR in the official pronouncements on Schiller was used as justification by the Federal Republic for excluding the results of GDR German research from their 'academic' discourse.

The genuine hope of 1955 that the Schiller celebrations would be able to bridge the political division were barely fulfilled at that time, and even less so four years later. The reason for this stemmed not only from the real political and social changes that deepened the divide but also from the lack of openness in the discourses which supplied the intellectual framework. In the climate of the Cold War the schemes and mechanisms of the discourses obstructed a dialogue in which each side could have accepted the other as a challenge to engage in self-examination.

Notes

1 Friedrich Dürrenmatt, *Theater-Schriften und Reden*, Zurich, 1966, pp. 214–33 (p. 215).

2 See Rainer Noltenius, *Dichterfeiern in Deutschland: Rezeptionsgeschichte als Sozialgeschichte am Beispiel der Schiller- und Freiligrath-Feiern*, Munich, 1984; Wolfgang Hagen, *Die Schiller-Verehrung in der Sozialdemokratie: zur ideologischen Formation proletarischer Kulturpolitik vor 1914*, Stuttgart, 1977; George Ruppelt, *Schiller im nationalsozialistischen Deutschland: der Versuch einer Gleichschaltung*, Stuttgart, 1979.

3 *Schiller – Zeitgenosse aller Epochen: Dokumente zur Wirkungsgeschichte Schillers in Deutschland*, edited by Norbert Oellers, 2 vols, Frankfurt am Main, 1970, Munich, 1976.

4 Benno von Wiese, 'Schiller-Forschung und Schiller-Deutung von 1937 bis 1953', *Deutsche Vierteljahresschrift*, 27, 1953, pp. 452–83 (p. 453).

5 *Frankfurter Allgemeine Zeitung*, 12 November 1959, p. 14.

6 'Erklärung des Schiller-Komitees der Deutschen Demokratischen Republik 1959', in *Der Menschheit Würde: Dokumente zum Schiller-Bild der deutschen Arbeiterklasse*, selected and introduced by Günther Dahlke, Weimar, 1959, pp. 319–26 (p. 325).

7 *Frankfurter Allgemeine Zeitung*, 18 May 1955, p. 9.

8 For the 'Western' view, see Ernst Nolte, *Deutschland und der Kalte Krieg*, Munich, 1974; for the GDR view see Hans Teller, *Der kalte Krieg gegen die DDR: Von seinen Anfängen bis 1961*, Berlin, 1979.

9 The difference between a 'pure' motive, which really deals with the writer and his work, and using the writer as a 'willkommener Vorwand zur Tarnung einer Demonstration' is stressed by Friedrich Beißner in his evaluation of the 1859 Schiller commemorations: 'Schillers dichterische Gestalt: Festrede bei der Schiller-Gedenkfeier der Universität Tübingen am 7. Juni 1955', in *Schiller: Reden im Gedenkjahr 1955*, edited by Bernhard Zeller, Stuttgart, 1955, pp. 138–61 (p. 139).

10 Compare Wolfgang Paulsen, 'Friedrich Schiller 1955–1959: ein Literaturbericht', *Jahrbuch des Deutschen Schilles-Gesellschaft*, 6, 1962, pp. 369–464.

11 'Zum 150. Todestag Friedrich Schillers am 9. Mai 1955: Beschluß des Politbüros der Sozialistischen Einheitspartei Deutschlands vom 25. Januar 1955', *Der Menschheit Würde*, pp. 277–81.

12 G. Mathieu, 'Schiller and the "Zentralkomitee"', *German Life and Letters*, 9, 1955–6, pp. 40–6 (p. 40).

13 Oellers, *Schiller – Zeitgenosse aller Epochen*, p. liii.

14 Paulsen, 'Friedrich Schiller 1955–59', p. 370.

15 Compare Wolfram Schlenker, *Das 'Kulturelle Erbe' in der DDR: Gesellschaftliche Entwicklung und Kulturpolitik 1945–1965*, Stuttgart, 1977.

16 Beißner, in Zeller, *Schiller: Reden 1955*, p. 138.

17 Wilhelm Emrich, 'Schiller und die Antinomien der menschlichen Gesellschaft: Festrede bei der Schiller-Gedenkfeier der Stadt Krefeld am 8. Mai 1955', in Zeller, *Schiller: Reden 1955*, pp. 237–50 (p. 237).

18 'Erklärung des Schiller-Komitees der DDR 1959', *Der Menschheit Würde*, pp. 319–26 (p. 324).

19 Gerhard Storz, 'Schillers Dichtertum: Festrede bei der Jahresversammlung der Deutschen Schillergesellschaft in Marbach a. N. am 7. Mai 1955', in Zeller, *Schiller: Reden 1955*, pp. 121–37 (p. 135).

20 Reinhold Schneider, 'Tragik und Erlösung im Weltbild Schillers: Festrede bei der Schiller-Gedenkfeier der Kölner Bühnen am 8. Mai 1955', in Zeller, *Schiller: Reden 1955*, pp. 276–302 (p. 300).

21 Paul Böckmann, 'Politik und Dichtung im Werk Friedrich Schillers: Festrede bei der Schiller-Gedenkfeier der Universität Heidelberg am 9. Mai 1955', in Zeller, *Schiller: Reden 1955*, pp. 192–213 (p. 212).

22 Emrich, in Zeller, *Schiller: Reden 1955*, p. 237.

23 'Die Schiller-Feiern in Marbach-Stuttgart und in Weimar 1955', *Goethe*, 17, 1955, pp. 315–18 (p. 315).

24 Karl Balser, 'Zum Ausklang des Schillerjahres', *Geist und Zeit*, 1956, pp. 137–42 (p. 140).

25 Max Mell, 'Aufblick zum Genius: Festrede bei der staatlichen Schillerfeier im Burgtheater in Wien am 5. Mai 1955', in Zeller, *Schiller: Reden 1955*, pp. 72–8 (p. 77).

26 *Der Spiegel*, 18 May 1955, pp. 34ff.

27 *Ibid.* In a speech to teachers in Düsseldorf on 9 May 1955, Fritz von Unruh attacked the 'große Männer' as follows: 'Heute sind sie durchschaut, wenn sie, das erhabene Wort "Freiheit" mißbrauchend, euch aufrufen zu neuen "Kreuzzügen" um Länderfetzen, Ölquellen, Weltberrschungsplänen! Denn, nicht wahr, wie bekämen sie wohl Millionen mal Millionen wiederum in Marsch und Massengräber, wenn sie nicht vor eurer Nase den ethischen Brocken einer "bedrohten" Freiheit hinhielten, für den ihr marschieren sollt'; Fritz von Unruh, *Mächtig seid ihr nicht in Waffen: Reden*, Nurnberg, 1957, pp. 273–301 (p. 285).

28 John Bourke, 'Schiller Year 1955: Commemorations in Germany', *German Life and Letters*, 9, 1955–6, pp. 85–90 (p. 89).

29 Paula Andersen, 'Seelenarzt für unsere Zeit', *Frankfurter Allgemeine Zeitung*, 9 May 1955, p. 6.

30 Dahlke, *Der Menschheit Würde*, p. 280.

31 Hans Kaufman, '"Denn er war unser!" Zu Friedrich Schillers 150. Todestag am 9.5.1955', *Einheit*, 10, 1955, pp. 458–66 (p. 458).

32 Johannes R. Becher, 'Denn er ist unser: Friedrich Schiller, der Dichter der Freiheit', in Dahlke, *Der Menschheit Würde*, pp. 298–316 (p. 313).

33 Theodor Heuss, 'Schiller: Ansprache bei der Schiller-Gedenkfeier der Deutschen Schiller-Gesellschaft in Stuttgart am 8. Mai 1955', in Zeller, *Schiller: Reden 1955*, pp. 79–89 (pp. 81 and 89).

34 Storz, in Zeller, *Schiller: Reden 1955*, p. 123.

35 Andersen, 'Seelenarzt', p. 9.

36 Alexander von Bormann, 'Der kalte Krieg und seine literarischen Auswirkungen', *Literatur nach 1945*, I, edited by Jost Hermand, Wiesbaden, 1979, pp. 61–113 (p. 102).

37 Compare Hans Karl Rupp, '"wo es aufwärts geht, aber nicht vorwärts . . .": Politische Kultur, Staatsapparat, Opposition', in *Die fünfziger Jahre: Beiträge Zur Politik und Kultur*, edited by Dieter Bänsch, Tübingen, 1985, pp. 27–35.

38 Werner Conze, 'Die deutsche Geschichtswissenschaft seit 1945: Bedingungen und Ergebnisse', *Historische Zeitschrift*, 225, 1977, pp. 2ff.

39 See also *Klassiker in finsteren Zeiten 1933–1945: eine Ausstellung des Deutschen Literaturarchivs im Schiller-National-Museum Marbach am Neckar*, edited by Bernhard Zeller, 2 vols, Marbach am Neckar, 1983.

40 Compare Jürgen Scharfschwerdt, 'Die Klassikideologie in Kultur-, Wissenschafts- und Literaturpolitik', in *Einführung in Theorie, Geschichte und Funktion der DDR Literatur*, edited by Hans-Jürgen Schmitt, Stuttgart, 1975, pp. 108–63 (pp. 111ff.).

41 Alexander Abusch, *Kulturelle Probleme des sozialistischen Humanismus: Beiträge zur deutschen Kulturpolitik 1949–1967*, Berlin and Weimar, 1967, p. 138.

42 'Beschluß des Politbüros', in Dahlke, *Der Menschheit Würde*, p. 280.

43 Becher, in Dahlke, *Der Menschheit Würde*, p. 298 and pp. 309ff.

44 Von Wiese, 'Schiller-Forschung', p. 452.

45 Compare Walter Müller-Seidel, 'Zum gegenwärtigen Stand der Schiller-forschung', *Der Deutschunterricht*, 1952, pp. 97–115.

46 Benno von Wiese, *Die deutsche Tragödie von Lessing bis Hebbel*, Hamburg, 1948; Kurt May, *Schiller: Idee und Wirklichkeit*, Göttingen, 1947.

47 Heuss, in Zeller, *Schiller: Reden 1955*, p. 80.

48 Fritz Martini, 'Tragödie und Humanität', in Zeller, *Schiller: Reden 1955*, pp. 251–75, p. 254.

49 Compare Wilhelm Heinrich Pott, 'die Philosophien der Nachkriegsliteratur', *Literatur in der Bundesrepublik Deutschland bis 1967*, Munich, 1986, pp. 263–78.

50 Martini, in Zeller, *Schiller: Reden 1955*, pp. 256ff.

51 Helmut Heißenbüttel, 'Literarische Archäologie der fünfziger Jahre', in Bänsch, *Die fünfziger Jahre*, pp. 308–25, p. 319.

52 Dahlke, *Der Menschheit Würde*, p. 24.

53 Compare Schlenker, *Das 'Kulturelle Erbe'*, pp. 155ff.

54 Otto Grotewohl, 'Wir sind ein Volk! Rede anläßlich der Schiller-Ehrung der deutschen Jugend in Weimar am 3. April 1955', in Dahlke, *Der Menschheit Würde*, pp. 281–98 (p. 292).

55 Becher, in *Der Menschheit Würde*, p. 315.

56 Grotewohl, in *Der Menschheit Würde*, p. 296.

57 Becher, in *Der Menschheit Würde*, p. 314.

58 Wilfried von Bredow, 'Geschichte als Element der deutschen Identität?', in *Die Identität der Deutschen*, edited by Werner Weidenfeld, Bonn, 1983, pp. 102–18 (p. 109).

59 Compare Helmut Peitsch, 'Die problematische Entdeckung nationaler Identität: Westdeutsche Literatur am Beginn der 80er Jahre', *Diskussion Deutsch*, 18, 1987, pp. 373–92.

60 On the question of identity problems after 1945 compare Maximilian Nutz, 'Restauration und Zukunft des Humanen: Zur westdeutschen Goethe-Rezeption von 1945–1949', in *Klassik und Moderne: die Weimarer Klassik als historisches Ereignis und Herausforderung im kulturgeschichtlichen Prozeß. Walter Müller-Seidel zum 65. Geburtstag*, edited by Karl Richter and Jörg Schönert, Stuttgart, 1983, pp. 457–81.

61 Carlo Schmid, 'Vom Reich der Freiheit. Festrede bei der Schiller-Gedenkfeier des Kuratoriums Unteilbares Deutschland in Berlin am 8. Mai 1955', in Zeller, *Schiller: Reden 1955*, pp. 99–120 (pp. 118ff.).

62 Dahlke, *Der Menschheit Würde*, p. 25.

63 Heuss, in Zeller, *Schiller: Reden 1955*, p. 76.

64 Thomas Mann, 'Schiller: Festrede bei der Schiller-Gedenkfeier der deutschen Schillergesellschaft in Stuttgart am 8. Mai 1955, wiederholt in Weimar', in Zeller, *Schiller: Reden 1955*, pp. 9–26 (pp. 23ff.). Compare also Mann's comment in his letter to Frido Mann on 11 April 1955, to the effect that he wanted 'zu den Roten nach Weimar und die westdeutschen Zeitungen werden schimpfen, weil ich finde, daß die Leute da *auch* Menschen sind und auch Deutsche', *Briefe 1948–1955 und Nachlese*, Frankfurt am Main, 1965, p. 392. *Die Zeit* criticised the fact that Thomas Mann accepted an honorary doctorate from Jena University and took part in the commemorations of a state 'der nachweislich innerhalb seines Territoriums schlimme Terrorakte duldet', 19 May 1955, p. 7.

65 *Süddeutsche Zeitung*, 11 November 1959, p. 1.

66 Walter Muschg, 'Die Tragödie der Freiheit: Rede, gehalten bei den Schiller-Feiern der Universität Basel am 5. November und des Senats und der Freien Universität von Berlin am 10. November 1959', in *Schiller: Reden im Gedenkjahr 1959*, edited by Bernhard Zeller, Stuttgart, 1961, p. 218–39 (pp. 239 and 227).

67 Alexander Abusch, 'Schiller im Staat der Arbeiter und Bauern', *Neues Deutschland*, 13 May 1959, also in Dahlke, *Der Menschheit Würde*, pp. 316–19 (p. 317).

68 *Ibid.*, pp. 317ff. Compare also Walter Ulbricht, 'Das Volk ehrt seinen Freiheitsdichter', *Neues Deutschland*, 11 November 1959, p. 1: 'Die Aufrechterhaltung der ausländischen Besatzung in Westdeutschland und der Militarismus lassen sich nun einmal nicht mit Schillers hohen Idealen von Freiheit und Menschenwürde vereinbaren.'

69 Teller, *Der kalte Krieg*, pp. 47ff.

70 'Erklärung des Schiller-Komitees', in *Der Menschheit Würde*, p. 320.

71 Alexander Abusch, 'Wir bewahren Schillers humanistisches Erbe für die ganze Nation', *Neues Deutschland*, 11 November 1959, p. 3.

72 Compare Scharfschwerdt, 'Die Klassikideologie' pp. 125ff.

73 *Weimarer Beiträge*, 5, 1959, special edition, p. 232.

74 Rudolf Winkler, Rolf Schultze, 'Das wahre Schiller-Bild', *Neues Deutschland*, 15 November 1959, p. 4.

75 Dahlke, *Der Menschheit Würde*, p. 9.

76 *Ibid.*, pp. 10ff.

77 Hans-Jürgen Geisthardt, 'Schiller mitten unter uns: die Arbeiterklasse verteidigt den Freiheitsdichter der Nation', *Neues Deutschland*, 10 November 1959, p. 4.

78 *Dokumente zur Kunst-, Literatur-, und Kulturpolitik der SED*, edited by Elmar Schubbe, Stuttgart, 1972, pp. 534ff.

79 *Ibid.*

80 *Neues Deutschland*, 7 November 1959, supplement.

81 *Ibid.*, 11 November 1959, p. 1.

82 Rudolf Hagelstange, 'Friedrich Schiller und die Deutschen: Rede bei der Schillerfeier der Stadt Marbach am 7. November 1959', in Zeller, *Schiller: Reden 1959*, pp. 53–75 (p. 74).

83 *Ibid.*, p. 57.

84 Muschg, in Zeller, *Schiller: Reden 1959*, p. 230.

85 Gerhard Storz, 'Friedrich Schiller: Rede bei der Feier der Stadt, der Universität und des Freien Deutschen Hochstifts Frankfurt am 10. November 1959', in Zeller, *Schiller: Reden 1959*, pp. 330–45 (p. 342).

86 Emil Staiger, 'Schillers Größe: Rede bei der akademischen Feier der Universität Zürich am 7. November 1959, wiederholt u.a. in Kiel, Bremen und Köln', in Zeller, *Schiller: Reden 1959*, pp. 293–309 (p. 306).

87 Herbert Marcuse, 'Über den affirmativen Charakter der Kultur', *Kultur und Gesellschaft*, I, Frankfurt am Main, 1967, pp. 56–101 (p. 66).

88 Dolf Sternberger, 'Macht und Herz oder der politische Held bei Schiller: Rede im Hessischen Rundfunk Frankfurt am 10. November 1959', in Zeller, *Schiller: Reden 1959*, pp. 310–29, p. 310. Compare Josef Hohnhäuser, 'Brecht und der Kalte Krieg. Materialien zur Brecht-Rezeption in der BRD', in *Bertolt Brecht*, II, edited by Heinz Ludwig Arnold, Munich, 1973, pp. 192–203.

89 Hans Mayer, 'Dem Wahren, Guten, Schönen. Rede bei der Eröffnung der Schillerfestwoche in Leipzig am 22. November 1959', in Zeller, *Schiller: Reden 1959*, pp. 159–69 (p. 163).

90 Dürrenmatt, *Theater-Schriften*, p. 224.

91 *Ibid.*, pp. 225 and 233.

92 Gerhard Storz, *Der Dichter Friedrich Schiller*, Stuttgart, 1959, p. 5.

93 This is in effect what Paulsen says in his research report (see note 10 above).

94 Rupp, in Bänsch, *Die fünfziger Jahre*, p. 29, sees in this view a way of dealing with the past: 'Gegen dieses System zu kämpfen – war das nicht Sühne für das eigene Versagen . . .?'

95 Werner Kohlschmidt, 'Tells Entscheidung. Rede bei der akademischen Feier der Universität Bern am 11. November 1959', in Zeller, *Schiller: Reden 1959*, pp. 87–101 (p. 99).

96 Fritz Martini, 'Der Erzähler Friedrich Schiller: Vortrag im Rahmen einer Vortragsreihe der Goethe-Gesellschaft Hannover am 10. September 1959', in Zeller, *Schiller: Reden 1959*, pp. 124–58 (p. 134).

97 Muschg, in Zeller, *Schiller: Reden 1959*, p. 229.

98 Benno von Wiese, 'Die Religion Friedrich Schillers: Vortrag im Rahmen einer Vortragsreihe der Goethe-Gesellschaft Hannover am 3. April 1959', in Zeller, *Schiller: Reden 1959*, pp. 406–27 (p. 410).

99 Compare also von Bormann (see note 36 above).

100 Helmut Holtzhauer, 'Eröffnung der "Wissenschaftlichen Konferenz über das Schaffen Friedrich Schiller. 6–9. November 1959 in Weimar"', *Weimarer Beiträge*, 5, 1959, special edition, p. 5.

101 *Süddeutsche Zeitung*, 12 November 1959, p. 1.

102 After a discussion of Muschg's speech, Karl Markus Michel asked: 'Schiller, der NATO-Dichter?' See Karl Markus Michel, '"Rinnen muß der Schweiß" oder wie wir Schillers 200. Geburtstag feierten', *Frankfurter Hefte*, 15, 1960, pp. 877–87 (p. 882).

103 Rainer Lepsius, 'Die Teilung Deutschlands und die deutsche Nation', in *Politische Parteien auf dem Weg zur parlamentarischen Demokratie in Deutschland*, edited by Lothar Albertin and Werner Link, Düsseldorf, 1981, pp. 419ff.

Travellers' tales from Germany in the 1950s

Helmut Peitsch

Gustav René Hocke singled out contemporary travel writing produced in 1945 and 1946 as heralding the dawn of a new age, a new realistic literature. In the periodical *Der Ruf* in November 1946 he concluded: 'Eine neue Gattung . . . ist in den Zeitschriften aller Zonen entstanden; der kaleidoskopartige Bericht über Deutschlandfahrten.'[1] Hocke did not seek to differentiate, in terms of its literary quality, between work which appeared in periodicals in the Western zones and that which was published in the Soviet zone. He drew a sharp distinction between all this work and non-Nazi work published up to 1945, insisting that 'Klarheit der Form und Unmittelbarkeit der Aussage' had replaced 'stilistische Esoterik' and 'Introversion', in other words the 'Kalligraphie' into which writers had been forced by the dictatorship.

Hocke's characterisation of post-war reportage, in which the reader from one zone could discover 'hell, scharf, klar' the reality of another 'in guter Sprache', echoed the programmes put forward at that time by Ernst Schnabel in the British publication *Die Welt* and by Wolfgang Weyrauch in the Soviet *Aufbau*. Like them, Hocke stressed a 'Realismus des Unmittelbaren', placing the courage to state the simple truth, and thereby to emancipate oneself from ideology, above the now suspect notion of beauty: 'Das Umfassen von Wirklichkeit macht . . . nicht nur klar und einfach; es macht auch rein.' Hocke's praise of reportage as the epitome of 'geistige Freiheit' ignored what Brecht had described as the 'Schwierigkeiten beim Schreiben der Wahrheit'. Hocke appeared to believe that it was quite a straightforward matter to achieve a 'reine Übereinstimmung von Aussage und Wirklichkeit'. Yet the occupation of Germany and the markedly different ideological approaches to re-education on the part of the victorious powers, their conflicting interpretations of Germany's collapse and divergent plans for the country's future, provided a context for Hocke's view which he failed to acknowledge:

> Je mehr man diese Wirklichkeit schildert, wie sie eben ist, desto mehr schwindet das Gefühl, man sei auch heute geistig doch noch nicht frei ... Fortschreitend erringt man die geistige Freiheit ebenso gefahrlos wie loyal, indem man aus echter Erschütterung, im Bewußtsein der wahren Ursachen und der klaren Konsequenzen, nicht über fragwürdige Ideologien schwätzt, sondern ganz einfach sagt, was ist und was nicht ist.

Hocke's preference for this form of reportage both precluded certain lines of enquiry concerning the German Question and implied simultaneously anti-ideological, existentialist answers.

A year later, Anna Seghers, a communist who had written in exile, chose reportage as a vehicle for the discussion of 'geistige Freiheit' when she spoke at the First German Writers' Congress. When she compared two reportage authors, she was seeking to distinguish between two traditions of German reportage, and, indeed, between two traditions of realism. Her examples were Ernst Glaeser, who had returned to Nazi Germany from exile and had become one of Hitler's war correspondents (though she did not name him), and herself. After her return she had not felt able to supply a number of foreign journals with the 'Berichte über Deutschland' which they had requested.[2] In her view, Glaeser defined realism merely as style and regarded his own writing as accountable to only one authority, his own creative genius. For her, however, the key issue was the effect of what was written; writing was a 'Bewußtmachung der Wirklichkeit' (p. 730). Alluding to Brecht's 'Fünf Schwierigkeiten beim Schreiben der Wahrheit', she sought to commit the writer to a conception of truth which she defined as a dynamic process, a direction, an orientation to the future. In so doing, she was foreshadowing the theoretical problems that reportage would face in the GDR. In describing the effect of Glaeser's war reports Seghers adopted a theoretical argument, based on the reader's identification with the narrative authority of the text. Logically enough, Glaeser's Second World War reportage was read by Seghers as an incitement to commit the most cynical Nazi atrocities:

> Er hat vielleicht als der Realist, der er in seiner Kunst war, geglaubt: wenn er in dieser Art Bericht erstattet, dann wird er in etwa auslegen, deutlich machen, was sich eigentlich auf dieser Szene, die er in seinem realistischen Stil schilderte, abspielte. Sein Auftraggeber hat also Recht

gehabt, nicht er. Die Wirkung war umgekehrt, wie er gedacht hatte. Er hat die Gewissen der Leser nicht gerührt, nicht aufgeregt, sondern im Gegenteil beruhigt; denn sie sagten: das geschieht also, das machen die Menschen, und infolgedessen mache ich es auch. (p. 71)

The notion that readers would imitate the characters presented in fiction epitomised the writer's educative role in the Soviet zone, as later in the GDR. It also accounts for Anna Seghers's own difficulties with reportage. It was hard enough to find typical features of day-to-day life in Germany; what was worse was that 'andere nicht dieselben Assoziationen bilden, nicht dieselben Lasten eines ("historischen und sozialen") Erbes mit sich herumtragen wie wir' (p. 74). Seghers sees herself as an intermediary between German readers, whom she regards as corrupted by negative role models, and foreign readers, who, through bitter experience of the Germans, are forced to question whether positive models are authentic:

wenn ich . . . einige dieser furchtbaren, typischen korrupten Erscheinungen darstelle, denen wir bei jedem Schritt in Deutschland begegnen können – das ist noch nicht das Bild des deutschen Volkes – oder wenn ich die ganz großartigen, überraschenden Widerstandsmomente darstelle. Auch sie erwecken eine Unmenge von Fragen für den, der nicht dieselbe Umgebung, nicht dieselben Möglichkeiten der Orientierung hat wie wir. (p. 74)

Ironically, in the light of growing tensions, Stephan Hermlin, writing in Alfred Kantorowicz's journal *Ost und West* in 1948, commended both Hocke and Seghers (West and East) to young writers. He advised them to write reportage before embarking on novels. At the First Writers' Congress Hermlin had called into question 'high' literature because it made people afraid 'die Dinge in ihrer grauenhaften und merkwürdigen Einfachheit darzustellen'.[3] With the great Second World War reportage produced in the USA and the USSR he contrasted a tedious obsession with form. It is clear that Hermlin's concern with clarity and immediacy is close to Hocke's, despite the fact that Hermlin goes on to imply a hierarchy of literary values when he writes that he does not rule out the possibility that reportage 'später einmal Material für eine Erzählung abgibt' (p. 39). In October 1948, at the Leipzig congress of young activists and writers, Hermlin once again outlined his views on reportage. The framework for the Congress was a discussion of Socialist Realism and the Soviet model, and hence of the contradiction between a working political aesthetic and one derived from the classical tradition. This aesthetic debate mirrors the contradiction between conflicting aims: that of constructing a socialist economy in the Soviet zone (although that was not yet fully articulated) and that of preventing the division of the German nation. Hermlin could not reconcile this fundamental contradiction, especially as it was exacerbated by his desire to distinguish the professional writer from the amateur, the creative writer from the journalist. He addressed aspiring authors thus:

> Aber warum muß es gleich ein Roman sein? . . . Nein, es gibt eine Stufenleiter der Formen. Das bedeutet nicht, daß die Reportage überhaupt unter dem Roman steht. Eine Reportage von Kisch und ein Roman der Seghers haben das gleiche spezifische Gewicht. Aber ich bin überzeugt, daß man vom Bericht und von der Reportage aus an die Gestaltung von Menschen und ihrer widerspruchsvollen Entwicklung erst herankommen muß.[4]

But if one were to assume that Hocke's enthusiasm about reportage and the GDR difficulties acknowledged by Seghers and Hermlin might imply a blossoming of reportage about the GDR in West Germany and conversely a dearth of travel writing about West Germany in the GDR, such a conclusion would be erroneous. The following analysis of hitherto neglected texts paints a different picture.

Surveys of post-war literature compiled shortly after the building of the Wall seem to suggest that the attempts at realism practised in the Western zones had not succeeded in capturing what the early GDR was like. They also indicated that GDR Socialist Realism of the 1950s produced not the expected great novel of the divided Germany but much reportage. Surveys published in the autumn of 1961 in both East and West reveal that contemporaries failed to see the decisive break that the Wall represented. With their references to the various forms of reportage in the two German states they demonstrate, too, that Hocke's 'Deutschlandfahrt' of 1946 had found no echo in the Cold War. The vast majority of travel writing in West Germany and the GDR was made up of reportage about those countries with which the two German states had entered political and, from 1955, military alliances.

West German travel literature treating the GDR as a lost homeland could be seen as supporting government demands for a re-unification of the German Reich within the borders of 1937. In the 1950s these texts are complemented by other West German versions of the same stamp: autobiographical stories of escape, either from east of the Oder–Neisse line or from the GDR. This ideological bias no doubt springs from the autobiographical authenticity of the accounts; personal experience clouds objectivity and wider social awareness. By focusing on a GDR located in the past, these autobiographies helped to create an atmosphere in the West German media which Gerhard Schoenberner described as 'Schizophrenie der "Nachrichten aus der Zone"', making 'das Land zwischen Elbe und Oder zu einer wahren terra incognita'.[5] Travel literature amounted to little more than memories of childhood and escape accounts. The GDR was passed off as a lost homeland. West German readers learned little about everyday life in the GDR, except about those who were engaged in final preparations for escape to West Germany, as little as they could from the press, radio and, increasingly, television news, in which, according to Schoenberner, one 'grundsätzlich nur von Versorgungsschwierigkeiten und Zuchthausurteilen hört' (p. 65).

It was less the problems associated with travel between the zones than the non-recognition of the existence of a second German state that accounts for the conflation of Germany and West Germany in Bertelsmann's *Praktisches Reisebuch*. In 1954 the author managed to depict Germany as an undivided whole, even including Berlin among 'Zonenrandgebiete':

> Die Bundesrepublik Deutschland (245292 qkm mit rund 48000000 Menschen) ist, gemessen an der ganzen Erde, ein kleines Land. Doch Gott hat diese Erde geschaffen und seine Gaben gleichmäßig verteilt. Dem einen gab er Größe, dem anderen Schönheit. Deutschland hat er dabei mit Schönheit bedacht, und Schönheit ist in dieser Welt, damit sich der Mensch an ihr erfreue.[6]

The publisher's foreword draws attention to the economic function of recreational delights afforded by West Germany: 'Jeder versucht auf seine Art, Kraft und Arbeitsfreude für ein ganzes Jahr aus seinem kurzen Urlaub mit heimzubringen' (p. 5). The traveller, secure in the knowledge that he can be satisfied with the beauties of West Germany, is confident that the truth about the GDR can be known from memory. Reportage about the current realities of the 'other' German state is rendered superfluous.

From the late 1950s onwards the publication of travel books about the GDR signalled that this wholly unrealistic attitude was gradually being abandoned. While volumes like Horst Mönnich's *Das Land ohne Träume* and Eberhard Schulz's *Deutschland heute* had, with their concentration on autobiography and cultural history, consigned the GDR to the margins, reportage by Erich

Kuby and Rudolf Walter Leonhardt began tentatively to shift the focus to the present. Kuby made the following telling point:

> Während die Großmächte Rußland und Amerika den äußersten Punkt des Kalten Krieges überwunden zu haben scheinen und den mühsamen und opferreichen Kompromiß unter der Drohung atomarer Vernichtung suchen, gewinnen bei uns die Kräfte die Oberhand, die die Suppe ihrer revisionistischen und nationalistischen Politik am antikommunistischen Feuer kochen wollen.[7]

Kuby described what historians have called the 'Spätblüte des Kalten Krieges' in West Germany.[8] The Bonn government's posturing over re-unification contrasted ever more markedly with the US policy aim of détente in Europe. West Germans reporting on the GDR opposed the dominant (and specious) propaganda which fed off the Khrushchev ultimatum and the building of the Wall. These writers constituted a section of the 'Anerkennungspartei', a rainbow alliance mainly made up of journalists and just a few politicians drawn from non-conservative parties. Even then, it should not be forgotten that following a 'Reise in ein fernes Land' undertaken with Leonhardt and Theo Sommer, Marion Gräfin Dönhoff, editor of *Die Zeit*, proposed a middle way between the Cold War and détente, arguing for 'keine Anerkennung der DDR, aber auch nicht diese geradezu hysterische Angst vor ihrer "Aufwertung"'.[9]

In the GDR the relationship between government policy on the German Question and GDR reportage about West Germany was quite different. From 1955 SED and GDR government documents referred to the existence of two German states, and the term détente was used as early as 1953. Yet, quite explicitly from 1952 onwards, the building of a socialist order in the GDR was propagated as a model for the whole of Germany. The terms 're-unification' and 'Gesamtdeutschland' muddied the waters for the various initiatives intended, by the GDR, to open negotiations between the West German and GDR governments. Doubts remained despite express commitment to the neutrality of a re-unified Germany or its integration within a collective European security system. The fundamental contradiction is revealed by Walter Ulbricht's accusation that, on the one hand, the West German government was betraying the nation by integrating West Germany into the Western alliance, while, on the other hand, they were planning the military annexation of the GDR and parts of Czechoslovakia and Poland.[10] Similarly, in 1950 Konrad Adenauer publicly declared GDR propaganda on re-unification to be preparation for military expansion, and he described the construction of a socialist society in the GDR as 'sovietisation' and contrary to the German character and traditions.[11] For all the parallels in each side's perception of the other's aggressive re-unification rhetoric,[12] there was also a certain lack of congruence: West Germany considered the idea of liberation as a matter of foreign policy for the major powers, while the GDR emphasised the significance of internal West German politics. The West German government encouraged the hope that the military superiority of the USA and NATO would combine to force the USSR to abandon the GDR. Meanwhile, the SED initially supported KPD rhetoric of the revolutionary overthrow of the Adenauer dictatorship, but then, after the banning of the KPD in 1956, demanded a change of government and, finally, the elimination of militarist and revanchist elements in West Germany. Irrespective of the sincerity and realism of the SED's re-unification propaganda,[13] all Walter Ulbricht's keynote speeches addressed the current situation in West Germany in terms of the relations between the two states and possible re-unification. The unremitting focus on internal developments in West Germany was reflected by the continuing interest in GDR newspapers and magazines in the early post-war reportage tradition of 'Deutschlandfahrten'. One of the consequences of governmental interest in the genre was that much of the published reportage in the GDR about West Germany strove to illustrate points made in party documents.

Reportage produced by two prominent authors may serve characteristic examples. One of them, Hans Mayer, later left the GDR; the other, Robert Havemann, stayed on to become the archetypal dissident. Havemann's 'Begegnungen in Deutschland' appeared on 16 April 1950 in *Sonntag*, the weekly journal of the Kulturbund. As in so much reportage from the immediate post-war period, a third-class railway compartment was the setting. The portraits of the passengers were confined to details about their background and politics, the dialogue to a statistical comparison of living standards. Havemann's account switches to the present as he astounds the West German passengers: 'Was sie hören, steht im schärfsten Gegensatz zu allem, was in ihren Zeitungen zu lesen ist.' Havemann has a former Soviet prisoner-of-war recount his participation in the work of reconstruction, 'die das ganze sowjetische Volk mit bis zur Aufopferung gehender Begeisterung vollbringt'. A Social Democrat is moved to rise from his seat 'als einfacher Deutscher' and to characterise 'die antisowjetische Politik meiner

Parteiführung in Hannover als den größten Feind allen Strebens zur deutschen Einheit'. Hans Mayer's piece, 'Westdeutsche Reiseerlebnisse', which appeared in *Sonntag* on 22 October 1950, also begins by linking the political awareness of the individual West German citizen with the SED position: 'Das Besatzungsstatut sorgt dafür, . . . daß sich der Westdeutsche in jedem Augenblick bewußt wird, einer amerikanischen Kolonie anzugehören.'[14] With scant regard for the consistency of his argument, Mayer juxtaposes specific events (the banning of works by Jaroslav Hasek and Günther Weisenborn, or Elisabeth Langgässer's death due to 'Entkräftung und Entbehrung') and commentary intended to stress the 'Mischung aus Nazigeist und Wildwest, aus formalistischen Snobs und Kulturbarbarei' in the West and the suppression of all progressive movements: 'Wer aus der DDR kommt und Westdeutschland mit Bewußtsein erlebt, muß Übelkeit verspüren'. As in all reportage from the GDR, Frankfurt, Heidelberg and West Berlin were singled out as particularly offensive to GDR sensibilities.

Anna Seghers delivered a timely warning against the danger of taking SED resolutions as blueprints for a picture of reality.[15] The first representative collection, *Menschen und Werke* of 1952,[16] demonstrated that this danger was not confined to reportage dealing with West Germany; it was rooted in the general understanding of literature in terms of cultural politics, with the problem at its most acute in relation to realism. Yet the collection pointed up a paradox: if GDR reportage concentrated on the model socialist reconstruction in the GDR as a blueprint for a future united Germany, what of everyday West German realities? If these were excluded, then literature could not claim to offer what was typical. If they were included, then travelogues about West Germany need not be measured against the norm of the typical and hence acquired an unusual status. The link between the construction of socialism in the GDR and an image of a future German state had a liberating effect. The collection *Menschen und Werke* was intended to mark a new beginning:

> Verstehen unsere Schriftsteller, sich noch tiefer mit der Wirklichkeit unseres neuen Lebens . . . zu verbinden, so wird ihnen bald auch deren Darstellung in Romanen und Schauspielen gelingen. Der Stellvertreter des Ministerpräsidenten Walter Ulbricht hat bei der Begründung des Fünfjahrplans darauf hingewiesen, daß die Hauptaufgabe unserer Literatur gegenwärtig darin besteht, diesen Übergang zur Gestaltung des Neuen in großen literarischen Formen zu erreichen. (pp. 9–10)

In 1958 Christa Wolf's survey of the development of GDR prose writing appeared. Commissioned by the German Writers' Union, it formed part of a collection entitled *Deutsche Literatur der Gegenwart*; significantly, GDR literature did not yet recognise itself as such. Wolf criticised the fact that since 1953–4, when as many as twelve titles had appeared, little reportage dealing with the GDR had been published.[17] Without going so far as to identify herself with a hierarchy of narrative and descriptive prose, she supported her argument that reportage (and reportage not confined to the GDR) should be promoted by arguing that 'es eine operativ wirksame Literatur ist, in der sich auch junge Autoren Verdienste erwerben können' (pp. 55–60).

It was established GDR novelists, rather than young authors, who produced reportage about West Germany. A comparison with West German authors of GDR reportage demonstrates that visitors from the GDR were returning to the world of their childhood. The routes taken by the Rhinelander Maximilian Scheer, the Westphalian Eduard Claudius and the Swabian Wolfgang Joho were organised around the visit to their home. It is significant that the GDR reviewer of their work noted: 'Alle drei Autoren sehen übrigens bei dieser Gelegenheit ihre alte Heimat wieder, aber merkwürdigerweise ist ihnen auch gemeinsam, daß gerade die entsprechenden Abschnitte zu den schwächeren Teilen ihrer Berichte gehören.'[18] The accounts exclude mention of re-union with relatives, reflecting the low priority accorded by Claudius, Joho and Scheer to the autobiographical dimension in their choice in 1945 of the Soviet zone, which they chose as their 'home' after exile in the West or time spent as British prisoners-of-war. While they repeatedly emphasised that they were travelling in Germany as Germans, they seemed to be propagating a GDR model for a re-unified Germany. Yet their search for common ground between the two German states, their desire to establish, through their reporting, the irrelevance of the border, proved precisely the opposite: they depicted an increasing estrangement from a West German way of life. In doing so, they gained insights which ran counter to the task entrusted to them by cultural politicians, insights which, moreover, were the more piquant because these authors were well acquainted with the geography, history, people and traditions of the areas through which they travelled in West Germany.

Joho, Scheer and Claudius discovered two things not foreseen in party documents, discoveries made possible only because they eschewed what could be termed the 'aesthetic of anticipation'. They discerned the continuing influence of the past on everyday life, a past which the GDR, perhaps too quickly, declared that it had overcome. Joho alluded to Stephan Hermlin's travelogue about the People's Republic of China, *Ferne Nähe*, in his introduction to his own volume of West German reportage *Zwischen Bonn und Bodensee*, which appeared in 1954 from Aufbau-Verlag, as did Claudius's *Paradies ohne Seligkeit* and Scheer's *Spieler*, which appeared the following year. For Joho, the journey 'Zwischen Bonn und Bodensee' revealed West Germany as a 'nahe Ferne'. While in Hermlin's reportage on China geographical distance had belied a closeness in 'geistiger und menschlicher Art', the opposite was the case with the two Germanies. In his 'nüchternen Rechenschaftsbericht' Joho set himself the task 'mit eigenen Augen und Ohren [zu] prüfen und erforschen, wie es denn in Wirklichkeit steht mit diesem einen und unteilbaren, wenn auch geteilten Deutschland' (p. 5).

In line with SED policy Joho, like Scheer, saw the indivisibility of Germany embodied in culture, especially in literature. This explains the prominence he gave to conversations with intellectuals in his reportage, in order to establish the climate of opinion and to bridge the political divide. It also accounts for the shock which he felt on discovering that divisions and differences existed, 'obwohl drüben wie hüben Deutschland liegt und ich mich aufgemacht habe, das Gemeinsame zu suchen und zu festigen. Bin ich so sehr infiziert von der verhängnisvollen Vorstellung der zwei Deutschland, daß ich sie schon im Antlitz der Höhenzüge, im Gesicht der Dörfer glaube erkennen zu können?' (p. 11). In Joho's conversations, his resolve to distinguish between illusion and reality – illusion is understood as the surface appearance and as the technological and economic spheres, while reality is equated with the inner world of intellectual and cultural values – produces some unusual effects. The GDR writer, because he or she 'knows better', slips into the role of story-teller or educator in conversation with people who are themselves not interested in a common German culture. Many of their conversations are therefore presented only very briefly in tems of the insights which they offer. The interest lies in whether or not they were successful, whether the interlocutors were 'von einer Reihe falscher Vorstellungen über den anderen Teil Deutschland befreit' (p. 50) or whether they might be deemed sufficiently worthwhile 'daß man sich immer wieder mit ihnen beschäftigt' (p. 90). Joho does not report any success in gaining support for his criticism of the 'Americanisation' and 'colonisation' of West German architecture and municipal building. His criticism reappears, predictably enough, in his descriptions of cities: his first impression of Frankfurt is cast as a generalisation, and in every other city he finds confirmation of his shock at the levelling, monotony and desecration in these 'Goldgräbersiedlungen' (p. 27, p. 203). However, the people with whom Joho converses prove deaf to his calls for 'echtes Nationalempfinden' (p. 31), which has been scorned in favour of 'fremde Kultursurrogate' (p. 31). Nor is he afraid to play the nationalist card when he associates with Americanisation both the bombing of West German towns and their reconstruction.

Joho's discussions about literature demonstrate, too, that there is no common ground in the concept of a German national culture. He produces a woman in Munich, who confirms for him that the Americans have at least managed to help reduce the unproductive activity of reading, but mostly he can only note a divergence in literary tastes in the two Germanies. The low standing of Thomas Mann, the utter ignorance about GDR literature – confirmed by exceptions to the rule, such as Seghers and Brecht, whose work from the Weimar Republic is remembered – and the fixed idea that 'an die Stelle von Blut und Boden lediglich die Stahlwerke getreten seien' demonstrate to Joho 'wie sehr die Spalterpolitik das geistige Band schon zerrissen hatte' (p. 121). However much the reporter presents himself or herself as a cultural educator, taking the trouble to convey information about the GDR or to issue invitations so that people can find out about the country for themselves, the onesidedness of the conversation yields to dialogue when another matter is treated: Joho's political interest in the material situation of the intelligentsia, a subject which embraces the social function of literature. Here he does not invoke the idealistic notion of a common German culture deployed as national heritage against the USA. Instead, he explores the material conditions of writers and their readers. The idealistic and materialist dimensions are, however, reconciled in the concept of 'way of life'. Like Scheer and Claudius, Joho sees the motor car as symbolising the West German way of life: competition and individualist anarchy demonstrate the assimilation of American models. The materialism of the American way of life is dealt with in stereotyped fashion by reference to the extremely high book prices and the relatively low living standard of intellectuals and writers. The difficulty with this cultural reconciliation of idealism and materialism emerges when Joho's subjects cannot be moved to speak out against Americanisation, whether on materialistic or idealistic grounds. Joho summarises his meetings with West German artists and intellectuals as follows: 'Sie lebten in ihrer Mehrzahl unter kümmerlichen äußeren Bedingungen, diese fanatischen Verfechter ihrer individuellen Freiheit, aber sie trösteten sich darüber hinweg mit dem Bewußtsein, wenigstens geistig unabhängig zu sein, wenn sie es schon nicht materiell sein konnten' (pp. 219–20).

The metaphor of the border occupies a prominent position in Joho's accounts of travel in West Germany. It enables him to bring out different conceptions of freedom in conversation with people presented as the dupes of American influence or the SPD's policies. When he discusses freedom, Joho either quotes his interlocutors directly or offers detailed summaries of their arguments. In so doing, he includes biographies of those portrayed, attempting to explain their position historically and socially, so as to avoid any impression of manipulation. Most are sceptical and critical of the West German government. While they may reject the GDR, they do not, Joho insists, have a hostile attitude towards it. Joho accounts for the importance which they attach to the 'eigene Fasson, selig zu werden' and their dislike of the 'einheitliche Ausrichtung' of the GDR in terms of liberal traditions, the experience of National Socialism, and the apolitical attitudes struck in the wake of post-war disillusion. His own views are conveyed in the form of a commentary addressed to the GDR reader. He criticises the ivory tower attitudes inherent in the notion of 'geistige Freiheit', condemning it as élitist arrogance and as the abandonment of a resistance mentality; he feels justified in so doing since he relates the anti-ideological private stance of the West German citizen of his generation to the Nazi period:

> Er empfindet Unbehagen und wird eines Tages vielleicht noch größeres Unbehagen empfinden (wie damals, als er, gezwungen und mit Repressalien bedroht, in die NSDAP eintrat), aber er wird nicht mehr tun, als sich selbst zurückzuziehen, in jene passive und unfruchtbare sogenannte 'innere Emigration'. (p. 75)

Joho vaguely relates sceptical, apolitical values to the Nazi experience, but fights shy of making a causal connection. Maximilian Scheer, however, in his West German travelogue *Spieler* detects straightforward continuity. Since in every scene his third-person reportage shows his traveller, modelled on Heine and Seume, to be superior from the outset, there is no serious debate with non-conformist West German intellectuals. It is only at the Wednesday discussions at Cologne railway station that the author demands to know why West German intellectuals are absent from the world peace movement; for once, he does not find an answer exclusively in the way in which American psychological warfare takes up fascist propaganda. On this single occasion he reflects on one writer's experiences with communists who used and discarded him, and another's assessment of communist propaganda: 'Man übermittelt fertige Denkresultate, ohne den Leser oder Hörer logisch zu diesen Resultaten zu führen' (p. 170). Scheer's prime concern in his travelogue is, however, to attack the Germans for their perennial thoughtlessness, their congenital inability to employ reason and think politically. Throughout, Coca Cola and Volkswagen symbolise the combination of a new 'foreign influence' and old 'dreams and illusions'. In many details of everyday life Scheer gives prominence to the continuity of reactionary German traditions. Yet his own calls for 'healthy' sexual mores or for a German people modelled on Tacitus's image of them, as opposed to 'nationale Würdelosig-keit', 'Überfremdung' and 'Nachäffung von Ausländern', occasionally lapse into bombastic nationalism despite his patently satirical intention.

In his use of the metaphor of the Germans' 'Konstruktionsfehler' Scheer adheres closely to the 'Misere-Theorie' of German history, a theory which was criticised with increasing vehemence after 1951. There is an echo of it in Joho's reportage. Significantly, Joho does not merely criticise nonconformist West German intellectuals who talk about Germany and the Germans as if they themselves did not belong; his criticism is also directed at the West German government's ignoring history and choosing Bonn as a capital, a choice epitomised by the functionalist architecture of the Bundeshaus. As elsewhere, Joho here shows that anti-government intellectuals are actually in agreement with the very government which they criticise. Their weakness, he argues, is the fact that they place all the blame on the unchangeable German character, which absolves them of the responsibility of addressing major problems. West Germany, for Joho, mirrors the problems faced by some intellectuals in the GDR. He concentrates on the border between the ivory tower and socially committed literature, between the theory of intellectual freedom and a willingness to engage the fundamental conditions of social life. He goes on to appeal to those members of the GDR intelligentsia who are either still trapped in the reactionary traditions of the German educated middle classes or who tend 'sich vor all dem, was im weitesten Sinn mit Politik zu tun hat, zurückzuziehen': 'Insofern ist eine Reise nach Westdeutschland . . . keine Reise in ein anderes Land, sondern eine Reise von Deutschland nach Deutschland' (p. 226). Joho ultimately proclaims the idea of one Germany, yet he finds it difficult to reconcile the different ways in which German traditions have been assimilated in East and West, and among these are the different traditions of reportage.

Significantly, it was precisely those authors of travelogues about West Germany who, in 1955, collaborated in the German Writers' Union on the preparation of a conference entitled 'Die Reportage – gestern und heute'. The conclusions reached here differed markedly from the theoretical statements about reportage formulated in the 1950s in the 'Bitterfelder Weg' and canonised by GDR literary history. During the debate G. Just took up the point about reportage from the 'whole of Germany'. Seizing upon Scheer's definition of the reporter as a 'Gesellschaftsforscher', he demanded that every piece of reportage should be 'ein Stück Entdeckung'. Indirectly he was criticising the editor of *Neues Deutschland*, Günter Kertzscher, who had accused reporters of a 'Sucht nach Schönfärberei'. Just explained their failure to produce an authentic picture of contradictory social conditions by pointing to the mode of representation which they adopted. He criticised the tendency 'das bereits Erkannte und in Beschlüssen und Dokumenten Festgelegte auf mehr oder weniger geschickte Art und Weise noch einmal zu illustrieren'.[19] In his attack upon the the self-assured and arrogant reporter Just was making a psychological and moral issue of the problem which Kertzscher had identified. For there was more than a personal attitude at stake in the argument that

> viele unserer Reporter . . . das Leben nicht beobachten, um aus Beobachtungen Schlußfolgerungen zu ziehen und Lösungen zu finden, sondern daß sie die Lösungen (der Konflikte) schon in der Tasche haben, wenn sie an die Beobachtung des Lebens herangehen . . . Sie wissen schon, wie die ganze Geschichte ausgeht; es kann sie eigentlich nichts mehr überraschen. (p. 36)

Just's critique of a method of reportage which tempted the reporter 'nur das zu beobachten, was zu ihrer Lösung paßt und von vornherein vor bestimmten Dingen die Augen zu verschließen'

(p. 37) characterised most tellingly the definition of the genre later institutionalised in the GDR. Yet the conclusion is inescapable that the abstract warning against preconceived ideas was not so far removed from a naive juxtaposition of immediacy and objectivity, reality and truth.

A comparison of the avowedly partisan GDR reportage about West Germany with West German reportage about the GDR, which was committed to an aesthetic of immediacy and would-be objectivity, yields surprising results. West German travel writers appeared self-assured; for them GDR reality only confirmed preconceived notions. GDR reporters in West Germany, on the other hand, failed in their task of exemplifying SED political propaganda when they encountered West German reality. The different styles of reportage, East and West, underline two discoveries made by GDR reporters in West Germany: the continuing influence of the past and the divisibility of German culture. West German travel writers carried on the traditions of the war-time propaganda company report and the conservative essay without being aware of the problems inherent in this tradition.[20] GDR travel writers, when not operating in a socialist context, took up a tradition which had been discontinued: that of socialist reportage as an aesthetic weapon in the class struggle, as produced by Egon Erwin Kisch and continued in the GDR by F. C. Weiskopf. GDR writers also drew on the revolutionary travel literature produced by Forster, Seume and Heine.[21] The various traditions are revealed in the preference for different forms of discourse and different modes of representation. The resulting styles can be seen to operate between two contrasting tendencies: what Dieter Schlenstedt has called 'Pseudo-Konkretion' and the 'Herstellen komplexen sozialen Zusammenhangs'.[22] The former style tends to blend description of empirically observed documentary material with the observer's account of his thoughts, feelings, interpretations, evaluations, and reflections. The latter style raises the reader's expectations of 'verifiable truth' and 'historical and social insight'. Dieter Schlenstedt extrapolates the following from the 'Kisch tradition':

Die Reportage erhebt ihren Anspruch auf Wirklichkeitsübereinstimmung auf merkbare Weise, weil sie ein bestimmtes rezeptives Verhalten, einen bestimmten Umgang des Lesers mit der Darstellung herstellen will. Der Leser soll die Wirklichkeit des in der Darstellung Präsentierten *setzen* und sich so zu ihm in eine ernsthafte Beziehung, in die Beziehung zur Realität bringen. (p. 387)

'Merkbar' does not mean that report and comment were strictly separated; it means that a form of generalisation and evaluation was employed which was alien to that type of reportage which stressed immediacy. In the latter case a slice of reality was presented without any noticeable intervention on the part of a reporter, whose point of view was identical to the chosen perspective on reality. The reader's acquiescence was also automatically assumed: a different point of view was precluded by the fact that the chosen perspective appeared to be universally valid. In contrast, the combination of situation and reflection, of report interwoven with the reporter's comment, constituted a different, more problematic, genre. Further differences in the mode of representation complicated the issue. In West German reportage about the GDR the reproduction of the speech of others was generally via the method recommended in the 'Bitterfelder Weg'. Figures introduced by direct speech were usually the author's mouthpiece. If characters were introduced with differing opinions, they were to be treated ironically. GDR travel authors found it difficult to treat ironically, or dismiss as ideology, everything that West Germans said to them. Taking seriously the words of others led to dialogue playing a greater role, various ideologies being set against each other in relation to a contested reality.

The 1950 collection *Das ist Germany*, edited by Arthur Settel, head of the press department of the US high commission, reads like a compendium of core motifs for Cold War reportage. Reporting specifically about the GDR is confined to one chapter, 'Die Zone des Schweigens', which is placed for effect at the end. In his introduction the former Military Governor-General, Lucius D. Clay, defines reportage in a way which echoes the post-war realist theory of immediacy. He introduces his almost exclusively British and American authors as 'experienced reporters', inferring an 'objective depiction' from their 'Beobachtungsfähigkeit': 'Durch ihre Augen Deutschland sehen, heißt wirklich, Deutschland sehen' (p. vii). Logically enough, their GDR reportage is shot through with the contradictory assertions that, on the one hand, everything has become 'offenbar' (p. 353) and, on the other, that socialism is a 'Geheimnis' (p. 331), a 'ziemlich dunkles Geschäft' (p. 359), a 'höchst dunkler Vorgang' (p. 342), which has 'sich erst zum Teil enthüllt' (p. 358). This contradiction is resolved by reported conversations which support the author's judgement. Thus we are informed of the 'obvious similarities' between the Hitler Youth and the Free

German Youth: 'Junge Deutsche, die in beiden Organisationen waren, sagen, sie seien bis auf die Hemdfarbe und die politische Propaganda ein und dasselbe' (p. 353). Another witness, a prominent refugee, makes the following comment about 'concentration camps': 'Gleichwohl ist es nichts als fair, darauf hinzuweisen, daß die Gaskammern nicht wieder "in Betrieb" genommen worden sind und daß sich die Behandlung der Gefangenen nach den ersten drei Jahren anscheinend gebessert hat' (pp. 364–5). The distinction between appearance and reality is used as a stick with which to beat the SED as the 'gefährlichste politische Partei Nachkriegsdeutschlands' (p. 353). Indeed, reportage about the GDR is packed with metaphors of unmasking, which fail to be directed against a naive trust in appearances and a distrust of totalitarianism. Its 'täuschende . . . Vorarbeit', 'Maske', 'Deckmantel', 'Fiktion' and 'Schatten' are to be revealed as dangerous and induce the reader to assume the role ascribed to the Germans in the Cold War by Richard Löwenthal: 'Den Kalten Krieg ohne Pardon ausfechten' (p. 53). In the reportage bearing this title West Berlin is labelled the 'Ostmark der westlichen Demokratie', and the social democratic population is said to be ready to take up arms; Löwenthal makes the Mayor, Ernst Reuter, the mouthpiece of his own belief in the liberation of Eastern Europe, the 'Anschluß einer befreiten Ostzone' by a 'blühenden westdeutschen Staat durch unaufhörliche politische Kriegführung' (p. 52).

The fact that many travel writers were 'nicht nur neugierig, sondern auch mißtrauisch' by no means rendered them immune to the Cold War.[23] A rejection of ideology encouraged them to trust appearances, which in turn made them less sensitive to historical and social factors. In *Die Welt* G. H. Witter proclaimed the travel writer's credo: 'Hinsehen! Umhören! Aufschreiben! Ohne Reflektion und Kommentar! Die Sachen müssen für sich selber sprechen! Er verzichtet auf gefällige Redensarten und ist nur noch hart, klar und unparteiisch.'[24] In his 'Reportage über Reportage' in *Der Ruf* Ottmar Katz indignantly rebutted the editor's question as to how he intended to 'die Geschichte aufziehen': 'ich will sie gar nicht aufziehen und will sie nicht so oder so sehen, sondern ich will hinfahren und alles aufschreiben, was ich sehe, und mehr will ich nicht.'[25] The repudiation of authorial comment, which was suspected of ideology and of partisanship, implied the suppression of the possibility that different points of view might offer differing perspectives upon the world. Conscious construction of a complex picture consisting of description, authentic accounts and comment was replaced by what Katz termed the supposedly spontaneous lack of ambiguity in the 'Momentaufnahme, die . . . ein ganz besonders geprägtes Bild zeigt'.[26] It was in the way in which minor details acquired symbolic significance that one could detect the convergence of different traditions in Cold War reportage about East Germany. These were, as indicated earlier, the propaganda company report and the conservative essay.

Reifenberg supplies an example of the latter; his reportage from East Berlin on the occasion of the First German Writers' Congress deploys a variety of imagery in order to evaluate Anna Seghers's polemic against the notion of 'geistige Freiheit' and Elisabeth Langgässer's critique of ivory tower attitudes. The author adopts the image of the archaeologist to describe his technique, a metaphor intended to lend credence to his claims of critical distance and meticulous attention to detail: 'In dem unkenntlichen Schutt glänzt zuweilen dickes Spiegelglas auf. Berlin ist ein Objekt künftiger Archäologen.'[27] The fragments collected and put on display in Reifenberg's text are gestures juxtaposed in such a way that East–West contrasts acquire human significance. At the beginning it is a married couple at the zonal border, at the end a group of three men: 'Der Mann hatte die Rechte auf die Schulter der Greisin gelegt und wies mit der Linken das westliche Licht. Die Geste ergriff mich, es war, als hätten die letzten Menschen das Ziel erreicht' (p. 13). At the end the light in the West is contrasted with the darkness in the East: 'ein gefährlich fremdes Land' (p. 16). In the 'flash' of a 'navigational light' there is expressed the same danger and mystery which Reifenberg detects in Seghers's speech: 'Noch lange hatte ich den eigentümlich beschwörenden Klang dieser Dichterstimme im Ohr, die wie aus einer dunklen Wolke des persönlichen Lebens Gedanken gleich verwirrende Blitze herniederschleuderte' (p. 15). Reifenberg answers metaphorically the only explicitly political question posed in his text. He does so, significantly, by quoting Rudolf Hagelstange: 'sollen wir Deutsche auf der Suche nach der Menschheit für immer dem Westen den Rücken kehren?' (p. 16). The question is answered in the image of migration from East to West, from darkness into light, thus dispensing with the need for further comment.

Possible reasons emerge for his refusal to reflect on historial and social circumstances when Reifenberg employs this technique in relation to Elisabeth Langgässer. He may well have felt that he

was a target for Langgässer's criticism of authors who had remained in Nazi Germany and whose esoteric style was an
'anakreontische(s) Tändeln mit Blumen und Blümchen über den
scheußlichen, weit geöffneten, aber eben mit diesen Blümchen
überdeckten Abgrund der Massengräber'.[28] Instead of exploring the
historical reasons for Langgässer's comments on ivory tower attitudes, he clings to the imagery: 'sie nannte ihn ein Türmchen aus
weißem Horn, vergleichbar den Federhaltern, die in einer Linse
eine Miniaturaussicht bargen' (p. 14). The way in which Reifenberg
manipulates the image reveals just how easily historical subject
matter could be adapted to the conservative essay and its type of
reportage. He associates the quotation with his memories of the
exile writer Joseph Roth, with whom he had worked as an editor
on the *Frankfurter Zeitung* during the Weimar Republic. Personal
reminiscence is deployed as a defence against criticism directed
at the very same kind of behaviour which Reifenberg was himself
displaying years later. Not only does he reveal his excessively
apologist intention by twice projecting on to the exile writer his
own literary theory, he also lays claim to Roth's influence when
he seeks to obscure the distinction between the sufferings of the
victims of Nazism and those of the Germans themselves. When
Reifenberg speaks of 'Feueröfen', his choice of metaphor echoes
something that Langgässer had said, although Reifenberg omits to
cite it directly:

> Josef [*sic*] Roth, so fiel mir ein, hätte diesen Vergleich nicht gebilligt,
> denn der Dichter hätte in solch einem Federhalter den Zauberstab der
> Phantasie ergriffen und durch diese Kinderlinse alle Herrlichkeit der
> Welt gesehen. Schließlich entdeckte ich in einem Hof der Jägerstraße
> einen Haufen ausrangierter Briefkästen, verrostete und undichte Opfer
> des Bombardements. Da sehnte ich mir . . . den Dichter (Roth) herbei . . .
> – er hätte mir die zerbeulten Eisenbehälter zum Sprechen gebracht
> und mir anvertraut, was im Gluthauch einer letzten Nacht an Wünschen
> und Ängsten der Einwohner dieser Stadt für immer zu Asche geworden
> sein mag. Die zarte Seele von Josef Roth hätte aus diesen Feueröfen der
> Metropole den Menschenstimmen, den armen und unscheinbaren, noch
> einmal zum Laut verholfen und ihnen die Bangnis genommen. (p. 14)

Erich Kuby, dispatched to Berlin by the *Süddeutsche Zeitung* at the
time of the blockade, entitled his reportage 'An der Spree schlägt
das Herz Europas', the metaphor epitomising his perspective.[29]
Distancing himself from politicians both of the Western allies and
the Soviet zone, he stressed his own credibility. He assured a

mayor in the Soviet Zone: 'ich stünde im Geruch, keine Meinung zu haben, vor allem keine vorgefaßte. Ich sei ein völlig unbrauchbares Objekt für Propaganda jeder Art.'[30] The values of both sides were mocked and contrasted with such fundamental concepts as 'life' and 'German values': 'Aber in Berlin geht es ... nicht um Weltanschauungen, sondern darum, ob ich, unter anderem, darüber bestimmen darf, welche Bücher ich lesen will, was meine Kinder werden sollen und ob ich meine Gedanken ausdrücken darf ... wir haben überhaupt keine Wahl'.[31] This combination of anti-ideological distancing and overblown metaphor undermined the theoretical claim to objectivity and immediacy. Thus, the 'compelling image', with which, seven years later, Horst Mönnich concluded his 'Reise durch die deutsche Wirklichkeit' was not only a formal rejection of sober reportage, but also reflected his views about West Germany, 'Das Land ohne Träume'.[32] Clinging to the dream of re-unification – which figures in no reportage about West Germany – leads him into an emotive profession of faith. A female tractor driver on a collective farm, who is also a Sunday School teacher and derived pleasure from working on the former landowner's estate, is fed the following sentences: 'Aber nicht deswegen, weil sie zu uns sagen: "Dieses Land ist euer, euch gehört es!" – darauf muß ich antworten: "Nein, der Besitzer ist noch immer derselbe. Gott ist es. Ihm gehört die Erde. Vielleicht haben die Verwalter gewechselt. Nicht der Besitzer"' (p. 213). Mönnich extrapolates from this a common German, indeed universally valid, attitude, based on the religious content of the image, a process whereby private property is guaranteed by the spiritual realm.

Mönnich's sobriety as a reporter turns out to be just as problematic as that which he ascribes to West Germany. His gloss on the title of his travel work functions, too, as self-portrait of the former propaganda company reporter, who made his debut in 1943 with *Russischer Sommer*: 'Ich bin durch das nüchternste Land der Erde gefahren, und ich habe ein Volk getroffen, das seine Vergangenheit so vergessen zu haben scheint wie seine Zukunft. Ich sah, daß es von nur einem Gedanken bewegt wird wie von einem Motor: von dem Gedanken an seine Gegenwart' (p. 7). The comparison of West Germany with a car is an echo of Mönnich's novel of 1954 about the 'Autostadt' Wolfsburg. Interestingly, in his biographical sketch the author forgets where he has learnt the skill of writing reportage: 'Den Krieg erlebte er an der West- und

Ostfront vom ersten bis zum letzten Tage, flüchtete über See aus dem Kurlandkessel, war dann Landarbeiter in Holstein und 1948 als Redakteur in Hamburg tätig, wo er durch Hans Zehrers hohe und gute Schule des Journalismus ging' (p. 2). The reference to Zehrer betrays something of Mönnich's past: Zehrer, during his spell as editor–in–chief of the British *Die Welt* (and with the agreement of the British controller) regarded experience of writing propaganda company reports on the Eastern front as proof of journalistic competence.

This 'university' of West German reportage was attended by other authors of West German travelogues about the GDR, such as Rudolf Walter Leonhardt, Eberhard Schulz and even Erich Kuby, who had made serious efforts to gain entry to a propaganda company by submitting examples of his work. In contrast to Mönnich, who as a member of the 'Gruppe 47' continued to purvey a familiar image of the enemy without apparently causing offence to the group, Leonhardt, Schulz and Kuby show how differently the literary heritage of Nazism could be treated in the context of the Cold War: their liberal, conservative, and leftist development of the reportage tradition conformed to the pattern of lessons learned from authentic and bitter personal experience. Because of a marked reluctance to pass direct comment, the condemnation of ideology emerges only indirectly in this kind of reportage. Its political tendencies emerge in three characteristic, anti-socialist motifs: for the conservative Schulz it is the memory of pre-war Germany; for the liberal Leonhardt it is the appeal to intellectual freedom; for the left-wing Kuby it is the cynicism of his style, the fact that he takes on Western prejudice but at the same time refuses to present GDR realities from a GDR point of view.

Schulz's invocation of Germany in former times darkly hints at the danger for the future lurking behind everyday experiences in a GDR world, where so much is 'zwielichtig und schwer deutbar'.[33] His ironic comments on everyday life in the GDR are contrasted with the affectionate depiction of familiar scenery, in which the old days are brought to life again:

> Wir erreichten den Bach, wir gingen über den Steg, der immer noch kein Geländer hatte, wir grüßten einen Mann, der eine Sense auf der Schulter trug, und er grüßte zurück, als seien wir nur der oder jener, gingen unter einem Tor hindurch, erreichten die Kirche und erfuhren die Wahrheit, daß die Jahre auf dem Lande keine Zahlen haben. Der Schmied hämmerte. In das Haus daneben traten wir ein. (p. 66)

If for Schulz 'die alte stillstehende Zeit' (p. 90) represented a refuge for traditional humane values,[34] then for the liberal Leonhardt
it symbolised the continuation in the GDR of a German past with
which West Germany had broken. Leonhardt's travelogue *X-mal
Deutschland* (in which five of the sixty-three sections deal with the
GDR) marked the first use of dialogue in which GDR figures were
not employed ironically as the mouthpieces of Western viewpoints.
This is what gave the classical allusion employed by his Leipzig
professor its credibility. The latter contrasted the intellectual
freedom of West German 'Athenians' with 'Mitteldeutschland: Das
rote Sparta' (p. 113). The travel writer's urbane generosity of spirit
is an appropriate vehicle for a superior attitude deriving from an
awareness of the obvious disparity between a socialist theory and
everday experience; he and the professor, however, evidently see
quite different things. Georg, the Leipzig professor, says

> 'Du wirst diesen Staat nie verstehen, wenn du etwas anderes darin
> siehst als den letzten und daher gültigsten Versuch eines uralten
> Bemühens der Menschen: ihrem Sein einen Sinn zu geben'. 'Weißt
> du, Schorsch, ich habe gar nichts gegen das Bemühen. Aber – sieh
> mal zum Fenster hinaus! – das, was dabei herauskommt, ist doch
> furchtbar'. Draußen war Schichtwechsel. Aus Dutzenden von Eisen-
> bahnzügen und Omnibussen war eine graue, uniforme Masse von
> Arbeitern und Angestellten herausgequollen, die nun in Straßen und
> Gäßchen auseinanderfloß. Es wirkte alles so entsetzlich triste und
> trostlos. (p. 113)

The contrast between the masses and the individual, social
pressure and freedom (above all, the freedom of the car driver),
informs Leonhardt's definition of German literature. German literature is identified with West Germany, where writers can be
critical and novelists especially must be critical by dint of their
'enge Bindung an die Wirklichkeit': 'Dem genau entgegengesetzt ist
die Mäzenaten-Theorie von der Kunst. Sie lautet, auf die einfachste
Formel gebracht: Maecenas (der König, der Führer, der Staat, die
Partei) tut viel für die Dichter, darf also erwarten, daß die Dichter
auch etwas für Maecenas, den König, den Führer, den Staat, die
Partei tun' (p. 460). The juxtaposition of Nazi past and GDR present
replaces any description or reflection in Leonhardt's reportage.
Without mentioning other names than – in passing – those of Brecht
and Strittmatter, let alone a single work, the literary editor of *Die
Zeit* proclaims the inferiority and lack of independence of everything that is written, printed and read in the GDR, contrasting it

with *German* literature i.e. West German literature, three-quarters of which is the literature of the 'Gruppe 47': 'Es gibt kein Werk der DDR-Literatur, in dem der Sozialismus und seine Errungenschaft auch nur versuchsweise in Frage gestellt werden' (p. 461).

Identifying literature with social criticism, Leonhardt excludes GDR literature from the canon of German literature, which, for him, is represented by West German literature alone. Schulz goes even further, specifically attacking GDR literature for its claim that it represents the whole of Germany. Schulz, too, chooses a Leipzig professor to voice allegiance to a conservative canon of Western modern classics, such as Hemingway, Faulkner, Steinbeck, Huxley and Waugh:

> 'Bei unseren deutschen Autoren – da stört das politische Zusatzgewicht. Zwei neue Gesamtausgaben von Heinrich Mann, Lion Feuchtwanger soviel Sie wollen; Heinrich Mann war schon Klassiker, ehe sein großer Bruder bei uns einkehrte . . . Im Westen ist Thomas Mann schon in die wohltätige Schonzeit des Vergessens eingegangen – ich weiß es', winkte er mit der Hand ab, 'bei uns steht er in Goldschnitt und Pergament in jeder Buchhandlung und ist . . . der politische Bildungsklassiker unserer schwarzrotgoldenen Volksdemokratie geworden'.

The ironic tone of Schulz's educated middle-class mouthpiece could be guaranteed to confirm the prejudices of the readers of this reportage in the *Frankfurter Allgemeine Zeitung*. This ironic tone is absent from Kuby's reportage; he replaces it by cynicism and didacticism, as he sets out to explore what actually lay behind slogans used in the West German press such as 'Pankow', and why a subject like the 'GDR State' was taboo for 'free' journalists. Kuby differs from Schulz and Leonhardt in that he does not readily accept concepts such as 'Old Germany' and 'geistige Freiheit'. Moving between West and East Germany, the reporter adopts the motto 'Man muß sie hören alle beede', yet the sentence which follows: 'Mißtrauen ist unter Umständen die bessere Hälfte des Vertrauens' (p. 107), gives the reader a hint as to how Kuby's conversations with GDR citizens should be read. Through a final twist his reportage leads the reader to question what has just been depicted. In one instance a visit to a successful collective farm: 'Ja, sage ich, dann könnten wir uns vielleicht draußen umschauen. Gern, sagt er. Und jetzt bringt die Frau tadellose Gummistiefel und frisch gewaschene Überziehsocken. Sie haben wohl manchmal Besichtigung? Ohja, sagt die Frau' (p. 110). In a manner quite different from Mönnich, Schulz or Leonhardt, Kuby

employs this same technique to conclude all scenes in which GDR
citizens report as socialists on the construction of their country.
He does not permit the reader to equate National Socialism and
communism as totalitarian systems, but prevailing West German prejudices nevertheless emerge. This is well illustrated by the
final dialogue with a former prisoner in the report of a visit to
Buchenwald:

> Sieh an, sage ich, aber es haben doch ganz wenige Deutsche von den
> Konzentrationslagern gewußt. Nicht einmal die SS im ganzen, sondern
> höchstens ein paar hundert SS-Männer. Ja, meint Herr Eichhorn, und
> ganz Weimar zum Beispiel. Davon, daß Buchenwald bis 1950 unter
> russischer Regie weiter als KZ diente, sagte er kein Wort. (p. 63)

Kuby presents full portraits of GDR citizens suffering under
socialist conditions but he does not use them as mouthpieces to
attack the system. He is wary of any 'gesamtdeutsches Gespräch'
and stands by one of his major theses, namely, that the German
communists have made a radical break with the German past,
while West Germany, in the light of militant National Socialism and
Prussian nationalism, is reproached for its failure to address the
Nazi past. However, Kuby's alertness to differences and similarities between the two German states has its limitations, as the
concept of 'gesamtdeutsch' reveals. He tends to view social phe-
nomena as the expression of something unwholesome called the
German character. He is convinced that the German character
cannot be changed and, in the final analysis, approves of the
division of Germany by the great powers and rejects nuclear
weapons for the West German armed forces as a threat to peace.
His embittered and cynical characterisation of 'the German' de-
rives from a viewpoint to be found neither in West Germany nor
in the GDR, but which may be identified most readily with the re-
education policies of the victorious powers in the immediate post-
war years. Some of the similarities between the two German states
which Kuby attributes to their inability to think in terms of peace
anticipate later negative images of Germany on the part of West
German writers. His views on this central issue suggest that Kuby
played his part in the Cold War on the Western side.

Kuby's description of two Baltic resorts at which official loud-
speakers (East) and private transistor radios (West) provide the
entertainment closes with the comment 'Orwell ist überall' (p. 91).
The contrast between the 'Zwang, sich . . . erholen zu müssen' and

the 'Freiheit, sich . . . erholen zu dürfen' is first confirmed in
Travemünde: 'Ich verglich und bemerkte, daß ich nicht das Opfer
meiner Illusionen gewesen war; dieser Strand besaß etwas
Wohlgefälliges, das dem Ost-Strand gefehlt hatte' (p. 90). But the
contrast is then undermined after the reporter has counted eighty-
three radios on the beach and news bulletins interrupt the music:

> Ich konnte, am Strand promenierend, einen Kommentar zum Verbot
> der KP ebenso total hören, wie ich auf dem Ostseestrand drüben den
> Kommentar gegen das Verbot der KP gehört hatte. Die Übertragung
> hätte nicht besser sein können, wenn sich die Kurverwaltung von
> Travemünde ebenfalls die Mühe gemacht hätte, eine Allee von Laut-
> sprechern in den Sand zu pflanzen. Orwell ist überall. (p. 91)

By adopting an outsider's perspective, transcending the East–West
confrontation, Kuby manages to deflect attention away from his
Western involvement in issues like the myths of the Berlin blockade, the Volkswagen and the *Bild-Zeitung*. Looking back on his reportage from Berlin in the depths of the Cold War, he sets up a
contrast between this work and the conspiratorial nature of West
Berlin, a feature that it shares with the GDR, except that the city
is even less attractive 'weil es zu dem sonstigen Hauptstreben,
einen billig-smarten US–bundesdeutschen Wunderzauber
hinzulegen, so gar nicht passen will' (p. 29). It is no coincidence
that Kuby's characterisation of the Berlin of 1948–9 corresponds
precisely to his own reportage style at that time: 'Damals durch-
schlug das deutsche Pathos die Sicherungen des Berliner Witzes'
(p. 28). With some wit Kuby presents the Karmann Ghia car, with
which he causes a stir in the GDR, as a symbol of the Federal
Republic:

> Es gibt kein vollkommeneres Symbol der Bundesrepublik und des
> deutschen Wunders als dieses Wägelchen. Was man davon nicht von
> außen sieht, Motor und Fahrgestell, ist in der Ära Hitler mit deutscher
> Tüchtigkeit geschaffen worden: der robuste, zuverlässige, soziale
> fahrbare Untersatz, made in Germany, für den kleinen Mann aller Länder.
> Was man sieht, die Karosserie, ist von einem Italiener: die elegante,
> bequeme, formschöne Blechhülle für den deutschen Bundesbürger.
> (p. 84)

A more serious point emerges in Kuby's approval of the Springer-
Verlag slogan 'Seid nett zueinander'. He contrasts its neutrality
positively with the Cold War motto of Bonn politicians, 'Haßt sie!':

> Ich bin davon überzeugt, daß die Veränderungen, die wir im Verhalten
> der Westdeutschen feststellen können: eine den Deutschen früher nicht

eigene Urbanität, eine relative Zunahme der öffentlich geübten Höflichkeit und ein durchaus erträgliches Benehmen im Ausland einschließlich gewisser Geschmacksveränderungen zum Guten und Weltläufigen hin – daß diese Veränderungen mehr, als wir ahnen, auf den breiten unterirdischen Einfluß der unter der weißen Fahne erscheinenden Springer-Presse zurückzuführen sind. (p. 118)

His reportage on the Berlin blockade, Volkswagen and the *Bild-Zeitung* reveals how the essentially nonconformist figure among West German reporters was not at odds, but in agreement, with long-term changes. If he was not taken seriously by his readers, it was because of his obsession with foreign policy and with a stereotyped view of the unchangeable German character. These two components laid him open to attack by conservatives on two counts: his negative nationalism and his attempt to take up a vantage-point outside German history. It is a measure of public opinion in West Germany that such criticisms had more impact than Kuby's non-conformist insights.

The above examination of the reportage which appeared in the two German states during the Cold War suggests the following conclusions. Little enough appeared in West Germany, and, where it did feature in books, it tended to be consigned to a marginal position. The case of the GDR reveals a fundamental contradiction: on the one hand the theoretical aim of demonstrating the indivisibility of a national culture, especially in the sphere of literature; on the other hand the reality than from the late 1940s to the early 1960s literature did not function as a medium for the preservation of the unity of the German nation.

Notes

1 Gustav René Hocke, 'Deutsche Kalligraphie oder Glanz und Elend der modernen Literatur', *Der Ruf*, 1/7, 1946, pp. 9–10.

2 Anna Seghers, 'Der Schriftsteller und die geistige Freiheit', in *Über Kunstwerk und Wirklichkeit*, I, edited by Sigrid Bock, Berlin, 1970, p. 73.

3 Stephan Hermlin, *Äußerungen 1944–1982*, Berlin and Weimar, 1983, p. 39.

4 Stephan Hermlin, 'Ja und Nein', *Ost und West*, 3/11, 1948, pp. 93–4.

5 Gerhard Schoenberner in *Information oder Herrschen die Souffleure?*, edited by Paul Hübener, Reinbek, 1964, p. 65.

6 Bernd Boehle, *Das praktische Reisebuch: ein Nachschlagbuch für Reisen in der deutschen Bundesrepublik*, Gütersloh, 1954, p. 20.

7 Erich Kuby, *Das ist des Deutschen Vaterland: 70 Millionen in zwei Wartesälen*, Reinbek, 1961, p. 5; first edition: 1959.

8 Wilfried Loth, *Die Teilung der Welt: Geschichte des Kalten Krieges 1941–1955*, Munich, 1983.

9 Marion Gräfin Dönhoff, Rudolf Walter Leonhardt and Theo Sommer, *Reise in ein fernes Land*, Hamburg 1964, p. 136.

10 See Walter Ulbricht's speech 'Die gegenwärtige Lage und die neuen Aufgaben der Sozialistischen Einheitspartei Deutschlands: aus dem Referat auf der II. Parteikonferenz der SED Berlin, 9. bis 12. Juli 1952', in *Zur Geschichte der deutschen Arbeiterbewegung: aus Reden und Aufsätzen IV: 1950–1954*, Berlin, 1958, pp. 390 and 393.

11 See Konrad Adenauer, *Erinnerungen 1945–1953*, Frankfurt am Main, 1967, pp. 362–4.

12 See Ernst Nolte, *Deutschland und der Kalte Krieg*, Munich, 1974, and Alexander von Bormann, 'Der Kalte Krieg und seine literarischen Auswirkungen', in *Literatur nach 1945 I: Politische und regionale Aspekte*, edited by Jost Hermand, Wiesbaden, 1979, pp. 61–116, or Christoph Kleßmann, *Die doppelte Staatsgründung: Deutsche Geschichte 1945–1955*, Göttingen, 1982, p. 300.

13 See Karl-Ernst Jeismann, 'Die Einheit der Nation im Geschichtsbild der DDR', *Aus Politik und Zeitgeschichte*, 13 August 1983, pp. 3–16, or Roland W. Schweizer, 'Die DDR und die Nationale Frage: Zum Wandel der Positionen von der Staatsgründung bis zur Gegenwart', *Aus Politik und Zeitgeschichte*, 21 December 1985, pp. 37–54.

14 Hans Mayer, 'Westdeutsche Reiseerlebnisse', *Sonntag*, 22 October 1950.

15 See Ingeborg Münz-Koenen, 'Zur Reportageliteratur der fünfziger Jahre', *Weimarer Beiträge*, 23, 1977, p. 49.

16 *Menschen und Werke: vom Wachsen und Werden des neuen Lebens in der Deutschen Demokratischen Republik*, edited by Deutscher Schriftsteller-Verband, Berlin, 1952.

17 *Deutsche Literatur der Gegenwart*, edited by Deutscher Schriftsteller-Verband, Berlin, 1958.

18 Hans-Jürgen Jessel, "Drei Autos rollten über die Zonengrenze', *Sonntag*, 17 July 1955.

19 *Die Reportage – gestern und heute*, edited by Deutscher Schriftsteller-Verband, Berlin, 1955.

20 See Helmut Peitsch, ' "Am Rande des Krieges"? Nichtnazistische Schriftsteller im Einsatz der Propagandakompanien gegen die Sowjetunion', *Kürbiskern*, 1984, pp. 126–49; Klaus R. Scherpe, 'Erzwungener Alltag: Wahrgenommene und gedachte Wirklichkeit in der Reportageliteratur der Nachkriegszeit', in *Nachkriegsliteratur in Westdeutschland 1945–49: Schreibweisen, Gattungen, Institutionen*, edited by Jost Hermand et al., Berlin, 1982, pp. 52–68.

21 This point is missed by Heinz Härtl, 'Entwicklung und Traditionen der sozialistischen Reiseliteratur', in *Erworbene Tradition: Studien zu Werken der sozialistischen deutschen Literatur*, edited by Günter Hartung et al., Berlin and Weimar, 1977, pp. 299–340, and Edelgard Schmidt, 'Zu einigen Entwicklungstendenzen der Reportage in der DDR-Literatur', *Weimarer Beiträge*, 19, 1973, pp. 133–40, as well as by the polemical thesis by Barbara Zwirner, *'Besseres Land – schöne Welt': Sozialistischer Patriotismus und Welterfahrung in der Reiseliteratur der DDR nach dem VIII. Parteitag der SED*, Phil. Diss. Freie Universität Berlin, 1986.

22 Dieter Schlenstedt, *Egon Erwin Kisch*, West Berlin, 1985, p. 37.

23 Ottmar Katz, 'Sagen Sie, wie macht man das? Reportage über eine Reportage', *Der Ruf*, 3/14, 1948, p. 2.

24 G. H. Witter, 'Interview mit einem Reporter', *Die Welt*, 1 April 1947.

25 Katz, *op. cit.*, p. 2.

26 *Ibid.*

27 Benno Reifenberg, 'In Quarantäne: Tagebuchnotizen aus Berlin', *Die Gegenwart*, 2/19–20, 1947, p. 16.

28 Elisabeth Langgässer, 'Schriftsteller unter der Hitler-Diktatur', *Ost und West*, 1/4, 1947, p. 39.

29 Erich Kuby, 'An der Spree schlägt das Herz Europas', *Süddeutsche Zeitung*, 24 April 1948.

30 Erich Kuby, 'Ein Ausflug an die Ostgrenze Europas', *Süddeutsche Zeitung*, 1 May 1948.

31 Erich Kuby, 'Die leidenschaftliche und tote Stadt Berlin', *Süddeutsche Zeitung*, 10 July 1948.

32 Horst Mönnich, *Das Land ohne Träume*, Munich, 1957, p. 213; first edition: Braunschweig, 1954.

33 Eberhard Schulz, *Deutschland heute: der Mensch der Nachkriegszeit*, Frankfurt, 1958, p. 70.

34 According to his conviction, 'Immer ist die Vergangenheit leuchtender gewesen als das, was ihr nachgefolgt ist', quoted in Schulz's obituary, *Frankfurter Allgemeine Zeitung*, 14 July 1982.

Literary conversations:
Hans Werner Richter's role in
the literary relations between
the two German states
Graeme Cook

Nowadays, Hans Werner Richter is known primarily for his work as manager and figurehead of the 'Gruppe 47'. It is a role for which he is still fêted, but one which tends to overshadow his manifold other activities before, after and during its twenty-year lifetime. Certainly, none of these activities shares the stature and durability of his achievement with the 'Gruppe 47', but, individually and collectively, they cannot be ignored. This is particularly true when it comes to a consideration of Richter's role in literary relations between the Federal and Democratic German Republics during the 1950s.

An examination of the history of the 'Gruppe 47' soon reveals that there was scarce involvement of East German writers in any form over this period. Such links as did exist – more of which in a moment – enjoyed faltering development only from the end of the decade onwards, and even then were destined to remain an obscure and inglorious facet of the group's overall make-up until its existence was suspended in 1967. In order to understand the reasons for this apparent lack of communication, in so far as they lie with Richter himself, it is therefore necessary to look beyond the confines of the 'Gruppe 47' and into the other spheres of his activity, not only in the 1950s but also in the 1930s and in the sensitive years immediately after the War ended, the experiences of which were central in shaping his attitudes for the decade to come.

The first noted visitor to the 'Gruppe 47' from the 'Zone', after the foundation of separate republics in 1949, was Peter Huchel, who came to Burg Rothenfels in 1954. Unfortunately, the spirits of the group were then at a low ebb and there is only scant account of the event, though Heinz Friedrich's report for the *Hessische Nachrichten* gives a clear indication of how he fared:

> Eine Attraktion der Tagung war der Besuch des ostzonalen Schriftstellers Peter Huchel, der die Zeitschrift *Sinn und Form* in Ostberlin herausgibt – einer der ernstzunehmenden Literaten aus dem Osten. Das literarische Ost–West-Gespräch blieb jedoch leider in den Anfängen stecken, dà selbst ein Mann wie Peter Huchel in starrer östlicher Meinungs-uniformität verharrt. Das war für die Teilnehmer der Tagung eine betrübliche Einsicht . . .[1]

This statement reveals a number of attitudes which set the tone for the years to come. Firstly, that there was an interest in writers from the East, and Richter took the initiative in inviting them,[2] but that it was also tempered by a scepticism towards the status of the writer within the apparatus of the GDR state, and by the prejudice that most writers from the East were not 'ernstzunehmen'. The consequent failure from the outset to establish any sort of common ground is also apparent from Friedrich's comments, as is the opinion that this failure lies with a characteristically Eastern bloc intransigence in Huchel's persona. It would be misleading to suggest, on the basis of this example alone, that these attitudes necessarily reflect Richter's own position with regard to the GDR writer, or indeed that Peter Huchel was an adequate representative of the sort of East German literature with which the 'Gruppe 47' envisaged communion. However, the attendance of Stephan Hermlin and Bodo Uhse in Berlin the following year was no more fruitful: 'Zwischen den beiden Fronten kam es zu keiner Verständigung, konnte es zu keiner kommen. Hier spiegelte sich innerhalb des Treffens der Gruppe 47 die ganze deutsche Tragik, die in der geteilten Stadt Berlin am reinsten zum Ausdruck kommt', wrote Peter Hornung in conclusion of his report on the meeting for the Regensburg *Tages-Anzeiger*.[3]

Apart from Alfred Kantorowicz, present as a guest at Niederpöcking in September 1957 shortly after his move to the West, the next East Germans to attend meetings of the 'Gruppe 47' were Uwe Johnson (newly settled in West Berlin) in 1959–60, Hans Mayer in 1959–60, and Johannes Bobrowski in 1960. This, as far as it is possible to tell from the readily available documentation, was the total extent of the East German presence until the building of the Berlin Wall in 1961.[4] It is clear from contemporary accounts also that literary relations with the GDR never figured as a significant issue in the life of the 'Gruppe 47' in the 1950s,[5] though to what extent this lack of contact can be attributed directly to Hans Werner Richter is more difficult to ascertain. There is a broad consensus of opinion that the 'Gruppe 47' owed its composition and continued existence exclusively to Richter, and that decisions on invitations, venue and the form of the proceedings ultimately lay in his hands.[6] Whilst this was technically the case, there is no doubt that he was also influenced in these decisions by the collective mood of the group itself, which by 1957 had shown clear signs of a departure from his original conception.[7]

This conception, rooted in the years of his internment as a prisoner-of-war in the United States, ought to have provided for a more vocal concern for German literature on the other side of the Iron Curtain. In *Der Ruf: Unabhängige Blätter der jungen Generation*, which Richter edited together with Alfred Andersch from August 1946 until April 1947, he occupied a middle ground between the politics of the American and Soviet occupiers. Richter's commitment to the idea of a 'third way' pervades *Der Ruf*, and is recorded in the programmatic article Deutschland–Brücke zwischen Ost und West' (4, 1 October 1946). Here, Richter put the case for a united Germany to act as a natural focus for the fusion of the most constructive quality of each superpower: of American democracy as representative of the Western liberal tradition, and of Eastern economic socialism as epitomised by the Soviet Union. It would, so he claimed, be the natural conclusion of a progressive historical convergence, wherein the West was shifting towards socialism and the East towards democracy. The consequences of ignoring this need would be dire:

> Indem man ein Volk zu trennen versucht, indem man versucht, diese Trennung im geistigen Sein dieses Volkes zu vertiefen, reißt man nicht nur die Kluft zwischen dem östlichen und dem westlichen Teil dieses Landes auf, sondern läßt diese Kluft zu jenem Abgrund zwischen dem westlichen und dem östlichen Teil Europas werden, der nicht mehr überbrückbar ist. Dies aber bedeutet den Untergang der deutschen Nation und ist der Zerfall des europäischen Lebens.

His relative optimism at this time can be gauged from the earlier two-part description of a journey into Soviet-occupied Germany,[8] which paints a positive picture of harmonious relations between the occupiers and the population and of the plans of the SED, though even this is qualified by the perception that the two sides of Germany are developing in different directions.

In the forefront of developments in Richter's ideal scheme of things would be the young generation to which *Der Ruf* specifically addressed itself. But Richter wanted not only to mobilise the political voice of the young generation, he also wanted to stimulate the literary one: in 'Literatur im Interregnum' (15, 15 March 1947), he exposed the inadequacies of emigrant and inner emigrant writers and appealed to 'die jungen Kräfte' as heir-apparent to the throne of German literature. The vision expressed in *Der Ruf* was short-lived, however, as Richter and Andersch stepped down from the editorship of the paper in April 1947 in a row over the pitch of their criticism of the American authorities. Richter turned towards literature as a means, he suggested, of exerting a far-reaching, though less overt, influence on Germany's political development. *Der Skorpion*, a cultural magazine, was the fruit of a summer's efforts to establish a focal point for the circle of writers who had rallied to *Der Ruf*. The enterprise was stifled in its early stages by the refusal of the Americans to grant a publishing licence, but by the time of this setback the 'Gruppe 47' had already begun to gather momentum.

There are indications, from accounts of the early meetings, that the group did attempt to embrace writers from all over the country, provided of course that they had the requisite political credentials. Friedrich Minssen reported on the second meeting of 1947 in Herrlingen that writers converged 'aus allen Zonen', and at the third meeting in April 1948 there were, according to Gunter Groll, 'Schriftsteller aller Zonen'.[9] It is in a report (also by Friedrich Minssen) on the Marktbreit meeting of April 1949 that a change in this trend can first be detected: the group is made up by 'ein Ausschnitt aus der jungen deutschen Literatur der Westzonen'.[10] An examination of the writers who attended in this and subsequent years also reveals a rapid Europeanisation of the 'Gruppe 47', with French, Dutch, Swiss and then, as it opened up to the East towards the end of the 1950s, Polish and Soviet guests. In *Im Etablissement der Schmetterlinge*, his collection of individual portraits of members of the group, Richter writes of the 'Gruppe 47' at the beginning of the 1950s: 'in dieser Zeit war es ziemlich gleichgültig, ob man Österreicher, Schweizer, Bundesrepublikaner oder sonstwer war. Für uns galt nur der deutsche Sprachraum und keine Staatszugehörigkeit.'[11]

The 'Gruppe 47', by its very nature, was also evidently not the vehicle best suited to conduct a sustained campaign of action in any one direction, such as an attempt to establish sound links with

GDR writers would have demanded. When Heinrich Böll penned his anatomy of the 'Gruppe 47', entitled 'Angst vor der Gruppe 47?', he characterised the group's pluralism by describing it as an 'immenser Brei von Schlamm'. This, moreover, reflected the political complexion of the Federal Republic: 'Die Gruppe gehört zu diesem Staat, sie paßt zu ihm, sie ist politisch so hilflos wie er'.[12] But the parallels between group and state had already become irresistible some years earlier: the *Spiegel* title feature of 24 October 1962, 'Richters Richtfest', talked of 'die Literaten-Konjunktur', and the commercial face of the group was elsewhere captured by the sobriquet 'Dichterbörse'. It was rather the formlessness, though, which would have directly hindered any impulse towards an initiative in East–West relations: this fundamental flaw, which was also paradoxically its chief strength, was built into the group's unwritten constitution by Richter from the very beginning. It was determined partly by a generation's profound mistrust of absolute premises, resulting from experience of totalitarian ideologies, and partly from Richter's self-confessed 'Neigung zur Improvisation'.[13] Whereas this inherent fluidity of structure was doubtless instrumental in ensuring the group's longevity, it also disabled systematic responses in matters of politics and aesthetics.

Richter did seem willing, as an article in *Hier und Heute* in 1951 indicates, to sanction other efforts towards contact with East German writers. In 'Wer spricht mit wem?', noted by Alfred Kantorowicz as 'ein bewahrenswertes Zeitdokument',[14] he reports on an initiative for talks between writers from both sides which received scathing treatment by the *Neue Zeitung*. A group of West German writers met to discuss a letter from Bertolt Brecht, Anna Seghers, Johannes Becher and Arnold Zweig (whose age and emigrant status, incidentally, rendered them unsuitable for invitation to the 'Gruppe 47'), and decided to respond by inviting them to Munich: 'Vielleicht ist ein solches Gespräch hoffnungslos, vielleicht sind auch Bert Brecht und Anna Seghers nur noch Lautsprecher (als welche sie Plievier bezeichnet hat)', concedes Richter, thereby expressing suspicions he betrays elsewhere, but nevertheless standing firmly on the side of dialogue. The meeting described by Richter appears in fact to have laid the ground for the 'Starnberger Gespräch' which took place on 26–7 March 1951, amid the crisis which led in October 1951 to the rupture between East and West in the German PEN club, and which was attended by an East German delegation made up of Willi Bredel, Peter Huchel,

Stephan Hermlin and Bodo Uhse. These talks also aroused hostility in the press, and laid the Western participants open to charges of collusion with agents of communism.[15] Richter's position with regard to the 'Starnberger Gespräch' is marked by the sort of scepticism which seems to have tainted the whole endeavour, as his report afterwards in the *Münchener Merkur* reveals:

> Das Gespräch zwischen westlichen und östlichen Schriftstellern in Starnberg war ein Versuch. Als Versuch war es von den westlichen Teilnehmern gedacht und als Versuch blieb es bestehen. Es brachte keine Ergebnisse, keine neuen Resolutionen und bedauerlicherweise auch keine klare politische Aussprache.
> ... Die zentralen politischen Probleme unserer Tage, die Frage einer Wiederherstellung der deutschen Einheit, freie Wahlen, Nationalversammlung usw. wurden nicht besprochen. Es blieb bei einer anfänglichen Diskussion über die Frage der Konzentrationslager, der Rechtssicherheit, der Freiheit und des Strafvollzuges in der Ostzone. Das Gespräch glitt dann zu literarischen und kulturpolitischen Fragen ab, die nach Ansicht einiger Teilnehmer nur dann gelöst werden können, wenn jene politischen Voraussetzungen gegeben sind, die in diesem Gespräch weder diskutiert noch geklärt wurden.... Der Wunsch, westdeutsche und ostdeutsche schöngeistige Literatur auszutauschen, die Absicht, eine gemeinsame literarische Zeitung herauszugeben, waren Wunschträume, die den gegebenen politischen Realitäten nicht Rechnung trugen. Skepsis und Mißtrauen blieben trotz menschlicher Fairneß bestehen.[16]

The essence of Richter's argument is that, if the East Germans would not state unequivocally their opposition to certain (stalinist) policies adopted by their state, then there could be no common basis upon which to pursue further discussion.

In 1951, in an interview with the Dutch writer Adriaan Morriën which has only recently been translated and published in Germany, Richter gave a bleak appraisal of the current state of relations between young writers in East and West Germany. Since Morriën attended the meeting of the 'Gruppe 47' in May of that year, it is most probable that Richter was speaking in the wake of the experience of the 'Starnberger Gespräch':

> Der Kontakt ist sehr mäßig, geringer sogar als der Kontakt zwischen deutschen und jungen französischen Schriftstellern. Ich bedaure das, aber der augenblickliche politische Zustand in Deutschland, von dem ein starker und nicht immer günstiger Einfluß auf die literarische Entwicklung ausgeht, läßt kaum ein anderes Verhältnis zu. Politische Propaganda, Intrigen und Verdächtigungen beherrschen das Leben in beiden Zonen so sehr, daß eine immer größer werdende Entfremdung

stattfindet, nicht nur im Volk, sondern auch unter den Intellektuellen. Trötzdem gehören für mich Huchel und Hermlin zur deutschen Literatur.[17]

The reasons for Richter's failure to establish concrete links with GDR writers during the Cold War are more than just political in a practical sense, however. There are also less obvious emotional grounds, bolstered by the popular perception of collaboration with an evil régime, but originating in personal experiences from the Third Reich. It has recently transpired that Richter himself not only published in Nazi Germany – an act which, in the context of the *Nullpunkt* and the credo of a renaissance headed by an untarnished young generation, smacked heavily of political compromise – but was also employed at one stage by the book trade section of the Reichsschrifttumskammer.[18] A knowledge of these facts makes it easier to understand why Richter was so obsessively opposed to co-operation with the American forces of occupation.[19] Having been lulled away from communist activism, and having succumbed to the temptation to write, even at the cost of his political integrity, it seems that he was now unable to differentiate adequately between different forms of authoritarian power. Anxious not to fall into a similar trap, he determined to engage in the sort of oppositional behaviour that he had failed to display ten years earlier.

If this was his attitude to the American military government 'und ihre Mitläufer',[20] then there was surely little hope for open-minded dialogue with those who accepted to co-exist with the Soviets, and later with the SED. The vigour with which Richter rejected even 'innere Emigration' after the war leaves no doubt as to his likely position with regard to 'SED-writers'. In an interview with me on 22 October 1987, Richter made the following judgement: 'Man mußte sich immer arrangieren mit den Nationalsozialisten, wenn man schrieb, irgendwie mußte man.' When we observe how he saw the East German system in terms comparable to National Socialism, it is logical to conclude that the status of the writer under each system was for him also comparable. This view of the GDR is explicit in the text of a report from 1952 about a visit made to Berlin.[21] As soon as he is over the border he finds himself in 'ein großes, unheimliches, dunkles Land' (p. 229), and comparisons with the Third Reich begin to accumulate: 'Schulungskurse . . . wie im Dritten Reich' (p. 231); 'die gleichen Säulen, die Hitler gestern baute' (p. 242); 'Gestern, denke ich, hatte der Führer immer recht und jetzt ist es die Partei' (p. 244); and there is the inevitable comparison between Stalin and Hitler (p. 235).

It is true no doubt that Richter's 'Kollaborationskomplex' derived not solely from his bad conscience over personal compromise but in part also from the pressure of contemporary opinion, for which dialogue would have been tantamount to admission of the legitimacy of the East German state (as response to the 'Starnberger Gespräch' illustrated): 'Da man befangen war in einem konservativen, legalistischen Denken, wurde jedes Miteinanderreden, jede Verhandlung, jeder mögliche Vertrag zu einer Art Verrat hochgespielt und hochstilisiert', Richter later wrote of the Cold War era.[22] What he fails to mention, however, is the extent of his own contribution to such attitudes. Its importance is such that his single most trenchant piece of criticism on conditions in East Germany was aired under a pseudonym. 'Dammbruch im Osten' was broadcast by the Nordwestdeutsche Rundfunk on 12 April 1953 under the authorship of a 'Hans Helmut Rehn'.[23] Designated a report, it took the form of a series of dramatic dialogues, punctuated by commentary from the 'Berichter', depicting scenes from life in East Germany. The portrayal is damning; it makes the anti-Sovietism of Richter's novel *Sie fielen aus Gottes Hand* (1951), which so incensed East German critics, seem anodyne by comparison. A brief overview of the content will demonstrate why.

The imaginary present, from which the reporter orchestrates the dialogues, is set in a camp for refugees from the East zone: 'Und da sitzen sie, vor mir auf den Strohsäcken in dem Flüchtlingslager in Berlin-Neukölln, die Verlierer von heute, betrogen und bestohlen um alles, gejagt, gequält, und geflüchtet, gebrochene und geschlagene Menschen. . . .' It is the function of the dialogues to dramatise the circumstances which have brought things to this pass: they enact the ruthless implementation of 1930s Soviet-style economic reforms aimed at 'Enteignung und Verstaatlichung des kleinen Besitzes'. Ordinary, honest citizens of moderate means are treated like criminals and divested of their property. None are spared: in an early episode, a man is taken from his sickbed and thrown in prison (like many others) on the flimsy pretext of a 'Verstoß gegen die Wirtschaftsstrafverordnung'. The total effect of these measures is evoked by reference to the title of the report: 'Und die Dämme brachen, die Dämme der Gewohnheit, der Sicherheit, des Besitz-und Heimatgefühls, und die große Flucht begann.'

These first scenes are clearly designed to excite the fears of the 'Kleinbürger', whose traditional conservatism and craving for security would be all the stronger after the upheavals and material privations of Germany's defeat. Subsequent scenes are targeted at other mass sectors of German society. The fate of the smallholder, backbone of the agrarian economy, is equally lamentable: he is driven off his land, where his family may have been farming for generations, by the 'psychologische Terror' of collectivisation or of impossible production quotas, and is replaced by town-bred agricultural technicians who do not have the necessary skills which come with being born and raised to local conditions. There is at this point more than a passing sense that the author is drawing on the 'Blut und Boden' cult promoted in the Third Reich, especially after earlier mention of the threat to 'Heimatgefühl'. Industrial workers are subjected to the same pressure of excessive quotas, old people are maltreated, and the young are pressganged into military service. The catalogue of terror concludes with the revelation of how a régime to which it is suggested that over 95 per cent of citizens are opposed can endure: 'die Diktatur ist nur noch ein Apparat, der in sich selbst läuft, mit tausend und abertausend gegnerischen Rädchen . . . ja, es ist ein Albtraum'.

'Dammbruch im Osten' clearly put Richter on common ground with those restorative forces to which, in the domestic political arena, he was so strongly opposed, and this contradiction explains his preference for a pseudonym. It also explains why he would later talk of 'ein konservativer Sog, dem leider auch Leute verfielen, die nach dem Krieg von einer anderen Konzeption ausgegangen waren'.[24] Those familiar with the post-war work of prominent National Socialist writers will not fail to recognize the association between the title of 'Dammbruch im Osten' and that of Edwin Erich Dwinger's epic novel *Wenn die Dämme brechen* (1950), which recounts the fate of the German people in East Prussia towards the end of the war. Dwinger was possibly the most distinguished exponent of literary anti-bolshevism and anti-Sovietism in the early years of the Cold War, so it is hardly surprising that when Richter surveyed the contents of a bookshop window display in 1951, he should have observed with such sarcasm: 'Links unten steht, ja wer steht denn da, Edwin Dwinger! In guten nationalen Schutzumschlägen reitet er immer noch quer durchs Baltikum, läßt Gott in Spanien schweigen und kämpft stetig noch mit Weiß gegen Rot. Er ist immer noch gängig, oder schon wieder gängig.'[25] The patently derivative character of 'Dammbruch im Osten' appears all the more impressive in view of this.

Richter had personal reasons for mistrusting the Soviet Union: these dated back to as early as 1932, when he was allegedly expelled from the German Communist Party – faithful to the Central Committee in Moscow – for holding 'Trotskyist' views. Later in the decade he witnessed the failure to mobilise a red front in response to the Spanish Civil War, and also heard about the Moscow show trials. Finally, with the Soviet–German non-aggression pact in 1939 he experienced the 'Zusammenbruch des Sowjetmythos', and a sense of betrayal and 'absolutes Ausgeliefertsein'.[26] Perhaps he later also saw these successive blows to his political morale as having driven him down the path towards the languid aestheticism of his Third Reich publications. Little wonder, then, that when the *Ruf* dispute blew up in 1947 he suspected Soviet as well as American intervention.[27]

In March 1952 a new fortnightly cultural magazine, backed by the Deutsche Verlags-Anstalt, Stuttgart, was launched: *Die Literatur: Blätter für Literatur, Film, Funk und Bühne* was edited by Hans Werner Richter, who also wrote the front-page essay which introduced it. In 'Courage?' (1, 15 March 1952) Richter proffered his own diagnosis of the condition of contemporary German literature, and outlined the means by which *Die Literatur* could assist in effecting a cure. Of principal interest to the present essay is his description of 'ein in Ost und West geteiltes und voneinander hermetisch abgeschlossenes literarisches Leben'. Accordingly, when he lays down the three points of the political, social and literary aims of *Die Literatur*, the task in the latter sphere is 'die Aufhebung der Zersplitterung der deutschen Literatur'. It is, however, portentous for the development of this ambition in *Die Literatur* that Richter seems more preoccupied with German literature in the Western world than with that in the Democratic Republic: 'Für uns gehört alles zur deutschen Literatur, was im deutschen Sprachraum erscheint – ob es in New York oder in Berlin, in Hamburg oder in der Schweiz herauskommt'; 'Das literarische Leben in Paris wird für uns genau so wichtig sein wie das literarische Leben in München oder in Hamburg', he writes, declaring his further intention of breaking down the linguistic and political barriers in modern world literature. As things turned out, the sixteen issues of *Die Literatur* contained little on the subject of East German literature. Moreover, the mood of the few articles relating to it was generally unfavourable, and although Richter personally contributed little, the programme he laid down for the magazine meant that he bore a degree of editorial responsibility for the content of what appeared.

'Bücher und Bücherlesen in der Zone' (10, 1 August 1952) paints a bleak picture of literary life over the border:[28] 'Die Ostzone: ein Gefangenenlager, und man greift nach dem, was man hat'; 'Die Antiquariate sind Oasen in der geistigen Wüste des Ostens'. Further images of the clandestine traffic in unofficial literature, and of the zeal with which quality literature from the West is consumed, are designed to kindle memories of the situation in Nazi Germany. The political significance attached to private acts must also invite comparison with the passive resistance of 'innere Emigration': 'alles hat seine Beziehung zur theokratischen Totalität des Regimes und die privateste Äußerung oder das persönlichste Schweigen ist nicht ohne Bedeutung.' In his review of Theodor Plievier's *Moskau* (' "Der Kampf um Moskau" ', 12, 1 September 1952), Richter himself also gives vent to the notion that Stalinism and Nazism are equal evils, a view he finds gratifyingly confirmed in the novel, which serves, he advises, as 'eine Warnung und eine Mahnung'.

The only significant article which casts East German culture in a favourable light is Gert Westphal's review of a book about the work of the Berliner Ensemble, though the title of even this – 'Vom Gegner lernen' (4, 1 May 1952) – implies the gulf to be bridged before the commentator can view his subject with a degree of dispassion. Between this and the demise of *Die Literatur* there was a further article which might have been expected to make some mention of new literature in the GDR, but the reference to 'das mißglückte Experiment des Stalinismus' in Gerhard Szczesny's 'Gibt es eine sozialistische Literatur?' (12, 1 September 1952) precludes any discussion of German socialist literature beyond the West. *Die Literatur*'s most prominent gesture in East–West literary relations was also its most destructive: the lead article of the final issue was Wolfgang Weyrauch's '13 Fragen an Bert Brecht' (16, 1 November 1952), which dispelled any lingering doubts that the state-sanctioned East German writer was anything less than a collaborator in an evil régime riddled with the traces of rehabilitated Nazism.

For the rest, *Die Literatur* fixed its gaze firmly westwards: to the modernistic influences of France, Italy and America, primarily. When I questioned Richter about the discrepancy between the declared intention of dealing with German literature as a whole in *Die Literatur* and the manifest failure to do anything of the sort, he replied: 'Die Möglichkeiten waren ja sehr gering, denn das war im Höhepunkt des Kalten Krieges. Die Absicht konnte man haben, aber man konnte es nicht durchführen' (interview on 22 October 1987). As to the reason for the negativeness of attitude towards the GDR, he stated: 'Man muß denken, man hatte die Diktatur hinter sich', a comment which confirms the trend detected in the magazine towards the equation of Nazi with Soviet totalitarianism. The significance of these observations on *Die Literatur* is heightened by the fact that it was widely perceived as being the organ of the 'Gruppe 47'.[29]

If Richter was to have achieved anything meaningful in literary relations between East and West Germany, then it was probably through the 'Gruppe 47' that he would have done it. A slight improvement in the situation came towards the end of the decade, but this was only really appreciable in quantitative terms in 1965, when a party of East German writers was permitted to attend the meeting in West Berlin. In 'Wie entstand und was war die Gruppe 47?', Richter mentions how Willy Brandt introduced him to the nascent concept of 'Ostpolitik' in 1959. Richter vigorously took up the idea two years later in an afterword to *Die Mauer oder der 13. August*, a political anthology he edited in response to the building of the Berlin Wall. He not only pleaded for a shift in foreign policy strategy but also called for more understanding towards East German writers:

> Es ist leicht, die Schriftsteller der DDR en bloc zu behandeln und sie als Stallburschen ihres Herrn zu bezeichnen, aber es entspricht nicht der Wahrheit.
> Dort wie hier gibt es Schweigende, dort wie hier sind die Ansichten differenziert, auch wenn das nicht seinen publizistischen Ausdruck findet oder finden kann.[30]

This conciliatory attitude even extends to those whom he does seem to regard as 'Stallburschen': Richter takes issue with the stance adopted by Günter Grass and Wolfdietrich Schnurre – who in an open letter exhorted East German writers to face up to their political responsibilities and speak out against the Wall – and explains, in apparent contradiction of his own earlier attitudes, why a comparison between the situation of writers in Nazi Germany and in the Democratic Republic is unjustified:

ein Jahrzehnt lang waren es nur ein paar U-Bahnteilstrecken, die man fahren mußte, um aus der Mitverantwortung für die Maßnahmen einer Diktatur in die Unverantwortlichkeit der demokratischen Freiheit zu entfliehen. Was also hält sie drüben – Stephan Hermlin, Bodo Uhse, Anna Seghers . . .? Ist es Bequemlichkeit, Gewohnheit, Untertanengeist, Opportunismus, oder ist es nicht vielmehr die Überzeugung, daß dem Kommunismus die Zukunft gehört? Und wenn es so ist, müssen wir ihnen dann nicht diese Überzeugung zubilligen, auch wenn wir dadurch zu ihren Gegnern werden?[31]

Indications of a readiness on Richter's part to look anew at the East German question can be seen in his contribution to a political anthology published in 1960: 'Zu spät?' describes a visit to his family in the GDR after an interval of five years.[32] What he finds, despite continuing severe restrictions, is an end to the immediate 'Terror' and a politically informed and inquisitive population enagaged in 'zähe Auseinandersetzungen' with its system. This contrasts with the indifference he encounters back in the Federal Republic to what he has to tell, which leads him to ask whether the 'Restoration' in the West is too far advanced for them to build upon the developments over the border.

Vestiges of the old mistrust endured, however: in 1963 he attended a congress of European writers in the Soviet Union, a country by then de-stalinised under a reforming Khrushchev. Here, Richter finds, 'nicht nur Rußland ist in Bewegung – alle Ostblockstaaten, mit Ausnahme der DDR, scheinen es zu sein'.[33] Richter expresses cautious optimism for progress of détente, but he had already had contact with Khrushchev in 1959, as president of the European Committee against Nuclear Armament, and in 1961 he had addressed an open letter to the Soviet leader (reproduced in *Die Mauer oder der 13. August*) in which he delivered a strong attack on Walter Ulbricht and asked Khrushchev to intervene and force the East German government to cease its intransigence in relations with the Federal Republic.

Richter's relations with the East German literary establishment were no less frosty in 1962, when leading members of the Deutscher Schriftstellerverband, including Bobrowski, published an open letter to the 'Gruppe 47' in protest against the arrest of Bruno Apitz in Dortmund, and appealing for solidarity in the interest of improved contact between writers on both sides. Richter's response expressed formal support, but drily pointed out the practical obstacles to such contact, not least of which being the continued internment of Wolfgang Harich and Erich Loest by the East German authorities.[34]

It was in 1965, when the 'Gruppe 47' met again in Berlin, that reconciliation finally became a serious, albeit fleeting, prospect for Richter. He later recalled the East German writers in the following terms:

> Sie unterschieden sich nicht von den anderen Vorlesenden, weder mit ihren Gedichten noch mit ihrer Prosa, noch in der Art, in der sie sich gaben. Es war die gleiche Literatur, dieselbe Sprache – es waren die gleichen Menschen. . . . für ein paar Stunden lang sah ich eine neue Aufgabe für die 'Gruppe 47': die Einheit der deutschen Literatur. Es war eine Illusion. Schon ein Jahr später setzten die Angriffe und Polemiken in der DDR-Presse gegen die 'Gruppe 47' wieder ein.[35]

Hans Werner Richter's activity in literary relations between the two German states, contrary perhaps to the expectations raised by his socialist commitment and by his image as a uniter of men, reveals itself to be remarkably insubstantial and, where existent, contradictory. This essay has sought to detrmine the personal and practical reasons why he never managed to follow through the aims he set himself even before the formal division of Germany. The 'Gruppe 47' ought, as far as it is possible to establish anything tangible with regard to its purpose, to have provided the stimulus to bridge the political divide, but in the end proved satisfied with its achievements at home, whilst East Germany remained, for the most part, out of sight and mind:

> Das wußten wir schon, was ungefähr literarisch vor sich ging. Aber die schlossen sich ja ab. Es waren zwei Staaten und zwei Gesellschaftssysteme. Oder man hätte sich ganz und gar natürlich dafür einsetzen müssen, daß man sich mit der Literatur, die dort erschien, beschäftigte. Aber wir hatten ja mit unseren eigenen Sachen zu tun.[36]

But the failure, as has also been shown, was attributable not only to the character of the 'Gruppe 47', or even to the considerable obstacle posed by the East German authorities, upon whom the realisation of plans ultimately depended; it can also be traced directly to Richter's individual experience – to his 'Kollaborationskomplex', induced to a degree by peer pressure, and by profound disaffection with the Soviet Union, but also by an anxiety to avoid the repetition of his earlier political misjudgement. Looking back on the failure, not only of his own periodical *Ost und West* but also of *Der Ruf* and of the 'Starnberger Gespräch', to bridge the divide between East and West, Alfred Kantorowicz offers an apology from whose reassuring pathos Richter also might draw some comfort:

> Waren die Männer, die den Kampf für die Einheit des Landes verloren, schuldig geworden, so war es eine tragische Schuld im Sinne der griechischen Tragödie: ein schuldhaft-schuldloses Versagen, ihnen auferlegt durch – man nenne es, wie man will – Zeitumstände, Entwicklungsgegensätze, höhere Bestimmung, Weltgeist, Vorsehung. Die Zeit selbst und gewiß das Land, in dem sie in der Zeit lebten, waren kein Humus, aus dem Ausgleich, Einheitsstreben, Verständigungsbereitschaft Wachstumskräfte hätten ziehen können. Der Vollzug der Spaltung war nicht aufzuhalten.[37]

Notes

1 Heinz Friedrich, 'Gruppe 47 am herbstlichen Main', *Hessische Nachrichten*, 21 October 1954. Also in *Die Gruppe 47. Bericht. Kritik. Polemik. Ein Handbuch*, edited by Reinhard Lettau, Neuwied and Berlin, 1967, p. 105.

2 In an interview with me on 22 October 1987, Richter stated that he consistently invited East German writers to meetings of the 'Gruppe 47', but that they were normally refused permission to attend by their authorities.

3 Peter Hornung, 'Die Gruppe, die keine Gruppe ist', *Tages-Anzeiger*, Regensburg, May 1955. Also in Lettau, p. 110.

4 Unfortunately, the archive of the 'Gruppe 47', which Richter has handed over to the Academy of Arts in West Berlin, and which ought to contain records of invitations and attendance, is not yet accessible at the time of writing. Its director, Dr Wolfgang Trautwein, stated to me in a letter of 10 August 1987: 'Aus dem derzeitigen Überblick über das Material nehme ich auch an, daß die für die DDR wichtigen Dokumente im Nachlaß nicht die Aussagekraft haben, die man erwarten würde.'

5 This assessment is based primarily on the wealth of material collected in Lettau.

6 Joachim Kaiser's comment on Richter's influence over the 'Gruppe 47' is typical: 'Alles, was in der Gruppe 47 geschieht, was so viel Widerhall, so viel Neid und so viel Haß provoziert, hängt von eines einzigen Mannes gruppenbildendem Genie, von seinem Temperament und seiner Laune ab.' 'Die Gruppe 47 in Berlin', *Das Schönste*, Munich, December 1962. Also in Lettau, p. 174.

7 See Hans Werner Richter, 'Wie entstand und was war die Gruppe 47?', in *Hans Werner Richter und die Gruppe 47*, edited by Hans A. Neunzig, Frankfurt am Main, Berlin and Vienna, 1981, pp. 27–110 (p. 79). The first edition was published in Munich, 1979.

8 Hans Werner Richter, '"Wo sollen wir landen, wo treiben wir hin . . .?" Skizzen von einer Reise in die östliche Zone', *Der Ruf*, 1, 15 August 1946; 2, 1 September 1946.

9 Friedrich Minssen, 'Notizen von einem Treffen junger Schriftsteller', *Frankfurter Hefte*, February 1948. Also in Lettau, p. 28; Gunter Groll, 'Die

Gruppe, die keine Gruppe ist', *Süddeutsche Zeitung*, 10 April 1948. Also in Lettau, p. 33.

10 Friedrich Minssen, 'Avantgarde und Restauration', *Frankfurter Rundschau*, 5 May 1949. Also in Lettau, p. 40.

11 Hans Werner Richter, *Im Etablissement der Schmetterlinge*, Munich and Vienna, 1986, p. 83.

12 Heinrich Böll, 'Angst vor der Gruppe 47?', *Merkur*, August 1965. Also in Lettau, pp. 389–400 (p. 398).

13 'Wie entstand und was war die Gruppe 47?', p. 81.

14 Hans Werner Richter, 'Wer spricht mit wem?', *Hier und heute*, 1/7, 1951, pp. 5–6. Kantorowicz's observations on the article and on the atmosphere of suspicion and hostility surrounding these contacts are contained in the entry for 5 May 1951 in his *Deutsches Tagebuch, Zweiter Teil*, Berlin, 1980, pp. 172–7. The first edition was published in Munich, 1961.

15 For more detail about the 'Starnberger Gespräch' in the context of declining literary relations between the two German states, see Helmut Peitsch, ' "Die Freiheit fordert klare Entscheidungen": die Spaltung des PEN-Zentrums Deutschland', *Kürbiskern*, 3, 1985, pp. 105–24 (pp. 118–21). The minutes of the meetings, as well as newspaper articles and other relevant documents such as invitation lists, are contained in the archive of the publisher Willi Weismann in the Deutsches Literaturarchiv, Marbach am Neckar.

16 Hans Werner Richter, 'Ost–West-Gespräch blieb ein Versuch', *Münchener Merkur*, 29 March 1951.

17 Adriaan Morriën, 'Interview mit Hans Werner Richter 1951', in *Dichter und Richter: die Gruppe 47 und die deutsche Nachkriegsliteratur*, Berlin, 1988, pp. 32–7 (p. 36).

18 For a detailed analysis of two of the stories published by Richter in the Third Reich, and their implications for his post-war status, see my article ' "Hinterwäldlerische Verlorenheit" ... Hans Werner Richter's literary work in the Third Reich', *German Life and Letters*, 42, 1989, pp. 312–27. A third story, 'Nur ein Flötenspiel', which displays overtones of National Socialist thinking and was first published in the *Hamburger Anzeiger* on 12–13 June 1937, is analysed in my Ph. D. dissertation *The Fiction of Hans Werner Richter* (University of Wales, 1989).

19 Richter describes his mood on his return from America: 'Ich ging so weit, jede Zusammenarbeit mit den Besatzungsmächten für eine Art von Kollaboration zu halten.' In 'Wie entstand und was war die Gruppe 47?', p. 33.

20 'Wie entstand und was war die Gruppe 47?', p. 39.

21 Hans Werner Richter, 'Berlin – Zentrum der deutschen Nachkriegswirklichkeit', in *Die Bundesrepublik heute; eine Bestandsaufnahme in Beispielen*, edited by Clemens Münster, Hamburg, 1965, pp. 227–73.

22 Hans Werner Richter, 'Bilanz! Bilanz? Zwanzig Jahre Bundesrepublik aus der Sicht eines engagierten Schriftstellers', *Die neue Gesellschaft*, 1 May 1969, pp. 67–74 (p. 72).

23 Hans Helmut Rehn (pseud.), 'Dammbruch im Osten', in the archive of the Norddeutsche Rundfunk, Hamburg. Tape number 61107/1–4; manuscript number 588.

24 'Bilanz! Bilanz?', p. 68.

25 Hans Werner Richter, 'Vor einem deutschen Buchschaufenster', *Hier und Heute*, 1/3, 1951, p. 6.

26 Hans Werner Richter, *Briefe an einen jungen Sozialisten*, Hamburg, 1974, pp. 82–3.

27 See 'Wie entstand und was war die Gruppe 47?', p. 43.

28 The authorship of this article is unclear. It was signed only '-er', apparently denoting the final letters of a name: the prerogative in employing this abbreviation would most likely be exercised by a member of the editorial staff, which indicates either Richter himself or Hans Georg Brenner. The style and content of the article, however, suggest the former. Alternatively, '-er' may represent 'der Herausgeber', in which case the article would definitely be by Richter.

29 For example, see Lettau, pp. 83, 98, 281.

30 *Die Mauer oder Der 13. August*, edited by Hans Werner Richter, Reinbek bei Hamburg, 1961, pp. 181–2.

31 *Die Mauer oder Der 13. August*, p. 182.

32 Hans Werner Richter, 'Zu spät?', in *Ich lebe in der Bundesrepublik*, edited by Wolfgang Weyrauch, Munich, 1960, pp. 60–6.

33 Hans Werner Richter, 'Der Weg der kleinen Schritte', *Neue Rundschau*, 74, 1963, pp. 600–12 (p. 609).

34 The letters, published in *Neues Deutschland* (4 November 1962) and *Die Zeit* (16 November 1962) respectively, are reproduced in Lettau, pp. 496–8.

35 'Wie entstand und was war die Gruppe 47?', p. 102.

36 Interview with Richter on 22 October 1987.

37 Alfred Kantorowicz, *Etwas ist ausgeblieben: zur geistigen Einheit der deutschen Literatur nach 1945*, Hamburg, 1985, p. 188.

Peter Huchel and *Sinn und Form*: the German Academy of Arts and the issue of German cultural unity
Stephen Parker

Following its launch in 1949 with the first Brecht Special Number, *Sinn und Form* rapidly became established as the 'literarische Prestigeorgan der DDR'.[1] During the period of Peter Huchel's editorship (1949–62), *Sinn und Form* came to enjoy a 'besondere Bedeutung, ja einzigartige Stellung'[2] in German literary life. By the mid-1950s influential Western circles had come to value its 'gesamtdeutsch' approach, and in the early 1960s Walter Jens was moved to describe it as 'so etwas wie das geheime Journal der Nation'.[3] Huchel's achievement over a decade with *Sinn und Form* was marked in 1959 by the award of the prestigious 'Plakette' of the Hamburg Academy of Arts. The award was made by Willy Haas, editor between 1925 and 1933 of the liberal Berlin weekly, *Die literarische Welt*. In his speech Haas suggested an affinity between the two journals, pointing out that Huchel had first developed his editorial skills on *Die literarische Welt*. With *Sinn und Form*, however, Huchel had outdone his mentor, since he had 'die von uns beiden so tief bedauerte politische Zweiteilung Deutschlands ohne viel Umstände zu einer geistigen Einheit zusammengeschweißt'.[4]

Official perception of *Sinn und Form* in the GDR during the late 1950s contrasted markedly with Haas's evaluation. Opposition to Huchel's editorship had existed from the outset, both because of his background as a non-marxist who had remained active in cultural life during the Third Reich and because he made little effort to accommodate the work of German Socialist Realists, above all those who had begun to publish after 1945, in a journal which from 1950 enjoyed a privileged status as the organ of the German Academy of Arts. With the death of the journal's most influential supporters in the Academy, Brecht in 1956 and Johannes R. Becher in 1958, *Sinn und Form* and its editor were exposed to the hostility of increasingly powerful SED figures, who were committed to the abandonment of the 'gesamtdeutsch' approach and to the introduction of more partisan literature. *Sinn und Form* was publicly censured for the first time in 1957, when Kurt Hager, Secretary of the SED Central Committee, criticised its 'ivory tower' attitudes.[5] In addition to Hager, those opposed to *Sinn und Form* included two highly influential figures: Alexander Abusch, who in the early 1950s was Secretary of the Kulturbund, from 1958 to 1961 Minister of Culture and then one of the Deputy Chairmen of the Council of Ministers with responsibility for culture and education; and Alfred Kurella, who after his return from the Soviet Union in 1954 was appointed Chairman of the Commission for Cultural Affairs set up by the Central Committee and from 1961 acted as Secretary of the Academy's Sektion Dichtkunst und Sprachpflege. In the late 1950s and at the beginning of the 1960s, these figures sought without success to pressurise Huchel, increasingly isolated from the Academy, into altering the journal's approach. The editor refused to modify an editorial line, in which undoubtedly the 'gesamtdeutsch' stance had been of vital importance in the growth of the journal's undisputed reputation. The construction of the Berlin Wall provided an opportunity for Huchel's opponents. The Academy leadership itself was subjected to intense pressure at an unprecedented 'Aussprache des Ministerrats der DDR mit der Deutschen Akademie der Künste', which took place in East Berlin on 30 March 1962. On this occasion the prominent Academy member Willi Bredel said of *Sinn und Form*: 'Diese Zeitschrift war, wenn ich das einmal ganz zugespitzt sagen darf, trotz ihres hohen künstlerischen Niveaus eigentlich ein Wanderer zwischen zwei Welten. Deshalb ist es erforderlich, daß jetzt endgültig eine Änderung herbeigeführt wird'.[6] The Academy proposed measures that it apparently viewed as compromises, including the introduction of either Bodo Uhse or Kurella's assistant Scherner as a second editor alongside Huchel. Huchel, however, remained intransigent, stating that he would resign in such an event. The affair rapidly escalated into an East–West scandal as the Academy moved to force the issue: Uhse's appointment was confirmed and Huchel duly resigned. In the autumn of 1962, Bredel, by now President of the Academy, published a statement in *Sinn und Form* defining its future role and editorial arrangements as follows:

Sinn und Form wird die Teilnahme der Akademie an der Entwicklung der sozialistischen Nationalkultur widerspiegeln und dem künstlerischen Leben der Deutschen Demokratischen Republik auch durch die Erörterung kulturpolitischer Probleme dienen. ... Der bisherige Chefredakteur Peter Huchel scheidet auf eigenen Wunsch mit Jahresende aus. Die Leitung der Zeitschrift *Sinn und Form* liegt ab 1. Januar 1963 in den Händen von Bodo Uhse.[7]

When he was finally allowed to come to the West in 1971, Huchel argued that he had merely sought to continue doing the editorial job with which he had been entrusted on the terms originally agreed. In the view of Huchel's opponents, however, *Sinn und Form* had been conceived to fulfil a specific role in the immediate post-war climate, when uncertainty had existed concerning the future of Germany. By the late 1950s this climate had been replaced by one in which both German states had achieved a measure of stability as separate entities. The editorial policy of *Sinn und Form* should, they believed, be modified to accommodate this change, just as the Academy itself had been transformed into a socialist institution.

Sinn und Form had emerged from the shake-out of journals that took place in 1948–9. In 1948, the editorial policy of *Aufbau*, the organ of the Kulturbund and the principal Soviet-licensed journal, was altered from its initial Popular Front stance to a more partisan line in cultural politics. Alfred Kantorowicz's *Ost und West*, the second most significant journal under Soviet patronage, did not meet with the approval of influential SED figures and was discontinued in 1949. The need had long been perceived by Soviet cultural officers and Johannes R. Becher, the President of the Kulturbund, for a journal which would project the quality of German intellectual life in terms of continuity of progressive traditions. At the core would be the array of figures with a international reputation who had returned from exile to participate in the construction of a socialist Germany, In a manner similar to Brecht's Berliner Ensemble and Walter Felsenstein's Komische Oper, *Sinn und Form* was conceived as a prestige project designed to impress and influence opinion outside the Soviet zone. Huchel was entrusted by Becher with the task 'dieser Zeitschrift "eine hohe wissenschaftliche und literarische Qualität zu sichern und sie als führendes literarisches Organ auf dem Gebiet der Literaturkritik zu gestalten"'.[8] Werner Wilk, who was involved at the planning stage, later recalled the terms of the editorial policy:

> Es sollte die große, repräsentative deutsche Zeitschrift sein, die mit Gedicht, Novelle, Romanausschnitt und Essay die Strömungen der deutschen und internationalen Literatur aufzuspüren und zu dokumentieren hatte. Sie sollte keine Polemik, keine Manifestation (außer der künstlerischen Werte) und keine Kritiken enthalten. ... Sie sollte 'gesamtdeutsch' – wie man später sagte – sein, sich aus tagespolitischen Forderungen und Erörterungen heraushalten und Beiträge von Schriftstellern aus allen deutschen Besatzungszonen bringen, soweit sie den künstlerischen Anforderungen entsprachen und keine dubiose Vergangenheit hatten.[9]

This 'representative' approach reflects early confidence in East Berlin that, through the avoidance of an explicitly revolutionary policy, broadly-based support for a socialist Germany could be gained in the cultural sphere, as well as in the wider political arena. In the summer of 1948 prestigious figures were invited to submit contributions. Among the names to be found in the first three issues are those of established German 'inner' and 'outer' emigrants, some politically progressive, others more conservative, for example Ernst Bloch, Hermann Broch, Gerhart Hauptmann, Georg Kaiser, Gertrud Kolmar, Werner Krauss, Hermann Kasack, Osker Loerke, Ernst Niekisch and Anna Seghers. Stephan Hermlin alone represented the younger generation of writers. The German contribution was complemented by the inclusion of a wide array of progressive international figures such as Louis Aragon, Federico García Lorca, Georg Lukács, Vladimir Mayakovsky, Mao Tse Tung and Romain Rolland. Of a print run of initially only 2,500, later between 5,000 and 6,000, a significant proportion was distributed abroad.[10]

The choice of personnel, as well as of the title and the design of the journal, was also a product of this 'representative' thinking, the ambiguities in which would presently emerge in the polarisation of German intellectual life during the Cold War. Becher's name was balanced through the presence as co-founder of Paul Wiegler. In 1945 Wiegler was a founder member of the Kulturbund and was appointed to lead the Aufbau-Verlag's editorial team. Widely respected as the author of a distinguished history of German literature and through his long association with the Ullstein Verlag, Wiegler enjoyed 'einen angesehenen bürgerlichen Literaturnamen'.[11]

Not altogether unlike Wiegler, Huchel had an essentially 'bürgerlichen Literaturnamen' known in Berlin circles from the 1930s. An early reviewer of *Sinn und Form*, Alfred Andersch, characterised Huchel as 'eigentlich kein Marxist, sondern ein "burgerlicher"

Lyriker hohen Ranges, dem wohl am ehesten Absichten zuzutrauen sind, wie sie innerhalb des Nazi-Staates die sogenannte "innere Emigration" beherrscht haben'.[12] In his choice of Huchel, Becher had the support of Soviet cultural officers (if not of all returning German emigrants), who were looking for a non-SED figure. Huchel had been prepared for a leading role in post-fascist cultural life through his selection for a Soviet military administration course in August and September 1945 at the Rüdersdorf POW camp near Berlin. He had further gained Soviet officers' confidence through his work between 1945 and 1948 with the Berliner Rundfunk. There, his implementation of the Popular Front policy for the arts brought rapid promotion, until the SED assumed control and introduced stricter Party discipline, which effectively marginalised non-SED figures like Huchel. For the *Sinn und Form* project, however, Huchel commended himself as a reliable figure of proven organisational ability and with catholic taste, who was not associated with any particular political faction. Huchel was apparently wary after his experience with the Berliner Rundfunk, yet agreed to participate in Becher's project, which meant continued high-level involvement in cultural life with adequate financial reward.

Planning for the new venture proceeded throughout the summer of 1948. Though permission was not granted to use the title of Thomas Mann's exile journal *Maß und Wert*, the choice of *Sinn und Form* echoed its classicistic balance. The design, unaltered today after more than forty years, emerged from lengthy discussions which included Huchel and the Potsdam figures, publisher Ulrich Riemerschmidt of Rütten & Loening, printer Eduard Stichnote and Suhrkamp editor Hermann Kasack, all of whom were soon to move to the West. Comparing *Sinn und Form* with *Neue Rundschau*, Andersch noted, 'die klassisch-edle Typographie (Eduard Stichnote) erreicht, ähnlich wie Anna Simons seinerzeit in der *Corona*, im Bodoni-Satz von *Sinn und Form* einen Höhepunkt des statischen Klassizismus'.[13] The design of the first number drew admiring comments from Hans Paeschke, editor of the Baden-Baden journal *Merkur*. In a letter to Kasack he wrote: 'Das Papier ist freilich sowjeto-plutokratisch und der Druck einfach herrlich, das kann Stichnote keiner nachmachen'.[14] In the same letter, Paeschke confessed his surprise 'daß *Sinn und Form* überhaupt in soviel Repräsentationsexemplaren in den Westen kommt und noch dazu mit so repräsentativen Herausgebern'. Seduced by the design and attracted by the personnel involved, Paeschke saved face with

scathing comments about the content and the intentions behind
Sinn und Form:

> Was übrigens den Inhalt betrifft, so ist es ein höchst lauer Aufguss von
> zum Teil längst Erschienenem und ein recht schwacher Versuch,
> sowjetische Ideologie poetisch zu bemänteln, Zwei, drei Hefte weiter
> und man wird beim Stalinismus angelangt sein. Mir greifts halt ans
> Herz, Loerke und auch Sie in dieser Umgebung zu sehen.

A month later Paeschke describes *Sinn und Form* as a 'kulturpolitischen Versuch im Sinn des trojanischen Pferdes, vom
Kommunismus in unsere Mauer geschickt'.[15] The image, employed
too in a review by the West Berlin writer Wolfdietrich Schnurre,
indicates the extent to which even before the founding of the two
German states, attitudes towards products of the Soviet zone had
hardened among those active in the cultural sphere in the West.
Andersch's review two years later is similarly coloured by a
profound mistrust towards the stalinist GDR. Only in the slightly
more relaxed atmosphere following Stalin's death and the demon-
strations of 16–17 June 1953 would there be a tempering of this
mistrust.

Although thanks were forthcoming from Brecht to Huchel for
the latter's efforts on the Brecht Special Number,[16] *Sinn und Form*
did not enjoy undivided support in East Berlin. In June 1949 the
reviewer of *Tägliche Rundschau* commented:

> Wir erkannten und anerkannten im ersten Heft den Willen der Heraus-
> geber, die Literaturprobleme der Gegenwart real und durch konkrete
> humanistische Beispiele wie Romain Rolland, Wladimir Majakowski
> und Gerhart Hauptmann, erhärtet im fortschrittlichen Geiste zu deuten.
> ... Die beiden letzten Hefte enthalten zwar gewichtige Beiträge, von
> guten Federn geschrieben, aber das Ganze ist (mit Ausnahme des Brecht-
> Sonderheftes) in eine dünne Höhenluft gesteigert, die die Gefahr in sich
> birgt, daß man vor lauter Ferne und Gehobenheit die Nähe nicht mehr
> sieht.[17]

The reviewer warned of 'formalistische(r) Tendenzen'. That and
similar charges would be repeated on many occasions over the
next decade. That *Sinn und Form* could become established and
could survive for so long with its original character intact was due
in some large measure to the support not only of Brecht and
Becher but also of Arnold Zweig, President of the German Academy of Arts from 1950 to 1953. The Academy was re-opened in
Berlin on 24 March 1950 as an institution to represent the arts

throughout Germany. Given the Academy's own 'gesamtdeutsch' approach, it was appropriate that *Sinn und Form* should in 1950 be taken under the Academy's wing. Zweig, who together with Becher was instrumental in this change in the journal's status, announced that *Sinn und Form* would in future act as the Academy's 'Sprachrohr und geistiges Visier'.[18] The extent to which *Sinn und Form* actually succeeded in fulfilling this role would be a matter of contention throughout Huchel's tenure of the editorship. The standing of *Sinn und Form* and its editor was none the less appreciably enhanced, and on 26 September 1952, on Becher's recommendation following Brecht's nomination, Huchel was elected to the Academy.[19] The one important change in content that ensued initially from the new arrangements for the journal was the inclusion of statements on cultural politics issued by the Academy. Significantly, with figures such as Brecht, Becher and Zweig, the Academy had a voice relatively independent of the SED. As President, Zweig was active in the promotion and, presently, protection of *Sinn und Form*.

Internal conflicts were at that stage of secondary importance when energies were being channelled into the construction of a new German state that would contrast with Adenauer's restoration. At a time when Adenauer was vigorously pursuing policies of re-armament and Western integration, prominent literary figures in the GDR voiced their opposition and their support for a GDR with policies for the construction of a socially just, united Germany. Zweig commented to Lion Feuchtwanger in a letter of 20 October 1951: 'da sehen Sie, wie die schriftstellerische Tätigkeit unsereiner zum Reisekaiser und zum aktiven Vertreter der Entspannungspolitik macht'.[20] For all its idealistic programme, *Sinn und Form*, too, was in the early 1950s on occasion deployed in the propaganda struggle. Thus, in 1951 the fourth number was dedicated to 'den III. Weltfestspielen der Jugend und Studenten für den Frieden in Berlin vom 5. bis 19. August 1951'. It opened with Stalin's 'Über den Frieden' and the special print run of 40,000 copies was distributed to participants.

Huchel, too, in these early years of the Cold War, performed the public duties commensurate with his position, representing GDR policies in Berlin and West Germany. At Easter 1951 Huchel travelled with Bodo Uhse, Stephan Hermlin and Willi Bredel to the 'Starnberger Gespräch', the first official meeting of GDR and West German writers outside the PEN framework. Huchel later addressed all those who had attended the Starnberg meeting in an open letter.[21] In it he pleaded for cultural unity despite the political division and called upon all German intellectuals to oppose the ratification of the General Treaty signed by West Germany and the Western allies in 1952.

Such meetings also provided an opportunity to cultivate contacts. At Starnberg Huchel met Hans Henny Jahnn, President of the Hamburg Academy of Arts. In Jahnn Huchel found a regular contributor to *Sinn und Form* and an opponent of the Adenauer government, who was prepared to support GDR writers' initiatives in the cause of German unity. Jahnn's letters to Huchel testify to the difficulties which this stance brought. In a letter of 27 March 1952, for instance, Jahnn wrote, 'Für alle Schriftsteller und Schaffende schlechthin, die den Kurs der Bonner Regierung nicht bejahen, wird das Dasein in ökonomischer Beziehung hier im Westen immer schwieriger.'[22] Jahnn sought, not always successfully, to respond to the calls for solidarity among intellectuals against Bonn, which were issued by Berlin Academy members and published in *Sinn und Form* during the early 1950s.

A case in point was Brecht's open letter of 26 September 1951,[23] which ended with the famous lines: 'Das große Karthago führte drei Kriege. Es war noch mächtig nach dem ersten, noch bewohnbar nach dem zweiten. Es war nicht mehr auffindbar nach dem dritten.' Brecht's letter also contained a call, clearly directed at the West, for freedom of publication and performance for all works with the exception of 'Schriften und Kunstwerke, welche den Krieg verherrlichen oder als unvermeidbar hinstellen, und für solche, welche den Völkerhaß fördern'. Jahnn, faced with repeated difficulties, apparently from the GDR authorities, in having his books published there, responded:

> Natürlich weiß ich von mir selbst, daß ich ein Individualist bin; aber den Krieg habe ich seit jeher abgelehnt, und daß mein Ziel die Verständigung ist, folgt als Selbstverständlichkeit daraus. Aber die Welt der Gegensätze ist nun einmal mit groben Waffen ausgerüstet. Das Gefühl, daß ich mitten zwischen den Fronten stehe, wird in mir immer deutlicher, so daß mein Unbehagen wächst.[24]

Brecht's open letter was treated with scorn in many circles in the West, and Huchel included an attack on those who had maligned Brecht in a speech delivered on 1 February 1952 before the 'Groß-Berliner Komitee der Kulturschaffenden'.[25] Huchel interpreted the attacks as evidence of 'eine maßlose, hinterhältige Hetze gegen den Frieden'.[26] He argued the case, as he would throughout the 1950s, for the preservation of cultural unity in Berlin despite the city's political division. Polemicising with untypical ferocity, Huchel drew a parallel between the actions of the Nazis in 1933 and those of the Western allies, especially the USA: 'Wir schreiben das Jahr 1952, und die ersten Vorboten der Barbarei sind schon lange wieder in die Mauern unserer Stadt eingezogen! Noch können wir sie zurückschlagen!.'[27] Undoubtedly, these words and others of a similar tone in the speech contributed to the image of Huchel as an orthodox cultural functionary, an image which enjoyed some currency in the West during the 1950s. Yet, although Huchel ascribed divisions in the cultural sphere exclusively to the 'tödliche Umarmung der amerikanischen Kulturpolitik',[28] the speech also contained a plea for an end to 'das Sektiererwesen in der Literaturkritik'[29] in East Berlin caused by those eager to uncover wherever they looked evidence of Western formalism. Thus, while Huchel's anti-Western comments placed him firmly in the GDR camp, he identified himself with those Academy members, including Brecht, Zweig and Hanns Eisler, who put up strong, if not always ultimately effective, resistance to SED attempts to undermine their position with charges of formalism.

During a period which saw him awarded the GDR National Prize, Third Class, in 1951 and election to the Academy the following year, Huchel could generally count on the support of the Academy for his editorial line, yet relations were not without tension. Members understandably wished to exert some influence and to ensure that the work of Academy members was included in the Academy's own organ. This imposed certain constraints on Huchel's editorial freedom, and in a letter of 26 March 1952 he complained to Jahnn:

> Dazu kommt, daß ich seit der Übernahme der Zeitschrift durch die Deutsche Akademie der Künste nicht mehr die volle Aktionsfreiheit besitze, die ich vorher hatte.... Ich blicke oft mit Schmerz auf die ersten beiden Jahrgänge zurück. Ich hoffe aber, daß eine endgültige Aussprache mit Becher manches klären wird.[30]

Yet, as Huchel was no doubt aware, Becher was a man of divided loyalties, whose support for *Sinn und Form* was contingent on other factors. The formalism debate demonstrated how Becher could be manipulated into abandoning Huchel, and how fragile, despite support from other quarters, the latter's position could become.

An excerpt from Ernst Barlach's papers, part of the drama *Der Graf von Ratzeburg*, was published in *Sinn und Form* in 1950, followed in 1951 by two pages of *Aufzeichnungen aus einem Taschenbuche von 1906*. When in 1952 the Dresden Barlach exhibition became the focus of the formalism campaign launched the previous year by the SED, *Sinn und Form* published Brecht's defence of Barlach. At the beginning of 1953 Hanns Eisler, Academy member and veteran communist, became the butt of criticism. In 1952 an excerpt appeared in *Sinn und Form* from Eisler's *Doktor Faustus* together with an essay by the Austrian marxist, Ernst Fischer, 'Doktor Faustus und der deutsche Bauernkrieg'. These publications were attacked by Alexander Abusch and Friedrich Wolf. In a rare statement in *Sinn und Form*, Abusch wrote of Eisler, 'Unter seiner formenden Hand verwandelt sich Faust in einen Renegaten, einen "negativen Helden"'.[31] Brecht's 'Thesen zur Faustus-Diskussion' were set alongside Abusch's piece, Brecht arguing that 'In einem geschichtlichen Augenblick, wo die deutsche Bourgeoisie wieder einmal die Intelligenz zum Verrat am Volk auffordert, hält Eisler ihr einen Spiegel vor'.[32]

It was in the highly charged atmosphere of debate surrounding the role of intellectuals in the GDR that the first serious attempt was made to remove Huchel. In 1975 he described the sequence of events as follows:

> Nach fünfjähriger redaktioneller Tätigkeit delegierte man mich nach Moskau, um während meiner Abwesenheit F. C. Weiskopf als Chefredakteur einzusetzen. Auf Betreiben maßgeblicher Kulturfunktionäre wurde zudem ein Text verfaßt, in dem ich mich schwerer ideologischer Verfehlungen beschuldigte. Der Text, in Ich-Form geschrieben und mit meinem Namen unterzeichnet, sollte in der nächsten Nummer von *Sinn und Form* erscheinen. Brecht, der von dieser Manipulation hörte, erhob Einspruch und erwirkte, daß es nicht zu einer Umbesetzung der Redaktion kam. Nach meiner Rückkehr aus Moskau sagte ich zu Brecht, ich wolle die Chefredaktion niederlegen und mich anderen Aufgaben – auf Grund bestimmter Angebote aus dem Ausland – zuwenden. Aber Brecht bestimmte mich, weiterhin Chefredakteur zu bleiben.[33]

If the weight of Brecht's intervention is indisputable, then the shock to the East Berlin system caused by the events of 16–17 June clearly worked to Huchel's advantage. Friedrich Wolf, who had taken exception, too, to the publication of Oskar Maria Graf's poems and Marceli Ranicki's (*sic*) essay on Erich Weinert, declared in a letter of 25 March 1953 to Abusch, Secretary of the Sektion Dichtkunst und Sprachpflege, that, in his opinion, the editorial staff of *Sinn und Form* were simply not equal to the political and aesthetic demands generated by the Academy's journal. Wolf's letter was discussed at a plenary session attended by Huchel on 26 March 1953, when it was agreed that a commission including Brecht, Bredel and Wolf himself should examine the editorial policy and personnel of *Sinn und Form*. The commission would be convened by Abusch. In response Huchel indicated a willingness to resign. Meanwhile, at a meeting of the Präsidium on 8 April it was agreed that the journal's editorial arrangements required fundamental change, which should be undertaken at the earliest possible opportunity. Günter Caspar of Aufbau-Verlag and F. C. Weiskopf were discussed as possible replacements. At a further meeting of the Präsidium on 13 May it was agreed that in the light of the editorial staff's grave errors and ideological unreliability they should be required to submit to the Academy leadership all plans for articles and proofs. Before the commission had met and while Huchel was still in Moscow, a dismissal letter dated 15 May 1953 was sent to him from the Academy, whose President Becher had become in April. It was signed by the Director of the Academy, Rudi Engel. The minutes of the plenary session of 26 June, the next record of events, testify to the dramatic turn that events had taken. Not only Brecht but also Eisler, Herbert Ihering and, indeed, Becher himself supported Huchel against attacks from Abusch and Wolf. When the commisson finally met on 2 July it comprised Paul Dessau, Huchel, Herbert Ihering and Eisler, as well as Abusch, Brecht and Wolf. The meeting was chaired by Arnold Zweig. Huchel announced that he would continue in his post only if the Academy withdrew its instruction that all plans for articles and proofs should be submitted for approval. Huchel's condition was accepted, as was his proposal that an advisory board should be formed. Brecht's proposal that Huchel should be free to choose his advisers met with agreement. Brecht, aware of the role in the affair played by certain members of the Präsidium, argued that its membership did not match the needs of the present situation in cultural politics; elections should therefore be held for the post of secretary to each section of the Academy. He would argue the case further at the next plenary session. A second meeting of the commission on 29 September confirmed the agreements of the earlier meeting. The commission also took into account the view of many Academy members that the journal needed a broader editorial base to accommodate the whole spectrum of the Academy's aesthetic and cultural interests. *Sinn und Form* should include, too, more work by young GDR intellectuals. It was agreed that the advisory board should include representatives from each of the Academy's sections.[34]

In the event editorial practice remained essentially as before. In fact, in a letter to Louis Fürnberg of May 1954 Arnold Zweig outlined continuing problems and sought, without success, to win him for the idea of editing *Sinn und Form* together with Huchel:

> Wir brauchen Dich, lieber Louis, in Berlin, und zwar in der Akademie der Künste und mit Huchel als Hauptherausgeber von *Sinn und Form*. Von Weimar aus ist das nicht zu machen, unsere Zweimonatsschrift krankt schon daran, daß Huchel in Wilhelmshorst sitzt und ebenda seine Redaktion und er nur zweimal wöchentlich in Berlin ist. ... Die *Neue Deutsche Literatur* hat aber durch Weiskopf einen solchen Aufschwung genommen, daß sich *Sinn und Form* nur halten kann und seinen Standard sogar verbessern kann, wenn es seine redaktionellen Kräfte verdoppelt.[35]

The debates concerning the future of *Sinn und Form* took place in the rapidly changing climate of cultural politics following the death of Stalin and 17 June 1953, in which the Academy sought to re-assert its position *vis-à-vis* the SED. At an extraordinary meeting on 30 June 1953 the Academy membership approved a list of proposals, which were published in *Sinn und Form*. They were presented to the government as measures designed to support the GDR in its efforts to secure re-unification and peace.[36] Acutely aware that restrictions in freedom of expression imposed by the bureaucracy were damaging to the GDR's reputation abroad as well as inhibiting debate at home, the Academy made a plea for greater independence from the government in all the media. Huchel underscored this collective appeal with an open letter published in September in *Neue Deutsche Literatur*, organ of the GDR Writers' Union. In his letter Huchel criticised the dogmatism of some GDR commentators during the formalism debate:

> Was allein die Barlach-Affäre angerichtet hat, als man es wagte, in so herabsetzendem Sinne über diesen großen deutschen Bildhauer zu schreiben, ist leider noch nicht in seinem ganzen Umfang erkannt. Es was ein Glück, daß es damals nicht bei dem Pyrrhussieg des flachsten kritischen Journalismus blieb und daß die Stimme der wirklichen Autorität, die Stimme Bertolt Brechts, auch für Westdeutschland hörbar wurde.[37]

The open letter ended with Huchel's accustomed call for unity among German intellectuals in the face of political division.

The concerted efforts of Academy members were not without effect in the new climate of cultural politics, and *Sinn und Form* was able to take advantage of the somewhat more relaxed relations between the two German states that existed until autumn 1956. In these years, through the expenditure of much energy in travel and in the cultivation of contacts, the journal and its editor achieved something of a breakthrough in West Germany. While in January 1953 Huchel had to report to Jahnn that Hamburg had 'mein Einreisegesuch für Westdeutschland abgelehnt',[38] in a letter of 23 February 1955 to Ludvík Kundera Huchel wrote that during the previous few months he had spent more time in the West than at his desk.[39] Venues in 1954 included Düsseldorf and the International PEN Congress in Amsterdam. A measure of Huchel's growing standing in West Germany was the invitation to attend the meeting of the 'Gruppe 47' at Burg Rothenfels in October 1954. Hans Werner Richter's invitation paved the way for Huchel to win young West German writers for collaboration on *Sinn und Form*, as well as to re-establish contact with old acquaintances like Günter Eich. Whatever hopes might have been invested in Burg Rothenfels, Huchel's first and only meeting with the 'Gruppe 47' turned out to be a most unfortunate experience. His participation was reported as follows in the West German press:

> Eine Attraktion der Tagung war der Besuch des ostzonalen Schriftstellers Peter Huchel, der die Zeitschrift *Sinn und Form* in Ost-Berlin herausgibt – einer der ernstzunehmenden Literaten aus dem Osten. Das literarische Ost–West-Gespräch blieb jedoch leider in den Anfängen stecken, da selbst ein Mann wie Peter Huchel in starrer östlicher Meinungsuniformität verharrt. Das war für die Teilnehmer der Tagung eine betrübliche Einsicht.[40]

The conflict was not forgotten, as Hans Mayer points out in his autobiography:

> Fast kam es zu Tätlichkeiten zwischen so alten und erprobten Freunden wie Peter Huchel und Günter Eich. Das war eine Schauermär. Später haben mir beide davon berichtet, unter Lachen. Ausgangspunkt des Krachs jedoch muß ein politischer Disput gewesen sein. Wobei es nicht nüchtern zuging. Trotzdem: Huchel hat nie wieder eine Einladung angenommen, oder erhalten. Mir riet er ab, als mich Richter . . . einlud.[41]

The débâcle of Burg Rothenfels effectively closed off relations between *Sinn und Form* and the 'Gruppe 47'. Despite agreement over the question of German cultural unity, re-unification and opposition to the Adenauer restoration, it would appear that, for influential members of the 'Gruppe 47', Huchel was too closely aligned with a communist system to which they were fundamentally opposed. Of those younger writers associated with the 'Gruppe 47' from the mid-1950s, only Helmut Heißenbüttel (1956) and Hans Magnus Enzensberger (1957) had work published in *Sinn und Form* in the period. Wolfgang Bächler had been associated with both ventures from an earlier stage, and the older Wolfgang Weyrauch contributed in 1955, although he, like Enzensberger and Heißenbüttel, had not been at Burg Rothenfels.

Despite the setback with the 'Gruppe 47', 1954 saw the publication of poems by Eberhard Meckel, on the face of it an unlikely figure until one considers the circles Huchel moved in before 1945. He also had the consolation that, in Alfred Döblin, he won a major name for *Sinn und Form* in the mid-1950s. Like Jahnn, Döblin was an established figure, who was disaffected with his treatment in the West and had many affinities with regular contributors to the journal. Indeed, the presence of such names as Brecht, Bloch, Ernst Fischer, Konrad Farner, Eisler, Ihering, Feuchtwanger, Zweig, Thomas Mann, Lukács and Anna Seghers, together with the inclusion of work by major international figures like Halldór Laxness, Louis Aragon, Mao Tse Tung and Pablo Neruda, guaranteed that as soon as the climate in East–West relations relaxed, the journal could gain acceptance in the FRG as a quality organ representative of major achievements in the literature of the first half of the century, a publication clearly at variance with other GDR literary magazines. Jahnn assured Huchel that

> *Sinn und Form* hier im Westen gelesen wird, und ich darf hinzufügen, daß ich über die Zeitschrift übereinstimmend gute Urteile höre. ... Mein Freund Hans Erich Nossack war jedenfalls von der letzten Nummer so angetan, daß er sich fest entschloß, Ihnen gelegentlich Arbeiten von sich zur Verfügung zu stellen.[42]

Nossack, again a somewhat older figure never closely associated with the 'Gruppe 47', duly sent Huchel the manuscript of his play *Die Hauptprobe*, the first two acts of which were published in 1955. Huchel further cultivated the Hamburg connection, travelling there the following spring for discussions, again with more senior figures, Günther Weisenborn, Hans Georg Brenner and Weyrauch. The inclusion of pieces by Weyrauch and Weisenborn added to the impression of *Sinn und Form* as a forum for figures whose horizons were not principally those of the post-war division and of the literary groupings that it had spawned. It is significant that Johannes Bobrowski, arguably Huchel's major 'find' in the mid-1950s, was then already in his late thirties and belonged to the same pre-war 'bürgerlich' tradition as Huchel himself. The GDR poet Erich Arendt, whose own work and whose translations were published, was, like Huchel, Brecht and Becher, of the older generation. It is true that Huchel gave early opportunities to Fühmann, Kunert, Kipphardt, Bienek and Hacks, but there was an emphasis on established names, whose work might be viewed as transcending the post-war division. This was not lost on those Academy members who wished to see greater representation of young GDR intellectuals. Until the mid-1950s Huchel's approach was underpinned by the marxist re-interpretation of the European tradition undertaken in major essays by Georg Lukács, Hans Mayer, Ernst Bloch, Ernst Fischer, Paul Rilla, Konrad Farner and Werner Krauss. As one might expect, the major focus was on the Enlightenment, Weimar classicism and nineteenth-century realism, although Mayer, Fischer, Farner and Bloch also treated writers associated with twentieth-century modernism.

Official recognition of Huchel's efforts was now forthcoming in the West as well as the East. Following the award of the GDR Fontane Prize in 1955, he was elected a corresponding member of the Hamburg Academy of Arts in 1957, the latter constituting a significant mark of acceptance in West Germany for the GDR editor. The representative, 'gesamtdeutsch' perspective of *Sinn und Form* was enhanced in these years by its use as a forum for celebration and commemoration. 1955 saw the publication of an excerpt from Thomas Mann's 'Versuch über Schiller', the speech delivered by Mann in Stuttgart and Weimar on the 150th anniversary of Schiller's death. The same number of *Sinn und Form* announced that Mann had been elected an honorary member of the Academy on his eightieth birthday, the event being marked by a number of specially commissioned articles. Later that year, mourning of Mann's death was led by Lukács's piece 'Der letzte große Vertreter des kritischen Realismus'. The same year witnessed the death of Rilla and of F. C. Weiskopf. Brecht was to follow in 1956, Döblin in 1957, Becher in 1958 and Jahnn in 1959. Special numbers of *Sinn und Form* were dedicated to Becher and Brecht.

These losses, moreover, coincided with renewed attempts by

the SED to assert its vanguard role *vis-à-vis* intellectuals following repression in Poland and Hungary. At the start of this new phase in GDR cultural politics a number of eminent marxist essayists and theoreticians who were regular contributors to *Sinn und Form* were attacked, the journal and its editor also coming in for criticism. Although Lukács had previously been a guarantor for critical orthodoxy in *Sinn und Form*, he was disgraced following his involvement in the deposed Hungarian government, and his writings criticised for their emphasis on the bourgeois tradition to the exclusion of proletarian–revolutionary achievements. Hans Mayer, too, was attacked on this count, as well as for his defence of the avant garde against the charge of decadence. In June 1956 Mayer had also publicly challenged the authority of the SED on cultural matters after having been debarred from speaking at the fourth German Writers' Congress in January of that year. Mayer's Leipzig colleague Ernst Bloch was accused of fomenting seditious activities and compelled to retire from his professorship. The same charge was levelled against Wolfgang Harich, a Becher protégé, who was imprisoned for ten years. Zweig commented to Feuchtwanger: 'Immer wieder sagt einer aus unserem Kreise: "Das müßte man dem Brecht sagen! Der würde sich einen Fall des Wolfgang Harich nicht haben gefallen lassen!"'.[43]

With Brecht's death, the waning of Becher's authority, the marginalisation of Zweig and the routing of the 'revisionists', orthodox cultural politicans such as Abusch, Otto Gotsche, Hager and Kurella were able to consolidate powerful positions in the hierarchy. From that time on they could exert considerable influence in the Academy where previously the balance of power had lain with the non-orthodox. The rise of these figures was, moreover, consistent with the flow of events in the struggle between the two German states. By the mid-1950s West Germany and the GDR had become integrated within their respective power blocs, each in practice pursuing a path of separate development. While there was still some propaganda value in the deployment of the ideas of re-unification and of cultural unity, their relevance was diminishing. In the GDR renewed efforts were made to focus attention on the task of the construction of a socialist society. A campaign was initiated in 1957 against residual bourgeois elements in the cultural sphere and contacts with the West discouraged. The campaign set the tone for the rest of the decade and beyond, the construction of the Berlin Wall in August 1961 representing its

logical conclusion. For the exponents of this strategy, an under-
taking such as *Sinn und Form* was at best a distraction, at worst
a pernicious influence. It is not without irony that *Sinn und Form*
had gone a long way to achieving its hoped-for status as a
'gesamtdeutsch' organ at a time when the GDR was in the process
of abandoning the policies from which the journal had originally
emerged. In Hans Mayer's view, the period from late 1956 onwards
represented 'sechs Jahre der Agonie'[44] for the journal and its editor.
Walter Felsenstein and Herbert Ihering were the only influential
voices in the Academy that could be counted upon to support
Sinn und Form.

In the new climate Huchel could not contemplate publishing
work by Harich, Bloch or Lukács, nor did Huchel find replacements of equivalent stature, so that *Sinn und Form*'s standing as
a forum for the marxist essay was undoubtedly diminished. All
three were attacked repeatedly, and, in a speech delivered at the
SED Kulturkonferenz held in Berlin on 23–4 October 1957, Hager,
for the first time, included an attack on *Sinn und Form*. It was
conducted in the following terms:

> Deshalb kämpfen wir gegen den Neutralismus, die unpolitische Haltung,
> die Selbstisolierung, die beschauliche Betrachtungsweise. So wünscht
> man sich als Leser der Zeitschrift *Sinn und Form*, die von der Akademie
> der Künste und angesehenen Schriftstellern herausgegeben wird, daß
> sie einmal aus ihrer feinen Zurückhaltung und Beschaulichkeit, die etwas
> von der Art englischer Lords an sich hat, ihrer noblen Betrachtungsweise
> und philosophischen Skurrilität heraustreten möchte und einmal
> parteilich zu den so nahen und wichtigen, so großen und erhabenen
> Problemen des Schönen in unserem sozialistischen Aufbau, des
> Heldenhaften im Kampf gegen den deutschen Imperialismus und
> Militarismus, des Sinns unserer Diskussionen über den sozialistischen
> Realismus, Stellung nehmen möchte.[45]

Hager's statement set the tone for the conflicts to come. Yet, if
Sinn und Form was now subject to public criticism, it did not yet
experience the radical changes which took place on other journals.
Between 1956 and 1958 the editorial staff of *Sonntag* were dismissed. Willi Bredel was sacked from his post as editor of *Neue
Deutsche Literatur*, and *Aufbau*, whose editor was Bodo Uhse, was
discontinued. It would appear that *Sinn und Form* escaped with a
warning because it was one of the very few GDR products that
enjoyed an international reputation at a time when the state had
few friends abroad.

Following Hager's attack there was no discernible change in editorial policy. Huchel evidently believed that the introduction of more Socialist Realism and the adoption of a decidedly partisan stance were incompatible with the journal's established identity as a high-quality 'gesamtdeutsch' organ. His refusal to incorporate such work did nothing to defuse the situation: his editorial line was open to intepretation – and was indeed so interpreted – as a snub not only to partisan Socialist Realists but to the state itself. For Huchel's opponents, his stance demonstrated that his loyalties lay not with the GDR and socialist art but with the 'bourgeois aestheticism' of the West. He had essentially remained the '"bürgerlicher" Lyriker' identified by Andersch at the beginning of the 1950s. The ambiguities inherent in the original conception of *Sinn und Form* were now forced into the open by the stark ideological alternative represented by the two German states.

If GDR cultural politicians believed that Huchel would yield to pressure, they underestimated the extent to which Huchel, stubborn and resourceful if not suited to the rigours of a protracted struggle, identified personally with the achievements of *Sinn und Form*. They also underestimated the extent to which the journal and its editor had become synonymous with German literature of the highest quality among influential circles in the West. Such was the journal's standing in that quarter that Huchel could now count on support in times of difficulty. For their part, West German pundits were eager to seize a stick with which to beat the GDR in the propaganda war. Thus, in the late 1950s Huchel continued to cultivate Western contacts, and he, in turn, was increasingly cultivated in West Germany. Irrespective of whether he hoped that pressure from influential Western circles would help him to survive what would be only a temporary climate of hostility towards *Sinn und Form*, or whether he saw his future in the West, he presently found himself in a Western embrace that would become ever tighter as the conflict escalated.

Among his trips to the West, in 1957 he attended a conference, 'Literaturkritik – kritisch betrachtet', organised by the Wuppertal Bund, the last Western outpost of the Kulturbund. Its organiser, Hans-Jürgen Leep, 'wollte auch den Lyriker Huchel dabeihaben, vor allem jedoch den Herausgeber der angesehenen Zeitschrift *Sinn und Form*'.[46] Huchel the lyric poet was also attracting increasing attention. Venues for readings in 1958 included Düsseldorf in June and Munich and Tübingen in September. Yet Huchel was by now engaged in a war of attrition at home. His correspondence with Jahnn shows that he felt under intense pressure. On 11 December 1958, following Becher's death, he wrote to Jahnn that 'ich gerade noch mein schwaches Segelschiff über Wasser halten kann'.[47] Huchel was later to describe the exchanges between himself and two of his principal opponents, Abusch and Kurella, in the following terms:

> Immer wieder gab es Sitzungen in der Akademie, mußte ich berichten, 1958 zum Beispiel über die ersten zehn Jahrgänge. Da stellte dann Alexander Abusch eine Frage, deren Antwort er selber schon kannte: Haben Sie den Geburtstag von Walter Ulbricht nicht wenigstens einmal gewürdigt? Ich verneinte, und dann nahm Herr Professor Kurella die Hefte in seine gepflegten Finger, hob sie hoch, ließ sie herunterfallen und rief: In den ganzen zehn Jahren wurde die Existenz der DDR nicht erwähnt (was übrigens nicht stimmte).[48]

In May the following year the first of many supportive articles appeared in the West German press. Marcel Reich-Ranicki observed.

> Zwar ist der Spielraum, den man dieser für das literarische Leben der Sowjetzone durchaus nicht typischen Zeitschrift gönnt, im vergangenen Jahr wieder wesentlich enger geworden, doch haben sich die Gerüchte, Huchel sei abgesetzt worden, erfreulicherweise als falsch erwiesen.[49]

While Huchel could derive from the award of the Hamburg 'Plakette' the sense of satisfaction that 'meine Arbeit ist nicht umsonst gewesen',[50] by September he was reporting to Jahnn the Berlin Academy's reluctance to acknowledge the prize. In the same letter he revealed,

> die letzten Monate, die ich mich mit der Zusammenstellung der ebenso umfangreichen wie zähen Sonderpublikation J(ohannes) R. B(echer) zu beschäftigen hatte, waren für mich in jeder Beziehung derart strapaziös, daß ich gesundheitlich wie nervlich völlig erledigt bin.[51]

The proposal for this second Becher special number had been made to the Academy by Huchel himself. Yet Huchel's distance from the cultural politics then being practised in the GDR is illustrated by his later comment on the Bitterfeld Conference of 1959: 'Ich wußte, daß die letzte Stunde für *Sinn und Form* geschlagen hatte'.[52]

The conflict dragged on through 1960, when the privilege of a family holiday in Italy was withdrawn, though the following year Huchel was not prevented from reading again in Düsseldorf and

Tübingen. By then, he was contemplating signing a contract with one of the major West German publishers, amongst whom he was in great demand. The editorial line of *Sinn und Form* remained essentially unaltered, with contributions in 1961 from Krauss, Mayer, Zweig, Fischer and Fühmann as well as Paul Celan's translations of Essenin. Something of an exception was provided by the inclusion in the second number of a short prose piece by Willi Bredel and an essay to mark Bredel's sixtieth birthday by Alfred Klein, head of the Academy's research project on proletarian-revolutionary literature. Numbers from later that year, however, reveal that there had been no change of heart. Ernst Fischer argued for a re-evaluation of Kleist, Mayer contributed an essay on Hofmannsthal and Richard Strauss, Jahnn, Bobrowski and Georg Kaiser all figured, while an opening was provided for the younger Reiner Kunze, Christoph Meckel and Klaus Wagenbach. Kunert published his first poems in *Sinn und Form* for over a decade.

The construction of the Berlin Wall in August 1961 produced a situation in which, in the eyes of GDR cultural politicians, a 'gesamtdeutsch' project like *Sinn und Form* was simply an anachronism. According to Hans Mayer, the first move was to subordinate the journal to a 'Gremium aus Mitgliedern der Akademie der Künste. Noch war es aus Leuten zusammengesetzt, die ihrem Akademiekollegen Huchel helfen wollten'.[53] Huchel later reported that his opponents then looked for a way of marginalising him: 'zu Beginn des Jahres 1962 erhielt ich Kenntnis von einem Ministerratsbeschluß, der eine "Neuregelung der ideologischen und personellen Lage in der Redaktion *Sinn und Form*" anordnete'.[54] After a number of increasingly bad-tempered exchanges, during which Willi Bredel, the new President of the Academy, 'vieles zu verhindern suchte',[55] Huchel was replaced by Bodo Uhse from January 1963.

Huchel, who retained editorial control until the end of 1962, arranged for an extremely demonstrative departure. The penultimate number contained Ernst Fischer's essay 'Franz Kafka', the final number Fischer's 'Entfremdung, Dekadenz, Realismus'. The latter was preceded by Sartre's speech at the Moscow World Peace Congress, 'Die Abrüstung der Kultur', with its plea for an end to dogmatism in USSR cultural politics. Essays by Mayer and Krauss were included, Huchel published some of his own poems, and, for the first time, poems were included by Paul Celan and Günter Eich, and a story by Ilse Aichinger. The final volume opened with

Brecht's 'Rede über die Widerstandskraft der Vernunft' written in 1936, which begins.

> Angesichts der überaus strengen Maßnahmen, die in den faschistischen Staaten gegenwärtig gegen die Vernunft ergriffen werden, dieser ebenso methodischen wie gewalttätigen Maßnahmen, ist es erlaubt, zu fragen, ob die menschliche Vernunft diesem gewaltigen Ansturm überhaupt wird widerstehen können.[56]

The use of Brecht to provide the scarcely veiled comparison between Nazism and the GDR was regarded as the ultimate insult by the SED. Abusch blocked Huchel's request to travel to Italy with his wife, following an invitation from his publisher, Gottfried Bermann Fischer. Attacks were launched on him and also on the Academy and its President, Willi Bredel, at the SED party conference in January 1963.

Bredel claimed that Huchel's final act as editor had demonstrated 'wes Geistes Kind er ist'.[57] The terms of an agreement with the Academy had obliged Huchel to present a plan of the final number. This he did, but then 'Leider hat sich der Chefredakteur Huchel nicht an seine eigene abgegebene Konzeption gehalten'. Bredel's speech provoked the following response from Kurt Hager:

> Aber bisher ging es in der Akademie der Künste, wie es nach den Ausführungen des Genossen Bredel scheint, offenbar zu wie im englischen Oberhaus, wo ein Lord dem anderen nicht wehtut und der Präsident keine Macht hat. (Heiterkeit und Beifall) Die erhabene, geradezu majestätische Isoliertheit im Elfenbeinturm hinderte aber weder Peter Huchel noch andere Mitglieder der Akademie, den Angriff gegen die Politik der Partei und gegen den sozialistischen Realismus zu führen.[58]

Hager repeated his attack on Huchel in a speech on 25 March. In the same month there was a further escalation in the affair with the West Berlin Academy's decision to award Huchel its Fontane Prize, a decision interpreted in East Berlin as a highly provocative political act. Huchel ignored attempts by Kurella and others in April to persuade him not to accept the prize, whereupon he was subjected to another attack by Hager at the end of May. Huchel's acceptance of the Fontane Prize was, in fact, the final straw for a number of people who had previously been not unfavourably disposed towards him. Until his departure to the West in 1971 he was ostracised by many colleagues.[59]

For all Huchel's important role in early GDR literary life, the events of the late 1950s and early 1960s ensured that he was consigned to the margins of GDR literary history.[60] Yet, as a key mediating figure between East and West during that 'period of transition', Huchel embodied a number of its contradictions and ambiguities, and it is significant that in the period shorly before the momentous events of 1989 GDR literary historians had begun to devote greater attention to the complexities of those years, including Huchel's own contribution.[61] During Huchel's lifetime, however, it fell to the West to honour his achievements: in his later years he was showered with prizes, including in 1976 West Germany's most prestigious award, *pour le mérite*.

Notes

1 Janet K. King, *Literarische Zeitschriften 1945–1970*, Stuttgart, 1974, p. 83.

2 Hans-Jürgen Schmitt, 'Literaturbetrieb als Staatsmonopol', in *Die Literatur der DDR*, edited by Hans-Jürgen Schmitt, Munich and Vienna, 1983, p. 74.

3 Walter Jens, 'Wo die Dunkelheit endet. Zu den Gedichten von Peter Huchel', *Die Zeit*, 6 December 1963, now in *Über Peter Huchel*, edited by Hans Mayer, Frankfurt am Main, 1973, pp. 22–7 (p. 22).

4 Willy Haas, 'Ansprache bei der Verleihung der Plakette an Peter Huchel am 7. 11. 1959', in *Kontraste: Jahrbuch der Freien Akademie der Künste in Hamburg*, Hamburg, 1960, pp. 11–15, now in *Über Peter Huchel*, pp. 160–3 (p. 160).

5 Kurt Hager, 'Den Dingen auf den Grund gehen', *Neues Deutschland*, 26 October 1957.

6 Bredel was quoted in 'Zwischen zwei Welten', *Der Spiegel*, 19 September 1962, pp. 86–7.

7 Willi Bredel, 'Erklärung', *Sinn und Form*, 14/5–6, 1962, p. 661.

8 Peter Huchel, 'Der Fall von *Sinn und Form*', *Europäische Ideen*, 35/12, 1975, pp. 5–6, now in Peter Huchel, *Gesammelte Werke* (GW), edited by Axel Vieregg, 2 vols, Frankfurt am Main, 1984, II, pp. 326–9 (p. 326). The quotation is taken from Huchel's personal contract with the Academy, a copy of which is deposited in Huchel's file in the Central Academy Archive, reference number A1.

9 Werner Wilk, 'Peter Huchel', *Neue Deutsche Hefte*, 9/90, 1962, pp. 81–96 (p. 89).

10 Elmar Faber/Franz Greno, 'Editorische Nachbemerkung', *Sinn und Form: die ersten zehn Jahre*, reprint, Berlin and Nördlingen, 1988, *Sonderhefte/Register*, p. 79. Some five hundred free copies of each number were distributed to individuals and institutions, almost half going to West Germany. See, too, Schmitt, p. 74, who estimates a print run of some 8,000, of which 3,000 were distributed abroad. From the outset *Sinn und Form* depended on heavy subsidies from the publisher Rütten & Loening and, from 1950, from the Academy. Both attempts to remove Huchel from his post, in 1953 and 1962, were preceded by threats of the withdrawal of the subsidy. See extracts from the minutes of meetings of the 'Präsidium' on 8 April 1953 and 3

February 1961 contained in Huchel's file in the Central Academy Archive, reference number A1.

11 Hans Mayer, 'Erinnerungen eines Mitarbeiters von *Sinn und Form*', in *Über Peter Huchel*, pp. 173–80 (p. 174). In footnote 20 on p. 676 of his informative article '*Sinn und Form: Beiträge zur Literatur* in den 50er Jahren' published in *Zeitschrift für Germanistik*, 11/6, 1990, pp. 667–77 Uwe Schoor writes, 'Das gesamte Projekt *Sinn und Form* läßt enge Beziehungen nicht nur zu den "Leitsätzen", sondern zum gesamten Anliegen des Kulturbundes erkennen, von den auch in bezug auf die Widerherstellung fruchtbarer Beziehungen zum Ausland'. In footnote 22, p. 676 Schoor draws attention to the fact that the journal's title 'wird im Entwurf zum Herausgebervertrag als geistiges Eigentum Bechers ausgewiesen'. Interestingly, on 21 December 1948 Becher in his capacity as President of the Kulturbund sent Wilhelm Pieck two copies of *Sinn und Form*, referring to it as an organ of the Kulturbund. The letter is among Wilhelm Pieck's papers in the Institut für Geschichte der Arbeiterbewegung in Berlin. It is deposited under reference number NL 36/676 in the file marked 'Entwicklung der SED zur Partei neuen Typs. Die Kulturpolitik der Partei. Kulturbund zur demokratischen Erneuerung Deutschlands. 1945–April 1946, 1946–49'. In 1949 Huchel was reporting to the Kulturbund's Kommission Literatur. At a meeting on 25 April 1949 he stated that he would not be able to publish Horst Lange's new novelle. This was regrettable since this extraordinarily gifted writer was in a desperate situation. Huchel and Lange were close friends from the Nazi years. The minutes of the meeting are deposited in the archive of the Kulturbund in Berlin in the file 'Büro Gysi. Kulturfonds. Berichte und Protokolle. Kommission Jugend und Studenten und andere Kommissionen, 1948–49'.

12 Alfred Andersch, 'Marxisten in der Igelstellung', *Frankfurter Hefte*, 6 1951, pp. 208–10 (p. 208).

13 Andersch, p. 208. Significantly, Andersch chose the same 'Bodoni-Satz' for the journal which he edited in the mid-1950s, *Texte und Zeichen*.

14 Hans Paeschke to Hermann Kasack, 8 February 1949, in '*Als der Krieg zu Ende war': Literarisch–politische Publizistik 1945–1950*, edited by Bernhard Zeller, third edition, Marbach am Neckar, 1986, p. 516.

15 Paeschke to Kasack, 5 March 1949, in '*Als der Krieg zu Ende war*', p. 517.

16 Bertolt Brecht to Peter Huchel, 1 July 1949, in Bertolt Brecht, *Briefe*, edited by Günter Glaeser, 2 vols, Frankfurt am Main, 1981, I, p. 613.

17 Ltz, 'Wesentlich – aber per Distanz', *Tägliche Rundschau*, 14 June 1949.

18 Arnold Zweig, 'Zur Übernahme der Zeitschrift durch die Deutsche Akademie der Künste', *Sinn und Form*, 2/5, 1950, p. 5.

19 At a meeting of the Academy's Sektion Dichtkunst und Sprachpflege on 30 January 1951 Brecht nominated Hermlin, Huchel und Kuba. Minutes of the meeting are deposited in the Central Academy Archive in the file 'Protokolle der Sektionssitzungen 1950–61', reference number 315. As Secretary of the Sektion Becher wrote his letter proposing Huchel for membership on 9 September 1952. The letter is in Huchel's file in the Central Academy Archive, reference number A1.

20 Arnold Zweig to Lion Feuchtwanger, in *Lion Feuchtwanger – Arnold Zweig Briefwechsel 1933–1958*, edited by Harold von Hofé, 2 vols, Berlin, 1984, II, p. 146.

21 Peter Huchel, 'Mahnung an die Schriftsteller', *Wege zueinander*, 1/1, 1953 p. 2, now as 'An die westdeutschen Kollegen und Freunde' in *GW*, II, pp. 288–9.

22 Hans Henny Jahnn to Peter Huchel, in *Hans Henny Jahnn – Peter Huchel: Ein Briefwechsel 1951–1959*, edited by Bernd Goldmann, Mainz, 1974, p. 40. Jahnn's letter of 12 May 1958, p. 91, indicates that in the late 1950s the pressure had by no means diminished: 'Wir sind hier in der ständigen Gefahr, daß jede Veröffentlichung in der DDR uns böse angerechnet wird.'

23 Bertolt Brecht, 'An die Künstler und Schriftsteller Deutschlands', *Sinn und Form*, 3/5, 1951, p. 5.

24 Jahnn – Huchel, 1 April 1952, p. 42.

25 Peter Huchel, 'Die gemeinsamen Anliegen', *Aufbau*, 8 (1952), pp. 235–40, now as 'Rede vor dem Groß-Berliner Komitee der Kulturschaffenden' in *GW*, II, pp. 269–82.

26 *Ibid.*, p. 279.

27 *Ibid.*, p. 270.

28 *Ibid.*, p. 283.

29 *Ibid.*, p. 282.

30 Huchel – Jahnn, p. 39. In fact as early as 26 February 1952 a plenary session of the Academy discussed the possible introduction of an additional editor alongside Huchel. Names mentioned were Paul Rilla, Heinz Lüdecke and Alfred Kurella. The meeting resolved to extend the range of *Sinn und Form* through the inclusion of 'kunstkritische Stellungnahmen' by Academy members. Huchel could not be expected to implement the resolution alone. The minutes of the meeting are deposited in the Central Academy Archive in the file 'Protokolle des Vorbereitenden Ausschusses zur Gründung der DAK sowie Protokolle der Plenartagungen 1950–53', reference number 118.

31 Alexander Abusch, 'Faust – Held oder Renegat in der deutschen Nationalliteratur?', *Sinn und Form*, 5/3–4, 1953, pp. 179–93 (p. 186). Wolf criticised Eisler and Fischer at a meeting of the Sektion Dichtkunst und Sprachpflege on 21 January 1953. At a meeting of 20 March 1953 it was agreed that *Sinn und Form* should lead the critical discussion of Eisler's work. The minutes of the meeting are deposited in the Central Academy Archive in the file 'Protokolle der Sektionssitzungen 1950–61', reference number 315.

32 Bertolt Brecht, 'Thesen zur Faust-Diskussion', *Sinn und Form*, 5/3-4, 1953, pp. 194–7 (p. 196).

33 Peter Huchel, 'Der Fall von *Sinn und Form*', GW, II, pp. 326–7.

34 Wolf's letter to Abusch of 25 March 1953 is in the Central Academy Archive in the file 'Dokumente zur Geschichte von *Sinn und Form*'. The minutes of the plenary sessions of 26 March 1953 and of 26 June 1953 are deposited in the file 'Protokolle des Vorbereitenden Ausschusses zur Gründung der DAK sowie Protokolle der Plenartagungen 1950–53', reference number 118. Excerpts from the minutes of the meetings of the Präsidium on 8 April 1953 and 13 May 1953 are contained in the document 'Angelegenheit *Sinn und Form*' compiled in the early 1960s by the Director of the Academy, Hossinger, The document is deposited in Huchel's file in the Central Academy Archive, reference number A1. Minutes of the meetings of the *Sinn und Form*

commission on 2 July 1953 and 29 September 1953 are deposited in the Central Academy Archive in the file 'Protokolle der Sektionssitzungen 1950–61', reference number 315.

35 Arnold Zweig to Louis Fürnberg, in *Der Briefwechsel zwischen Louis Fürnberg und Arnold Zweig*, edited by Rosemarie Poschmann and Gerhard Wolf, Berlin and Weimar, 1978, p. 206.

36 'Vorschläge der Deutschen Akademie der Künste', *Sinn und Form*, 5/3–4, 1953, pp. 255–7.

37 Peter Huchel, 'Antwort auf den offenen Brief eines westdeutschen Schriftstellers', *Neue Deutsche Literatur*, 1/9, 1953, pp. 89–91, now in *GW*, II, pp. 290–2 (p. 291). Huchel's open letter was in response to the Hamburg writer Herbert Lestiboudois' 'Offener Brief an den Schriftsteller Peter Huchel' dated 15 April 1953 and published in *Neue Deutsche Literatur*, 1/7, 1953, pp. 105–9. Lestiboudois himself had written in response to Huchel's 'Mahnung an die Schriftsteller' (see note 21 above). There is evidence in Berlin archives that through the exchange of letters Huchel's opponents were engineering a opportunity for him to exercise self-criticism following his dismissal from *Sinn und Form*. The archive of the Kulturbund contains papers of the Writers' Association from the early 1950s. Among them is a memorandum from W. Baum to Abusch dated 22 November 1951 reporting Lestiboudois's arrival in Berlin as a guest of the Writers' Association. Lestiboudois would be presenting himself to Abusch the following week. The memorandum is in the file marked 'Deutscher Schriftsteller Verband 1950–52', reference number 98. The 'Teilbestand *Sinn und Form*', reference number 56, deposited in the Academy contains a letter to Huchel dated 22 May 1953 from Günther Cwojdrak of *Neue Deutsche Literatur*. Cwojdrak offered comradely advice as to how Huchel might frame his answer to Lestiboudois. Huchel might telephone him for further discussion of the matter after his return from the Soviet Union. The same file contains a letter dated 31 July 1953 from Huchel to Günter Caspar, in which Huchel reported that he hoped he had now defused all his opponents' 'mines'. He was almost certainly unaware that Caspar had been discussed as his possible successor.

38 Huchel – Jahnn, 31 January 1953, p. 50.

39 The letter, excluding the opening paragraph which contains this information, was published in *GW*, II, pp. 335–6.

40 Heinz Friedrich, '*Gruppe 47* am herbstlichen Main', *Hessische Nachrichten*, 21 October 1954, now in *Die Gruppe 47*, edited by Reinhard Lettau, Neuwied and Berlin, 1967, pp. 104–5.

41 Hans Mayer, *Ein Deutscher auf Widerruf*, 2 vols, Frankfurt am Main, 1984, II, p. 230. Richter in fact invited Huchel to three meetings of the 'Gruppe 47' which took place after Huchel's dismissal from *Sinn und Form*. On each occasion Huchel was not permitted to attend.

42 Jahnn – Huchel, 22 February 1955, p. 72.

43 Zweig – Feuchtwanger, 3 December 1956, II, p. 332.

44 Mayer, *Über Peter Huchel*, p. 180.

45 Hager, 'Den Dingen auf den Grund gehen'.

46 Mayer, *Widerruf*, II, p. 226.

47 Huchel – Jahnn, p. 94.

48 Peter Huchel, 'Gegen den Strom: Interview mit Hansjakob Stehle', *Die Zeit*, 2 May 1972, now in *GW*, II, pp. 373–82 (p. 376).

49 Marcel Reich-Ranicki, 'Peter Huchel: ein mann ließ sich nicht irre machen', *Die Welt*, 23 May 1959.

50 Huchel – Jahnn, 4 June 1959, p. 102.

51 Huchel – Jahnn, 12 September 1959, p. 104.

52 Huchel, 'Gegen den Strom', *GW*, II, p. 377.

53 Mayer, *Widerruf*, II, p. 248.

54 Huchel, 'Der Fall von *Sinn und Form*', *GW*, II, p. 327. The meeting in question in fact took place only on 30 March 1962. See note 6 above.

55 Mayer *Widerruf*, II, p. 250. A record of Huchel's meetings with Bredel and Academy Director Dr Hossinger between mid-June and December 1962 was kept by Hossinger in a series of memoranda, which are deposited in Huchel's file in the Central Academy Archive, reference number A1. Bredel himself was subjected to intense pressure to effect the change required by the SED. In a letter to Bredel dated 30 August 1962 Hans Bentzien, Minister of Culture, described the content of the latest number of *Sinn und Form* as diametrically opposed to the Academy's cultural policy and mission. He found it full of scepticism, negation and a 'gesamtdeutsch' attitude. Bredel should therefore lose no time in implementing measures which would put a stop to the damage done to GDR cultural policy by *Sinn und Form*. The letter is deposited in the Central Academy Archive in the file 'Dokumente zur Geschichte von *Sinn und Form*'.

56 Bertolt Brecht, 'Rede über die Widerstandskraft der Vernunft', *Sinn und Form*, 14/5–6, 1962, pp. 663–6 (p. 663).

57 Willi Bredel, 'Wem dient die Kunst?', *Berliner Zeitung*, 19 January 1963. According to Hossinger's note, the Academy got sight of the final number only on 27 December 1962. Hossinger's note is contained in the document 'Angelegenheit *Sinn und Form*' deposited in Huchel's file in the Central Academy Archive, reference number A1.

58 Kurt Hager, 'Elfenbeinturm verlassen', *Berliner Zeitung*, 19 January 1963.

59 In 'Peter Huchel: Porträt eines Lyrikers', *Das Wort*, 11 (1968), pp. 65–77, now in *Über Peter Huchel*, pp. 36–48 (p. 38). Franz Schonauer writes that the sense of anger and bitterness was such that 'selbst liberalere Geister unter den DDR-Funktionären bei Nennung seines Namens fanatisch sich verhärten'.

60 Poems were published in *Sinn und Form* after his death and again in 1988, and attempts were made by the Aufbau-Verlag in the mid-1980s to publish a selection of his poetry.

61 Despite the fact that *Sinn und Form* continued to play a prominent role in GDR literary life, there was until the late 1980s no significant amplification upon the brief entry on page 511 of the *Geschichte der Literatur der Deutschen Demokratischen Republik*, edited by Horst Haase *et al.*, Berlin, 1977, which reads: 'Tendenzen des Ästhetizismus und der Versöhnung von bürgerlicher und sozialistischer Ideologie, wie sie in der Zeitschrift *Sinn und Form* zu finden waren, setzte man den Klassencharakter und die Volksverbundenheit sozialistischer Kunst und Literatur entgegen'. In a speech at the Tenth GDR Writers' Congress in 1987 Stephan Hermlin encouraged a re-appraisal of Huchel's role. Recalling his collaboration with Huchel on *Sinn und Form*,

Hermlin said: 'ihren Redaktionsbeirat verließ ich vor genau fünfundzwanzig Jahren, aus Solidarität mit dem damals abgesetzten Chefredakteur Peter Huchel' (Stephan Hermlin, *Neue Deutsche Literatur*, 36/423, 1988, pp. 35–40 (pp. 35–36)). Evidently alluding to the events surrounding Huchel's dismissal, Hermlin continued: 'Es gibt einige Künstler und Schriftsteller der DDR, die sich damals mit Ignoranten und dogmatischen Berserkern zu schlagen hatten für das Werk anderer und für ihr eigenes Werk' (*ibid.*, p. 38). He completed his speech with a warning that 'eine Gesellschaft, die der Zukunft zustrebt, sich ihrer Vergangenheit versichern muß' (*ibid.*, p. 40). In 1988 the Humboldt University accepted Uwe Schoor's doctoral dissertation, Sinn und Form *unter der Chefredaktion von Peter Huchel: Konzeption, ausgewählte Konturen und Wirkungen. Untersuchungen zu den Jahrgängen 1 bis 14 (1949–1962).*

Women and peace in literature and politics: the example of Anna Seghers

Cettina Rapisarda

Anna Seghers, who in 1947 returned from exile to a Berlin divided into four sectors, is an exemplary figure in the development of literary life in the two post-war German states. The author's reputation and the reception of her works were decisively shaped by the East–West conflict. Immediately after her return she found recognition in all the occupied zones. A clear sign of the esteem in which she was held in the West came when she was awarded the Büchner Prize in Darmstadt in 1947. Published in 1946 by the Aufbau-Verlag and in various Western editions up to 1948, the novel *Das siebte Kreuz*, which was written in exile and was already a success in the United States, established the author's reputation in the early post-war period. The reason for the fundamental change which soon took place in Anna Seghers's standing in the West was to be found almost purely in her politics, and not in her literary production. The novel *Die Toten bleiben jung* was presented at the Frankfurt book fair in 1949, but met with little response in the West. For several years books by this author, who had declared her allegiance to the newly-established GDR, were not available in the West. The work of Anna Seghers, who was chairwoman of the Writers' Union in the GDR from 1952 onwards, and who enjoyed great esteem in the literary life of her country, remained almost completely outside the literary public's awareness in the Federal Republic of the 1950s.

It is constructive to sketch the development of Anna Seghers's reception in the West over the period under investigation here. It was not until 1959 that the West again turned its attention to her, on the publication of her novel *Die Entscheidung*, which depicted the origins of the GDR and conditions in that country. Readers in the Federal Republic were unwilling to make a serious attempt to come to terms with this book, written as it was from the perspective of a female intellectual from the GDR. This unwillingness extended to a lack of objective literary examination of the work. The tone of its reception in the West almost unanimously echoed that of its first review, which spoke of 'intellectual capitulation' on the author's part and which disqualified the book in terms both of literary merit and of the ideas it contained.[1] The second part of the novel, published in 1968, met a similar fate. The image which West Germans had of Anna Seghers was, with some justification, described in terms of 'negative fascination'.[2] The development of this 'negative fascination' closely followed that of the Cold War itself.[3] The condemnation of her books, which were written for a GDR public and which were indeed difficult for Western readers, was not least an expression of anti-communist convictions and of a rejection of the GDR as a whole.[4]

That this condemnation derived from political as well as literary considerations is illustrated by the controversy over whether it was permissible for Western publishing lists to include works by authors from 'die Zone', a question which arose when a first Western edition of *Das siebte Kreuz* was announced in 1962.[5] Similarly, there were protracted discussions over the issue of Seghers being awarded honorary citizenship of Mainz, her home town.[6] Indeed, Seghers regularly became the subject of debate at decisive moments in the GDR's history, in 1961 for instance, when the Wall was built,[7] and in the autumn of 1989 upon the publication of a book titled *Schwierigkeiten mit der Wahrheit* by Walter Janka, telling of the injustice he suffered when he was sentenced at a show trial in 1957.[8] This book, in which Anna Seghers in particular is attacked for her involvement in one of the charges brought against Janka, and also because of her inactivity at the trial, has renewed discussion of the political stance of the author, who died in 1983.

At a conference in East Berlin in March 1990,[9] which was the first opportunity for students of German to address the question of Anna Seghers after the publication of Janka's book and the effective collapse of the SED, new insights into her thinking began to emerge, particularly with regard to the events of 1956–7. A story found among her unpublished work, written in that year and called *Der gerechte Richter*,[10] shows how critically Anna Seghers came to regard the system of justice and, more generally, the development of socialism in her country, at least for a certain time.[11] Furthermore, it was known that Anna Seghers had her reservations, despite her fundamental support for the policies of the GDR.[12] The critical content of novels such as *Die Entscheidung* and *Das Vertrauen* must be reassessed in the light of this short story.[13] Indeed, *Das Vertrauen* contains a passage which is, in sense, a continuation of *Der gerechte Richter*. Ulsperger, one of the characters, has kept silent on the persecution he suffered in the Soviet Union. His decision not to speak is explained as follows: 'Er hat nichts sagen können. Viele Leute hier wären erst recht wieder irr und wirr geworden.'[14] The Cold War and the pressure from the West which accompanied the GDR from its very beginning did nothing to encourage criticism. An author like Anna Seghers, whose hopes were set on the re-alisation of socialism in her country, would justifiably have feared speaking the same language as those who wished to condemn both the idea of socialism itself and the attempt to make it a reality by criticism of its shortcomings.

Anna Seghers's concern with the question of peace in the years following her return from exile will be examined here in the context of the difficulties experienced by GDR intellectuals who were fundamentally committed to socialism. In the immediate post-war period the issue was coloured not only by the concrete experi-ence of the destruction wrought by fascism and war but also by the renewed danger of hostilities in the wake of the East–West conflict. In the 1940s and 1950s Seghers frequently made her views on the question of peace known through the medium of articles and speeches. These statements appeared almost exclusively in the GDR and have generally been overlooked in the West. Explicit statements by Seghers on the role of women in society are of particular interest, since views on this matter are otherwise al-most completley absent from her writings. Following on from her anti-fascist work in exile, Seghers reflects on the possibility of bridging the East–West divide to secure peace, a venture in which women would play a significant role.

In 1952, at a meeting of the Council for World Peace, Seghers spoke in favour of 'eine Versammlung der Mütter der ganzen Welt', and recommended 'eine Konferenz zur Verteidigung ihrer Söhne'. She saw solidarity amongst women as an opportunity for broader co-operation moving beyond national and political boundaries. She cited the personal feelings characteristic of women or mothers, especially the loving and protective bonds with their sons: 'es gibt keine Frau, ob sie schwarz oder weiß order gelb ist, Deutsche oder Französin, Amerikanerin oder Sowjetbürgerin, die das

Teuerste, was sie besitzt, als Kanonenfutter hergeben will'.[15] In an open letter of 1955 she set her expectations of women in general in a historical context and argued that precisely because of the historical experiences of the World War, co-operation between women from lands with different political orientation is conceivable. She reported:

> Als ich kurz nach dem Krieg quer durch Europa fuhr, traf ich Frauen in jedem Land und an jedem Ort, in deren Gesichtern das Leid um ein teures verlorenes Leben eingeprägt war, das Leid um einen Mann oder Vater, um einen Sohn oder Bruder, um einen Bräutigam oder Freund. . . . Ihrer verzweifelten Frage 'Warum ist gerade mein Leben zerstört?' folgte immer der Ausruf: 'Wenn doch nur unsere Kinder glücklich werden!'[16]

The feeling of responsibility for future generations which characterises women as mothers is seen as a starting-point for political action. In the same text Seghers expresses the conviction that the role of women in the private sphere already supports peace in any case: 'Tiefen Anteil an der Kraft jedes Volkes, an der kriegsbremsenden, friedenhütenden Kraft, haben die Frauen, die zu ihm gehören, Mütter und Töchter, Schwestern und Bräute. Denn sie sind es, denen das Leben entspringt – das gerade, was unsterblich ist an den Völkern.'[17] In 1949 she had already spoken of 'eine große besondere Rolle' to be played by women in a peaceful union of all people extending beyond national boundaries: 'Nicht nur als Arbeiterin, als aktive Kämpferin, sondern in jeder Art menschlicher Gemeinschaft, als Mutter, als Ehefrau, als Schwester'.[18] These sentiments highlight the way in which women's influence in the private sphere can promote the cause of peace. Although Seghers supplies no further details, it seems that the allusion to a life-giving and life-maintaining female capacity is central; and thus motherhood seems, as it were, to supply the fundamental pattern for all women. In a further article she attributes to mothers a primeval force which should be turned to the benefit of the peace movement: 'Es gibt eine Kraft, die nie ermüdet, die immer in dem Maß wächst, in dem sie gebraucht wird. Es ist die Kraft der Mutter, die ihr Kind schützt. Für sie gibt es keine Abstumpfung'.[19] Here, however, moving beyond the traditional restriction of the mother to the private sphere, Seghers calls for political action in accordance with the Stockholm appeal to ban all nuclear testing:[20] 'Die Kraft einer Mutter wird unermeßlich in dem Augenblick wachsen, in dem sie begriffen hat, daß es ebenso möglich ist, die

Atomgefahr zu bekämpfen, die auf ihr Kind lauert, wie es möglich ist, Verbrechen und Seuchen zu bekämpfen.'[21]

The content of Anna Seghers's definition of motherhood, which in these texts serves to delineate the duties of all women, calls for some clarification. A definition of women in terms of biological motherhood or of an assigned motherliness is consistent with conservative dualistic gender definitions of womanhood, which, whether of ontological or characterological basis, carry with them the danger of becoming established in a way which is restrictive for women and legitimises the status quo.[22] It is, however, necessary to understand in individual cases in what context and in what form these patterns of thought are applied, to what extent they are understood as normative and repressive for women, or have innovative and emancipatory elements. This is all the more valid for the post-war years, since sexually dualistic ways of thinking experienced a new upturn at this time, and even the contemporary women's movement not only analysed but adopted them.[23] A characteristic feature of these years was that the new evaluation of traditional patterns of womanhood had to be carried out in such a way as to dissociate them from those of National Socialism. Seghers expressed her opinion on the National Socialist conception of motherhood in the service of militarism as early as 1942. In so doing, she expressed her belief in the existence of an indestructible, 'genuine', and thus apparently fundamental, sort of motherhood:

> Was Hitler auch immer mit dem Wort 'Mutter' gemacht hat, an wieviel Muttertagen, durch wieviele Mutterkreuze die deutsche Frau gepriesen wurde, dem niederträchtigsten Krieg Söhne geboren zu haben, der echte Begriff 'Mutter' hat deshalb nie ausgelöscht werden können, weil er zu den Begriffen gehört, die jeder Mensch, jede Minute durch eigene Erfahrung erneuert.[24]

It is clear from Seghers's views on how peace may be secured, cited above, just what an extra-historical definition of womanhood in the contemporary political context can achieve: since all women or mothers are held to be fundamentally life-giving and life-maintaining, it is precisely they who seem predestined to meet together on a common basis beyond political fronts and to show commitment to peace.

The notion that women, particularly mothers, had a role to play in the furtherance of peace is also a feature of Seghers's literary work. Indeed, Seghers was able to exercise more influence through

her literature than through political action. The question of the
form which the duty of women takes can be asked, in the more
general context of the author's image of women, of a novel like *Die
Toten bleiben jung*.

Die Toten bleiben jung, a less well known novel than, for example, *Das siebte Kreuz* or *Transit*, is especially instructive for the
peace question on the one hand because it contains a large-scale
treatment of the Second World War and militarism and on the
other because female characters in particular are given relatively
large scope. In two respects this novel occupies a transitional
place: firstly in so far as it was written in the period from 1944 to
1949, partly in exile and partly afterwards; and secondly in that it
was, as already mentioned, still available in published form in the
West. In this novel the author outlines her historical–materialistic
interpretation of epochs, and, by depicting the lives of individual
families from representative social groups, attempts to give a di-
verse picture of German history from 1919 to 1944. She portrays
the individual development of the separate figures from a humanist perspective: although they are all products of their differing
social backgrounds, this does not make them seem inextricably
linked to their similarly differing political orientations, a fact which
is strongly evident in the women characters. Starting with the
murder of a Spartacist fighter in 1919, different strands of the plot
describe the life of his girlfriend Marie and those of the four
members of the White Guard involved in the murder, former officers and soldiers who fought in the First World War, up to the
last years of the Second World War. In this depiction the author
consciously pursued an educational and didactic objective opposed
to fascist and militaristic ideology, which she characterised in
contemporary statements and in the essay 'Aufgaben der Kunst'
as the primary literary task for the present.

An analysis of the position of women in the interpretation of
war and militarism in the novel can proceed from a short scene
within the description of war. The text describes how, in Poland
shortly after the attack on the Soviet Union, an old peasant woman
is tormented by German soldiers:

> 'Tanz, alte Hexe', und alle klatschten und lachten und pfiffen. Sie stieß
> oft an und schlug oft um, denn sie war beinahe blind. Es glänzte in
> ihren erloschenen Augen; sie hatte vielleicht schon die Nachricht
> begriffen: Jetzt kommt es, jetzt ist es soweit. . . . Zum erstenmal zuckte
> ihr Gesicht, als sei es vom Lachen angesteckt. Ihr zahnloser Mund

verzog sich; ihre Brust schüttelte sich vor Lachen. Ihr Teufel habt bald
ausgeteufelt. Hans starrte ihr nach; sie kam auch ihm jetzt hexenhaft
vor; er spürte einen Bruchteil der eigenen Mutter in dieser Hexe und,
wenn er an seine Heimat dachte, einen Bruchteil der Hexe in seiner
sanften, schweigsamen Mutter.[25]

The woman in this scene appears as the defenceless victim of
arbitrary, inhumane violence on the part of the military. As a victim she represents not only the Polish people but also, in the
comparison to a German mother, the civilian population in general which has been affected by the War. In this way, an opposition
based on gender between perpetrators and victims is implicitly
created. The two women are placed in parallel in the subjective
perspective of the soldier Hans, who, in contradiction to his communist beliefs, belongs to the German army. From his point of
view the tormented woman becomes threatening because of her
laugh, and thus she appears as a witch. She arouses fear in that
she is able to foresee the future downfall of the enemy army –
following a mythological pattern of the blind seer in a state of
ecstasy – and in that she possesses a power which raises her
above her tormentors. At the same time, however, her threatening
quality seems to Hans to grow precisely through her affinity to his
mother Marie. This could be explained by the fact that this woman,
like his mother, becomes for him a surrogate conscience. The
image of the Polish woman still accompanies him later, as it pre-
dicts the victory of the Soviet Union over Germany, also reminding
him of the fact that he is on the wrong side.[26] The development of
his conscience, traditionally bound to a father-figure, is for Hans
tied to his mother; when, as a child, he takes part in a theft, his
mother explains the importance of conscience: 'Ich kann ja nicht
immer bei dir sein; das kann ich ja nicht. Das kann ja nur bloß
dein Gewissen.'[27] The mother, with her humanity and depend-
ability, also represents an ethical point of orientation later on, and
it is no accident that, on meeting her again, he is plagued by the
idea of the guilt which he bears as a soldier.[28]

Marie, who together with her son Hans stands at the centre of
the proletarian strand of the plot, can be regarded in Seghers's
novel as an exemplary mother. Through her motherhood she has
made possible a form of survival for her murdered lover in the
form of his son, an element on which the title of the novel plays.
The woman's achievement here consists in the first place in the
process of biological motherhood. The importance of the mother

is symbolically increased through secularised Christian imagery, which is carried consistently throughout the novel and which is suggested by the name Marie, a name frequently used by Seghers. This symbolism has reference to the continuity of the political work of the Spartacist and his son, who arrives at the same political beliefs as his father. The mother is not directly involved in the development of the basic political convictions of the son, which also include an anti-militaristic position; the influence of a friend of the father is decisive here. Although it is upon Hans's conscience, marked as it is by his mother, that his own political attitudes are based, the reverse influence takes place as far as his actual political position is concerned. Whereas the motif usually characterised as 'handing over the baton' ('Staffettenmotiv'), frequently used by Anna Seghers to describe the personal bestowal of political insights, is generally depicted as the initiation of a younger person by an older one, here the son influences his mother in a reversal of this mechanism.[29] Supported by her ties to him, she develops her own political convictions. These finally find their expression in Marie's act of sabotage in an armaments factory. She feels strengthened by the son whenever she fights against the production quota, and by thinking of him she can decide on well-planned and cunning sabotage.[30] Years later, Seghers used the motif of a mother becoming politically aware through her son as the central point of her story 'Agathe Schweigert'. The love of the mother for her politically active son allows her to achieve a qualitative change in maternal love itself, although in the end she no longer devotes herself to her son personally but to his friend and to his comrades-in-arms.

The model for this story, the authenticity of which the author affirms in a postscript, is Maxim Gorky's well-known novel *The Mother*, as it is for the development of Marie. In the 1940s, Anna Seghers repeatedly mentions this book in her reflections on an ideological response to fascism. She emphasises the political development of the mother figure who 'aus einer unwissenden armen Frau zur Trägerin einer Fahne wird'.[31] Even apart from this political development, she describes the mother elsewhere as a model character, 'die auf der tiefsten Stufe der Not höchsten Begriff von menschlicher Würde verkörpert'.[32] According to the writer's theories, the dulling influence of fascist ideology is countered by the description of such figures, for in this way it can be shown 'was das unteilbare, das unverletzliche Individuum bedeutet'.[33]

Anna Seghers wanted to incorporate in Marie both the aspects of the female figure in Maxim Gorky's novel which she identified: human greatness and the capacity to develop. On the one hand, she shows through Marie how a proletarian woman who has had neither education nor support comes to refuse to take part in the production of weapons, and how this process of development is augmented not only by Marie's emotional ties to her son but also by her independence from him. On the other hand, as a character and as a mother she embodies a principle opposed to war and becomes the upholder of humanist values. Concerning Marie's humanity, which even extends to a woman fanatically holding out for National Socialism who is still working in the armaments industry towards the end of the war, one of the last sections of the book reads:

> Der Soldat mit dem Stumpf sagte: 'Mutter!' Wo seine eigene jetzt war, wußte er nicht. . . . Sogar die Kläber hielt sich weniger stramm, ihre Augen glänzten weniger, sie sprach weniger munter. Das alles machte sie weniger gespensterhaft, als ob sie, sobald Marie da war, das Recht der Menschen begriff zu leiden.[34]

A glance at the whole of Seghers's novel shows that by no means all women are depicted as peace-loving purely on the grounds of their sex. Certainly, an exemplary gulf opens up between the peasant woman Liesel Nadler and her husband who enthuses about war: the woman carries out all the work involved in mortherhood and the home, both during the War and later in peacetime, whilst her husband despises the labour of daily life and awaits the adventure of war, which would heighten his sense of self-worth. At the same time, the Prussian nobility with its militaristic tendencies is personified by a woman, the ossified Amalie von Wenzlow. In her whole manner she strives to live up to her physical similarity to Friedrich II. Through Amalie, whose life is marked by a renunciation of her own wishes, the author also presents the lack of freedom in the life of women, even if they are from a socially privileged background; indeed, perhaps that background restricts their freedom even more, in accordance with Seghers's notion of class. Much more clearly than the biographies of the men around them, the development of such women in the novel can be read as 'Tragödien unentfalteter Möglichkeiten des Menschenseins',[35] and it is by reference to women that the author lays down an 'Ansatzpunkt für die Frage nach Glück und wirklicher Befreiung des Menschen'.[36]

Just as Walter Benjamin wrote that the figure of Katharina in the novel *Die Rettung* is 'nicht unbehauster als Melusine',[37] so several female figures are characterised by alienation from a world in which they have no chance to speak. Lenore, the wife of one of the officers, von Klemm, with whom she has an unfulfilled marriage, no longer feels any attachment to her husband, and is disowned after the discovery of her infidelity. Lenore encounters injustices time and again in her daily life.[38] In this she resembles the young Anneliese von Wenzlow, a woman who frees herself from the paternal home and the Hitler Youth, seeks her own path in life, and develops a critique of National Socialism from a Christian standpoint. In these figures, women's moral independence is suggested, but generally does not reach the point at which it would be socially effective. The same applies to Elisabeth, who is married to the SS man Ernst von Lieven, but who mentally renounces him the more she learns of his part in the deportation of Jews. She married him in the hope that he would enable her to return to her Baltic homeland, to the place of her childhood, where she could become a mother herself. From her viewpoint she rejects various National Socialist terms and instead generates her own set of opposing values. It is not a National Socialist 'Vaterland' but the 'Heimat' that has value for her, and her brother's comment that 'Du bist in Deutschland daheim' does not satisfy her. She replies:

> ich bin denn doch noch immer nicht erwachsen genug. Für mich kleines Mädchen ist ein Vaterland etwas gar zu Gewaltiges. Und wenn man noch also Kind gleich zwei solche Bauklötze rechts und links gehabt hat wie Rußland und Deutschland. Ich habe genug an dem, was ich mit meinen Augen umfassen kann: den Garten, den See, ein paar Wälder.[39]

In the same way she defines her child from her personal perspective as 'Erdenbürger' and not with the abstraction of her husband as 'Volksgenosse'. The term 'Erdenbürger' has the following meaning for her: 'Ein Kind, Ernst, braucht die Erde. ... Ein Kind hält einen mit der Erde zusammen; ein Kind, das verpflichtet.'[40] Described as a mother who is close to nature and to life, Elisabeth sympathises with abused women and children, and thus her own life loses its meaning, for she realises the disdain in which her environment holds all morals.[41] With characters like Elisabeth, the author turns specifically to her female readers and outlines startingpoints for positions opposed to National Socialism which arise out of her conception of a female perspective.

In *Die Toten bleiben jung* it is thus particularly women and mothers like Marie who are raised to the status of upholders of humane values opposed to militarism and Nazism. To what extent this moral revaluation has emancipatory or restrictive implications for the image of women is a matter of dispute in the secondary literature.[42] One criticism is directed at the fact that Marie's life is full of privation and at the extent to which she is at all entitled to her own happiness. Does, for Anna Seghers, a moral concept also apply which subordinates the private spheres allocated to women to political ones, and thereby regards the question of individual happiness and sexuality[43] as of secondary importance, as was established by criticism in the proletarian novel of the 1920s?[44] The credo of the Spartacists at the beginning of the novel is frequently interpreted in this manner: 'Das richtige Leben, zu dem auch die Liebe gehört, fängt ja erst später an, wenn das Wichtigste getan ist.'[45] Although it is true that this quotation does not allow us to conclude directly that the author was convinced of a hierarchy of the political and personal, the exemplary Marie subordinates her personal happiness to her duty, just as her lover does.[46] Overall the structure of the novel, in which political events are related through private lives, balks at a clear and classified division of the two spheres. It is through Marie's role in the novel as a whole and through her very personal political course that the author attempts to achieve a synthesis of the two areas. But to what extent does the character of Marie, the 'sanfte, schweigsame Mutter', possess normative and anti-emancipatory implications in that she corresponds to ontological definitions of femininity?

Whilst Marie as a mother is stylised and turned into a hero,[47] her characteristics of passivity and self-sacrifice, traditionally defined as feminine, remain unexamined in respect of historical origins and legitimacy. In fact, the independence of Seghers's female characters is frequently to be attributed to unhistorical, sexually ontological patterns of femininity, such as that of women's relationship to nature, or their closeness to a life force. In this authorial intention two inconsistencies can be identified as far as the figure of the gentle Marie is concerned. In the symbolic passage quoted earlier, she has been attributed with a hidden, potentially 'hexische' side which can be regarded as a confirmation of the Hebrew meaning of the name Marie/Mirjam (contrariness).[48] Marie is an example of Seghers's motif of the hidden 'Kraft der Schwachen' – this being the programmatic title of a collection of stories – which was to emphasise the unrecognised capacities of women in particular. In her ability to cope with life Marie is only apparently weak, and after the sabotage she is able to make use of her supposed naivety as camouflage. The second inconsistency in the character lies in her capacity to change politically, which has already been described,[49] and which restricts the extent to which female characteristics are predetermined and thus their normative valency.

It should be noted, however, that this capacity to change is itself actuated and guided predominantly by men; and thus once more the active part in political action falls to male characters, to the murdered Spartacist and his friend, or to Hans. In this respect one can speak of a 'männlichen Blick der Anna Seghers' which satisfies itself 'mit jener Fremdbestimmung der Frau, die dieser allenfalls den Platz an der Seite des Mannes einräumt'.[50] On occasion 'das unbedingte gegenseitige Verständnis' of the sexes has been praised as 'die große Menschheitsperspektive' of the author.[51] In its consequences for the position of women, this changing relationship probably needs to be judged more critically, as other examinations have done: 'Die Existenz der Frau wirkt gegenüber der des Mannes abgeleitet'; out of this, however, there arises 'bei Anna Seghers gegenüber dem, was Frauen leisten und leiden, keine Geringschätzung', asserts Eva Kaufmann, for example.[52] Complete independence for a women like Marie is not depicted, her development is only described in its beginnings and it never reaches a point at which the social primacy of the male figures would be called into question. Although motherhood leaves its mark on Marie's political development, her political work is in itself sexually specific, albeit in a novel manner.[53]

To explain the traditional elements in Anna Seghers's image of women, reference is frequently made to her non-autobiographical way of writing, to the absence of the author in her text.[54] Indeed, the central female figures in Seghers's work can in general hardly be read as literary representations of the author herself. On the contrary, the course Elisabeth Endres identifies for the author is perhaps more likely: 'Sie identifizierte sich sehr häufig mit der geläufigen Identifikationsfigur, dem Mann. ... Eine Frau hat die Gleichberechtigung gefunden, indem sie den Mann reden läßt, als wäre er ein Stück von ihr'.[55] In the reception of her works, Seghers, who was not generally assigned to the special category of 'Frauen-literatur', reached an equality of status with her male colleagues.

Typically, this is evident in the mostly positive criticism of her 'männliche Schreibweise'; for example, a contemporary review of *Die Toten bleiben jung* speaks appreciatively of 'einer – bei Frauen – bewundernswerten Objektivität, Sachkenntnis, Logik und Präzision'.[56] In evaluating this attitude it is worth considering that, whilst on the one hand it was the basis for a retention and propagation of gender roles, on the other it took a step towards equal rights in the form of the far from easy violation of a taboo. The author thus conquered for herself a domain belonging to the opposite sex, an element which could also be perceived by the readership as emancipatory for women. This course, on which the author herself embarked, was diametrically opposed to that followed by the women characters in her works as their female roles are explored.

In Seghers's early works, motherhood itself is an autobiographical theme, through which she deals with her own experience as a woman. The years in which she herself became a mother – her son Peter was born in 1926 and her daughter Ruth in 1928, from her marriage with Laszlo Radavanyi – were decisive for her career as a writer. On completion of her doctorate, she gave up the study of the history of art in favour of literary work and, in 1928, with the Kleist Prize, she received her first, very important recognition as a writer. In these years she took the decision to become politically committed, a commitment which was also to shape her activities as a writer: in 1928 she joined the KPD and in 1929 the Bund proletarisch-revolutionärer Schriftsteller. In a story of 1929–30, 'Auf dem Wege zur amerikanischen Botschaft', she describes the political action of a woman who is a mother. She is presented as one person in a series of demonstrators, but her political action stands in conflict with her motherly duties. She must reject the images of her children which keep coming to her mind when the demonstration becomes highly dangerous: 'Alte Gedanken rieben sich an ihrer Stirn, um nochmals ausgedacht zu werden; aber so kam sie nie auf den Platz, so voll und schwer. Wegstoßen mußte sie endlich diese Kinder und verlassen. Durchbeißen alle Nabelschnüre'.[57] The conflict between maternal responsibilities and socio-political work, in which Seghers would also include her literary work, is heightened in the portrayal of a proletarian woman with her difficult living and working conditions, but is nevertheless founded on autobiographical experience. The incompatibility with politics not so much of the mother's role as demanded by society, which is not under discussion here, but of her own wishes and real duties, finally transpires to be insoluble. For, as Friedrich Albrecht put it: 'politisches Handeln und Sorge um die Kinder werden als schroffe Alternativen begriffen, nicht als widerspruchsvolle Einheit aufgefaßt und unter einem höheren Gesichtspunkt versöhnt'.[58] It is probably to this aspect of the story that the author was referring when she volunteered her dissatisfaction with it: 'In diesen Geschichten gibt es viele verzweifelte und untergehende Menschen. Wenn man schreibt, muß man so schreiben, daß man hinter der Verzweiflung die Möglichkeit und hinter dem Untergang den Ausweg spürt'.[59] A few years later, in 1932, she presented the conflicts involved in motherhood once again, in the story 'Marie geht in die Versammlung', in which an 'Ausweg' is presented figuratively. A motif from the earlier story reappears: the mother believes she sees her son walking in front of her in the street, rejoices at the sight, but is disappointed when she finally discovers him to be a stranger. In this second treatment of the theme, the moment of disappointment is tied to an insight into her responsibility even towards the stranger; she gives him the expensive fruit which was meant for her children. She formulates her belief as follows: 'Man darf nicht bei den Kindern hocken, man muß arbeiten, nicht für drei Kinder, sie sagt, für drei Millionen Kinder'.[60] Both stories legitimate the political work of a woman even when it comes into conflict with her duties as a mother, although the conflicts and disappointments of the mother are not glossed over in the process. In contrast to the first story, however, the second offers a reconciliation of the contradictions on a moral plane.[61] Political work is taken as an appropriate expression of a symbolically viewed motherhood, which is thus released both from the narrowly biological and from the private family contexts.

If the concepts of motherhood in the three areas examined – the post-war statements on women's duties in the name of peace, the novel *Die Toten bleiben jung*, and the two pre-war stories – are compared, both consistencies and inconsistencies are evident. The intellectual step to a political reinterpretation of motherhood, which underlies Seghers's theories on peace, is already present in an early story. Whilst the stories still display the pressure of actual biographical experience and represent clearly conflicts in the life of a politically active mother,[62] those sorts of conflicts are omitted from the novel *Die Toten bleiben jung* in favour of turning the mother into a hero.[63] Ideal images, in particular that of the proletarian mother depicted by Maxim Gorky, become decisive for the presentation of motherhood in the novel. The woman as an upholder of humanist ideals and in her potential for political development is placed in parallel with the figure of the revolutionary in opposition to fascism. This presentation of women, which can partly be understood as an interpretation of history, but predominantly as an ideal, is carried over in the post-war period directly into political work. Out of the earlier treatment of the theme of motherhood there develops in Seghers the idea of a specific political duty for women. To summarise, the task of women in the cause of peace is understood by Seghers not as being inconsistent with, but as congruous with, the characteristics and values normally described as motherly, the qualitative development and social expansion of which is called for.

Moreover, the idea of a duty for women and particularly for mothers in the name of peace as Anna Seghers formulated it in the post-war period was not purely her own work. It was in fact widespread in the early post-war years, particularly in the contemporary women's movement. The reflections of Anna Seghers are also to be understood in this context, for, although the author was not herself a member of such organisations and her work would presumably not have been produced at close quarters to them, their discussions cannot have been without influence. The year 1947 saw the foundation of such international peace organizations as the MMM (Mouvement Mondial des Mères) and the World Organization for the Mothers of all Nations (WOMAN), the latter established by the North American journalist Dorothy Thompson. The most important women's organisations founded in the four zones of occupation generally declared a belief in peace to be one of their primary tenets, and mostly identified it as a specifically female responsibility. To this extent it is legitimate to speak of a specifically feminist pacificism, which formed 'einen zentralen Bestandteil der neuen Frauenpolitik nach 45'.[64] It is therefore not surprising that the first large meeting of women's organisations from all the occupied zones in Bad Boll in May 1947 had as its theme 'Friedensbewegung, Völkerverständigung und Völkerversöhnung als Aufgabe der Frau'. However, in the same year it became clear that the desire of women's organisations for East–West co-operation was increasingly being jeopardised by the course of the Cold War.[65]

In the Federal Republic, criticism of the increasing GDR tendency to use the term 'peace' in an inflationary, propagandistic manner joined forces with the rejection of its critical usage in the Federal Republic itself, particularly with regard to the question of rearmament. It is constructive to look at the history of the Westdeutsche Frauenfriedensbewegung in this light. Founded in 1957, it was shaped mainly by people of Christian orientation, although it did not reject co-operation with GDR organisations. As a result, the West German peace movement was publicly and repeatedly characterised as a 'disguised communist organisation' in the Federal Republic.[66] By 1952, the year in which Anna Seghers spoke out for an international conference of mothers for the defence of their sons, the possibility of effective, wide-ranging congresses able to bridge the East–West gap and bring balanced and representative groups of women of varying political allegiance together under the common aspect of motherhood was already very faint. In Anna Seghers's later texts there are no indications of moves to set up such a conference.[67] But considering Anna Seghers's reputation in the West, one must assume that she would have been the person least likely to have her ideas listened to in the Federal Republic.

Notes

1 Marcel Reich-Ranicki, 'Die geistige Kapitulation der Anna Seghers', *Die Welt*, 3 September 1959. Reich-Ranicki had begun to write on the largely ignored literature of the GDR, including Seghers's work, some months before. See 'Deutsche Schriftsteller, die jenseits der Elbe leben', *Die Welt*, 7 March 1959.

2 There have been several analyses of Seghers's reception in the Federal Republic, including: Andreas W. Mytze, 'Von der negativen Faszination: das westdeutsche Seghers-Bild', *Text und Kritik*, 38, 1973, pp. 20–31; Valentin Merkelbach, *Fehlstart Seghers-Rezeption: Vom Kalten Krieg gegen die Autorin in der Bundesrepublik*, in *Anna Seghers Materialienbuch*, edited by Peter Roos and Friederike J. Hassauer-Roos, Frankfurt am Main, 1977, pp. 9–24; Christa Degemann, *Anna Seghers in der westdeutschen Literaturkritik 1946 bis 1983*, Cologne, 1985.

3 Following the reduction in tension between the two German states which was achieved by the *Grundlagenvertrag* in 1972, Seghers's works began to receive a fairer hearing as well as wider circulation in the West. See Werner Buthge, *Anna Seghers: Werk – Wirkungsabsicht – Wirkungsmöglichkeit in der Bundesrepublik*, Stuttgart, 1982, p. 251.

4 The divergent development of the two German states led to ignorance and prejudice about life in the GDR among Western readers. The resulting difference in expectations tended to complicate reception in the West. See Buthge, *Anna Seghers*, pp. 252–60.

5 Plans by Luchterhand to reprint *Das siebte Kreuz* in 1962 led to public protest on the part of Peter Jokostra and Wolfdietrich Schnurre.

6 Seghers was not awarded freedom of the city until 1981, although the proposal was first mooted in public in 1970. (See also the excursus on this subject in Degemann, *Anna Seghers in der westdeutchen Literaturkritik*, pp. 210–20.)

7 Wolfdietrich Schnurre and Günter Grass wrote an open letter to thirteen GDR writers, including Anna Seghers, demanding a statement on the building of the Wall.

8 Walter Janka, *Schwierigkeiten mit der Wahrheit*, Reinbek, 1989.

9 'Erfahrungen austauschen und Rat schaffen – Die Erzählerin Anna Seghers 1900–1990', 30–1 March 1990. Seghers's daughter, Ruth Radvanyi, told the congress that it had become evident from talking to colleagues and friends of her mother's that Anna Seghers had consulted with Walter Ulbricht both following Janka's arrest and after the sentencing (see also the interview in *Sonntag*, 13 May 1990). As far back as 1962, Peter Jakostra, in his protest at the publication of Anna Seghers's works, had referred to her behaviour at the trial of Walter Janka, Erich Loest and Wolfgang Harich. At the time Marcel Reich-Ranicki, who was certainly not uncritical towards Anna Seghers, responded as follows: 'es ist zu sagen, daß noch nie ein Schriftsteller in einem kommunistischen Land gegen die Verhaftung eines Kollegen *öffentlich* protestiert hat ... Ob Anna Seghers oder andere führende Schriftsteller der DDR in Sachen Harich und Loest inoffizielle Schritte unternommen haben, entzieht sich unserer Kenntnis. Darüber gibt es nur Gerüchte. Sollen westdeutsche Publikationen der DDR-Autoren von Gerüchten abhängig gemacht werden? Oder sollen sie als Preise für Tollkühnheit dienen?' The quotation may be found in Merkelbach, *Fehlstart Seghers-Rezeption*, pp. 15–16.

10 This text was first presented at the above congress by Sigrid Bock and Martina Langermann, and is due to be published by the Aufbau-Verlag and in the periodical *Sinn und Form*. The story concerns the unjust sentencing of a former fighter in the Spanish Civil War, a convinced socialist, and a 'just judge' who refuses to endorse the sentence and as a result is himself sent to prison. Despite the critical tone of the story it is marked by a note of reconciliation. The ending suggests that the two prisoners will be able to resume normal life as unsung heroes after release, as though nothing had happened. However, the author makes it plain that the conduct of a judge who refuses to endorse the sentence is an exception to the normal behaviour of that time, including perhaps her own.

11 One of the sentenced men tells of his despair, not during the struggles in the past but just at the moment when 'wie es heißt, die Verwirklichung unseres Traumes, und nicht nur unseres, uralter Menschenträume' came about. The very people who are persecuted become beacons of hope: 'Wir hier, wir sind im Recht. Es ist eine Bürgschaft, daß es uns gibt' (taken from a copy of the manuscript, Anna-Seghers-Archiv, p. 36).

12 The author's difficulties in adapting to the political and politico-cultural climate have been reconstructed by Alexander Stephan in his article ' "Ich habe das Gefühl, ich bin in die Eiszeit geraten ...": Zur Rückkehr von Anna Seghers aus dem Exil', *Germanic Review*, 62, 1987, pp. 143–52. Inge Diersen showed in a paper presented at the above-mentioned congress, entitled

'Problematische Heimkehr: "Das Argonautenschiff" ', how the use of themes from mythology and legend as well as the translocation of stories to Latin America were the expression of a flight from the politico-cultural demands of her own country. Anna Seghers's reservations with respect to the formalism debate are hardly surprising in view of her correspondence with Georg Lukács in 1939.

13 It has been pointed out more than once that both these novels are critical of the objectives of GDR society. The criticism is always well-founded and constructive, as Martin Straub and Frank Wagner emphasised at the Berlin congress. See also Mytze in *Text und Kritik*, pp. 23ff.

14 Anna Seghers, *Werke in zehn Bänden*, 10 vols, Darmstadt and Neuwied, 1977, VIII, p. 301. This passage may be understood as an attempt to explain the behaviour of all those who kept silent about their experiences because they did not wish to have them publicised in the West.

15 'Beitrag zur Außerordentlichen Tagung des Weltfriedensrates in Berlin (DDR) 1952', in *Über Kunstwerk und Wirklichkeit*, 4 vols, edited by Sigrid Bock, East Berlin, 1971–, III, pp. 82ff. (p. 84).

16 'Offener Antwortbrief an eine sowjetische Mutter', *Über Kunstwerk*, III, pp. 110ff. p. 110.

17 *Ibid.*

18 'Bericht zum "Ersten Weltkongreß der Kämpfer für den Frieden" (Paris/Prague, April 1949)', *Über Kunstwerk*, III, pp. 51–5 (p. 55).

19 'Aufruf zum "Berliner Appell des Weltfriedensrates für die sofortige Einstellung aller Kernwaffenversuche"' (1957), *Über Kunstwerk*, III, p. 112.

20 The Stockholm appeal reads: 'Der Atomkrieg würde Millionen Menschen vernichten und ganze Kontinente verwüsten. Kein Land, kein Volk will diesen Krieg. Trotzdem wird er in aller Öffentlichkeit vorbereitet, und viele Menschen sehen dem tatenlos zu. Die Vereinigten Staaten und die Sowjetunion setzen ihre Wasserstoffbombenversuche fort; auch Großbritannien will nun damit beginnen. Wir fordern die sofortige Einstellung der Versuche. Das Leben unserer Kinder muß geschützt werden', *Über Kunstwerk*, III, p. 303.

21 *Über Kunstwerk*, III, p. 112.

22 Compare Karin Hausen, 'Die Polarisierung der "Geschlechtscharaktere" – eine Spiegelung der Dissoziation von Erwerbs– und Familienleben', in *Sozialgeschichte der Familie in der Neuzeit Europas*, edited by W. Conze, Stuttgart, 1976, pp. 363–93.

23 See Annette Kuhn, 'Frauen suchen neue Wege der Politik', in *Frauen in der deutschen Nachkriegszeit II: Frauenpolitik 1945–1949: Quellen und Materialien*, Düsseldorf, 1986, pp. 12–35 (p. 18).

24 'Volk und Schriftsteller' (1942), in *Über Kunstwerk*, I, pp. 191–7 (p. 192).

25 Seghers, *Werke*, VI, p. 357.

26 Seghers, *Werke*, VI, p. 371.

27 Seghers, *Werke*, V, p. 228.

28 Paradigmatically, this concerns the guilt he feels with respect to a Soviet mother whose child he snatched away (Seghers, *Werke*, VI, pp. 416ff.).

29 A woman is hardly ever given the task of passing on the baton in Anna Seghers's work. An exception is to be found in the collection of stories *Der erste Schritt* of 1953, in which several people describe their paths towards work in the name of peace. Amongst them a mother, Francesca of Turin, receives the stimulus for this work from her daughter.

30 Seghers, *Werke*, VI, pp. 430ff.

31 'Kulturelle Brücken zu anderen Völkern (1946/47)', in *Über Kunstwerk*, I, pp. 208–11 (p. 210).

32 'Die Aufgaben der Kunst' (1944), in *Über Kunstwerk*, I, pp. 197–201 (p. 199).

33 *Ibid.*

34 Seghers, *Werke*, VI, p. 432.

35 See Inge Diersen, 'Kritik des Militarismus und Gestaltung der nationalen Perspektive in Anna Seghers Roman *Die Toten bleiben jung*', *Weimarer Beiträge*, 7, 1961, pp. 80–98 (p. 94ff.).

36 Angelika Pöthe, *Zum Figurenaufbau ausgewählter Frauengestalten im epischen Schaffen von Anna Seghers*, unpublished dissertation (available in Anna-Seghers-Archiv, Berlin), 1976, p. 25

37 'Eine Chronik der deutschen Arbeitslosen: zu Anna Seghers Roman *Die Rettung*', in Walter Benjamin, *Gesammelte Schriften*, III, edited by H. Tiedemann-Bartel, Frankfurt am Main, 1980, pp. 530–8 (p. 536).

38 For example, the fact that around her only baby sons are wished for gives her a new, even stronger feeling of disquiet (see Seghers, *Werke*, V, p. 12).

39 Seghers, *Werke*, V, pp. 192ff.

40 Seghers, *Werke*, VI, p. 347.

41 See Seghers, *Werke*, VI, p. 397 and pp. 401ff.

42 Fritz J. Raddatz first sharply criticised Seghers's image of women in his book *Traditionen und Tendenzen*, Frankfurt am Main, 1972, second expanded edition 1976, pp. 215–40 (pp. 230ff.).

43 The criticism that Seghers's female characters lack sensuality and have an aversion to sex can be found in Fritz J. Raddatz (*ibid.*) and, for example, in Irene Lorisika, who even draws biographical conclusions regarding the author (see Irene Lorisika, *Frauendarstellung bei Irmgart Keun und Anna Seghers*, Frankfurt am Main, 1985, p. 118). In general it must be said of such biographical extrapolations that, if for male authors representations of women are examined as a surface for sexual projection, then in the context of a female author like Anna Seghers the male figures must necessarily be brought into the interpretation. Only in this way can a psychoanalytical interpretation of female authorship be taken properly into account.

44 See Michael Rohrwasser, *Saubere Mädel, starke Genossen. Proletarische Massenliteratur?*, Frankfurt am Main, 1975.

45 Seghers, *Werke*, V, p. 42.

46 Doubts concerning the necessity of the superiority of political aims are to be found in the story 'Crisanta' of 1950. In it the author chooses the point of view of a Mexican girl whose life is destroyed because her boyfriend leaves her in favour of his own development and political work.

47 Margret Iversen, in her unpublished dissertation *Präsentationsformen des Weiblichen in Anna Seghers Romanen 'Das siebte Kreuz', 'Transit', und 'Die Toten bleiben jung'*, West Berlin, 1980, has pointed out that the figure of Marie can be traced back to various mythological patterns beyond the Christian Madonna figure to that of a saint, for example, or the bride in a 'Hohes Paar' such as Ernst Bloch has written of. Margret Iversen has also argued that Seghers's women are the victims of a male ideology despite or indeed because of the idealisation in mythological terms to which they are subjected. (See 'Zum Frauenbild bei Anna Seghers', in *Spuren*, 4, 1979, pp. 38–40.)

48 See Rolf Schneider, 'Nachdenken über A.S.', in *Über Anna Seghers: ein Almanach zum 75. Geburtstag*, East Berlin and Weimar, 1975, pp. 245–53 (pp. 248ff.).

49 The changing relationship between ontological determination and Marie's capacity to change is examined, for example, by Sigrid Tölpelmann *in Autoren – Figuren – Entwicklungen: zur erzählenden Literatur in der DDR*, East Berlin and Weimar, 1975, pp. 49ff.

50 Erika Haas, 'Der männliche Blick der Anna Seghers – das Frauenbild einer kommunistischen Schriftstellerin', in *Notizbuch*, 1980, pp. 134–49 (p. 148).

51 Ilse Nagelschmidt, 'Die Frauenbildgestaltung bei Anna Seghers in den Romanen und Erzählungen der 50er und 60er Jahre' (manuscript of a lecture delivered in 1986, available in the Anna-Seghers-Archiv in Berlin), p. 13.

52 Eva Kaufmann, 'Anna Seghers: Drei Frauen aus Haiti', in *Weimarer Beiträge*, 26, 1980, pp. 151–61 (p. 158).

53 To this extent one can hardly speak of Seghers's female figures representing a model of a converging equality of rights leading to 'die vermännlichte Frau', as Erika Haas does in 'Der männliche Blick der Anna Seghers', p. 148.

54 This criticism may found in Fritz J. Raddatz and, later, for example, in Irene Lorsiska, *Frauendarstellungen*, pp. 115ff. In other contexts, the indirect biographical perspective and her more universally valid and more objective aims in writing are often regarded positively (see, for example, Inge Diersen, *Seghers-Studien*, East Berlin, 1965, pp. 121ff.).

55 Elisabeth Endres, 'Über das Schicksal der schreibenden Frauen', in *Neue Literatur von Frauen*, edited by Heinz Puknus, Munich, 1980, pp. 7–19 (p. 17).

56 Review by Ernst Reissig in *Ost und West* 3, 1949, pp. 117ff.

57 Seghers, *Werke*, I, pp. 79–94 (p. 92).

58 Friedrich Albrecht, *Die Erzählerin Anna Seghers: 1926–1932*, East Berlin, 1965, p. 93.

59 *Über Kunstwerk*, II, p. 11.

60 Anna Seghers, *Gesammelte Werke in Einzelausgaben*, East Berlin, 1981, IX, pp. 188–90 (p. 189).

61 Peter Beiken sees in the figure of the woman in 'Auf dem Weg zur amerikanischen Botschaft' Anna Seghers's decisive model of woman as historical subject. A more dominant position in Anna Seghers's work as a whole is occupied, however, by the numerous later female figures, whose traditional attitudes, for example in rejecting abortion, Beiken has described

as strength (See Peter Beiken, 'Eintritt in die Geschichte: Anna Seghers's Frauen als Avantgarde', in *Die Horen*, 4, 1981, pp. 79–93). The figure of a woman who does not break completely with the maternal role but develops it further, a process we can follow in 'Marie geht zur Versammlung', is typical of Seghers's later concept of the political task of the (proletarian) woman.

62 The author again takes up this theme of the politically active mother in her story 'Die Tochter der Delegierten' (1951), which is told from the point of view of the daughter. She carries the burden of the political work of the mother, yet in this way a special partnership between mother and daughter arises, and the daughter grows to political responsibility.

63 The murder by the Nazis of Seghers's own mother might help to explain the modified representation of the mother. The autobiographical story 'Der Ausflug der toten Mädchen' (1943–4) deals with this theme.

64 See Annette Kuhn, *Frauen suchen neue Wege der Politik*, p. 25.

65 There were no delegates from most of the Western organisations at a 'Tagung deutscher Frauen aller Zonen' called in the Eastern sector of Berlin in 1947, whilst at an interzonal Congress in Frankfurt am Main representatives from the Soviet zone were not admitted as speakers.

66 See Elke Nyssen, 'Die Westdeutsche Frauenfriedensbewegung', in *Feministische Studien*, 3, 1984, pp. 66–77.

67 Anna Seghers apparently took part neither in the Kongreß der Frauen und Mütter für den Frieden in 1951 in Velbert/Rheinland, nor in the Weltkongreß der Mütter in July 1955 in Lausanne.

The literary critic Hans Mayer: from West to East, from East to West

Franziska Meyer

> Wann immer ich mich befrage nach Augenblicken des Lebens, wo ich ganz bei mir selbst war, stellt er sich ein: der Blick vom Katheder in den einstigen Hörsaal 40 der Leipziger Universität . . . *Mein Ort war der Hörsaal 40 in Leipzig. Er ist es geblieben.*[1]

Reading these sentences occasioned some emotion for one of Hans Mayer's former students, as she made clear in a speech given at the Berlin Akademie der Künste to mark the eightieth birthday of her former examiner.[2] Christa Wolf went on to say: 'Wir begannen zu empfinden, wie dringlich wir Lehrer wie Sie brauchten'.[3]

> Daß es hart werden würde, hätte jemand uns damals schon voraussagen können, der imstand und willens gewesen wäre, alle Seiten aller Widersprüche zu überblicken, die in jenem geschichtlichen Augenblick beschlossen waren. Sie, verehrter Hans Mayer, haben ihre volle Schärfe zu spüren bekommen: allen Zerreißproben ausgesetzt, die ein deutscher Schriftsteller in den beiden deutschen Staaten erfahren konnte.[4]

The 'Zerreißproben' which Christa Wolf mentions here will be explored in detail later in this essay. They can easily be lost from sight, if 'alle Seiten aller Widersprüche' – contradictions to which the marxist Hans Mayer found himself exposed in the welter of cultural and literary conflict in the GDR during the late 1950s – are passed over in favour of fixation on his later move to the Federal Republic.

Hans Mayer was born in Cologne in 1907 as the son of upper middle-class Jewish parents. After studying law and gaining his doctorate in 1930 he studied history and philosophy, and had to emigrate in 1933. Mayer spent the years of exile in France and Switzerland. In 1938 he was deprived of German citizenship. His parents were murdered in the concentration camps. After the war Mayer went first to Frankfurt am Main and worked for the

Americans as an editor at DENA (Deutsche Nachtrichtenagentur) and later – with Stephan Hermlin – for Radio Frankfurt. A collection of critical essays on literature, written by Mayer and Hermlin for radio, appeared for the first time in 1947 under the title *Ansichten über einige Bücher und Schriftsteller* from Limes Verlag in Wiesbaden. Mayer soon broke with his American employers, who had become more and more displeased with his 'Kommentare zur Außenpolitik', and who consequently suggested that he should resign 'voluntarily'. In this way he became, in the spring of 1947, 'ein erstes Opfer des kommenden kalten Krieges, noch bevor er ausbrach', as his memoirs put it.[5] As chairman of the VVN Hessen (Vereinigung der Verfolgten des Naziregimes) Mayer participated in the first – and last – Pan-German Writers' Congress in Berlin, in October 1947.[6] In August 1948 he was the only participant from the Western zones to accompany a delegation of East German and West Berlin writers to the International World Peace Congress in Breslau.[7]

Finally, in October 1948, Hans Mayer was offered, and accepted, the Chair of the History of World Literature in the Faculty of Sociology (known in the GDR as GEWIFA – gesellschaftswissenschaftliche Fakultät) at the University of Leipzig; later he also took on the Chair of Comparative Literature in the Faculty of Arts. Here Mayer encountered Ernst Bloch, along with Werner Krauss, one of the most important marxist scholars of Romance studies, and Walter Markov, an expert in the history of revolution. Together they were to make a decisive contribution to the history of literary studies and historiography in the GDR. Mayer commented on these years in his memoirs: 'Hier konnte ich fünfzehn Jahre lang nützlich werden'.[8]

As director of the Institute of Literary History in Leipzig he occupied for more than a decade an exceedingly influential academic post and moulded generations of GDR Germanists and authors. From 1955 Mayer edited the series 'Neue Beiträge zur Literaturwissenschaft' together with Werner Krauss, and received the GDR's annual award for academic achievement, the Nationalpreis, in the same year. Christa Wolf was not the only student of Mayer's who was later to make literary history; others included Uwe Johnson, Irmtraud Morgner, Jochen Ziem and Kurt Batt, as well as a number who later became theatre directors, such as Harry Kupfer, Adolf Dresen and Götz Friedrich. The Germanists Klaus Schuhmann, Günter Mieth, Klaus Pezold, Wilfried Hartinger and Claus Träger were Mayer's students, as was Wilhelm Girnus, who later became editor of *Sinn und Form* and Mayer's opponent. On his many journeys abroad in East and West the GDR Germanist earned an international reputation, and, particularly after his first contact with authors of the 'Gruppe 47', was regarded with increasing respect by West German colleagues in the world of literary criticism.

In the wake of changes in literary and cultural policy in 1956, Mayer became caught in the crossfire during a series of heated debates, which created an atmosphere of tension which lasted over a year. The occasion was the ideas he expressed in 'Zur Gegenwartslage unserer Literatur', collectively labelled 'Opulenztheorie' in the GDR. In 1959, the year he was first invited to a meeting of the 'Gruppe 47', Mayer began publishing his works, many of which had already appeared in the GDR, in the Federal Republic. He came in for renewed attacks when, in 1962, he published the volume *Ansichten über einige Bücher und Schriftsteller* with Rowohlt. It was Mayer's interpretation, and rehabilitation, of Boris Pasternak's novel *Doctor Zhivago* which aroused hostility in this instance. In the autumn of 1963 Mayer failed to return to the GDR after a stay in the Federal Republic. In a letter to the university authorities he explained that he reached this decision after 'nahezu alle Voraussetzungen weggefallen sind, die mich vor fünfzehn Jahren veranlaßt hatten, von Frankfurt am Main aus dem Ruf der Leipziger Universität Folge zu leisten'.[9] Two years later, in the summer of 1965, Mayer continued his university career at Hannover, having spent the intervening period in Tübingen.

In view of the many individual publications Hans Mayer produced, which include almost fifty titles, not to mention his innumerable contributions to books, journals and newspapers as well as editorial work and translations of Sartre and Aragon, and in view of the range of his works – they embrace not only numerous writings on East and West European literature, but also almost the whole of modern German literature, as well as studies on the history of music and opera – in view of all this it would be tempting to describe the writer Hans Mayer as one of the few universal literary historians. Mayer's *Außenseiter* (1975) and his two volumes of memoirs *Ein Deutscher auf Widerruf* (1982 and 1984) reached a particularly wide audience. An investigation into the secondary literature which touches on the 'Fall Mayer' reveals a measure of the cost of the Cold War. For years Western and Eastern depictions of this conflict in the annals of literary history have given rise to a series of quite uncomplicated accounts marked by their very uniformity, reproducing – consciously or unconsciously – contemporary Cold War patterns. The simplified perceptions fit only two moulds; 'dissident' or 'renegade'. In this way either Mayer's years in the GDR are condensed to a camouflaged existence under the strictures of stalinist cultural policy or they are explained away in the undifferentiated accusation of relinquishing socialist principles or of class betrayal.

Wolfgang Emmerich's *Kleine Literaturgeschichte der DDR*[10] omits to consider the works Mayer produced while in the GDR, and disregards their influence on marxist literary criticism there. Emmerich dwells exclusively on standpoints Mayer occupied at a considerably later date – after his fall from grace – and quotes this 'dissident' as a contemporary witness, in order to give definitive authority to his line on the development of GDR literature. Later accounts produced in the GDR also draw a line under Mayer's case; either they reproduce without commentary the debates of the late 1950s, or the name Mayer fails to appear even in the index of surveys of GDR literary history. It was Ursula Wertheim in 1969 who made the harshest and most uncompromising judgement on Mayer:

> Hans Mayer kam theoretisch nie über eine vulgärmaterialistische Position hinaus, seit 1956 ging er mit seiner 'Opulenztheorie' über die zwanziger Jahre sogar hinter diese Position wieder zurück; wo er schließlich auch politisch landete, beweist seine Republikflucht.[11]

Mayer's own account is hardly more reliable. In the second volume of his memoirs he recollects the Leipzig years in great detail. The unevenness of his depiction is striking; in particular the mixture of resentment, justification, and occasional shows of confidence with retrospective identification which precludes a simplistic anti-communist reading, but which also exposes a wound which clearly remains unhealed. Only a naive reading which confuses Mayer's own testimony with the actual events can expect to discover from him the authentic key to a very complex and contradictory chapter in the history of GDR literature and literary criticism. Many of Mayer's later interpretations of his own career, which follow the pattern of permanent 'dissidence', cannot easily be reconciled with his contemporary views. They conflate the various phases in the development of cultural policy and ignore the extent to which he was integrated (or not integrated, as the case may be) in the changing consensus on literary and cultural policy. An example of such an approach may be found in a passage from the *Frankfurter Vorlesungen* (1987):

> Meine erste Illegälitat, als Außenseitertum zu verstehen, bestand darin, daß ich mein sozialistisches Denken und Fühlen einzubringen hatte in ein System der totalen Gleichschaltung. Die war für mich ausgeschlossen: vor allem weil ich rasch erkannte, daß jeglicher Versuch einer Propagandaschwätzerei auf dem Universitätskatheder, im Sinne des in Moskau theologisierten Marxismus–Leninismus, meine Glaubwürdigkeit als akademischer Lehrer beendet hätte. Gerade dies durfte nicht eintreten.[12] ... Ich mußte zum Außenseiter und Dissidenten werden im Machtbereich einer stalinistischen normativen Kunstlehre.[13]

The relevant documents on cultural and literary policy which relate to the discussions of the 1950s reveal an extremely bitter, extremely dogmatic and acrimonious dispute, which took the social role of literature inordinately seriously and drastically overstated that role. The conflict at issue here cannot be understood either by reference to the dictum of 'totale Gleichschaltung' nor that of 'normative Kunstlehre'. Neither may Mayer's image of his own role, that of an 'am Boden hingekauerte Existenz'[14] be easily reconciled with his reputable position in the academic world. It is precisely the vehemence of the official verdicts which were later pronounced on him that shows how far his influence was recognised.

In order to do justice to the complexity of the 'Fall Mayer' during his fifteen years as a GDR Germanist, it is essential to bear in mind the various phases of debate in cultural policy, with their internal contradictions. Christa Wolf's recollections serve as an example:

> Das waren die fünfziger Jahre auch: eine Zeit heftiger Diskussionen. Dogmatismus? Ja. Wenn du die Zeitungen jener Jahre nachliest, dir können die Haare zu Berge stehen ... Und wir Jungen waren in alles verwickelt. Wir nahmen Anteil, es war unsere Sache. Wir waren in einer Stimmung übersteigerter Intensität, alles, was 'hier und heute geschah' war entscheidend, das Richtige mußte sich bald und vollkommen durchsetzen, wir würden den Sozialismus, den Marx gemeint hatte, noch erleben.[15]

Here a very complex picture emerges; continuities and disruptions are exposed which by no means lead seamlessly to 1956, the year in which Mayer got himself into hot water with his much-quoted essay on contemporary literature. Later, too, Mayer held views which might be described quite uncontroversially as typical

GDR views, and which could not have been integrated into the kind of literary studies prevalent in the Federal Republic, where the emphasis was largely on the history of ideas and on intrinsic analysis. We look first at Mayer as a student of Lukács.

During the early years of the GDR, literature was assigned an extraordinary, educative, and consciousness-shaping role. In this context literary debates drew heavily on those conducted during exile. After the War the majority of exile writers had gone to the Soviet zone (later the GDR) and there took up the marxist discussion on socialist realism and the national tradition. This discussion had been set in train at the end of the 1920s in the Bund proletarisch–revolutionärer Schriftsteller and continued later in the pages of exile newspapers. The nature of political alliances during the early years of the GDR was such that particular value was placed on the preservation of the classical, humanist tradition. The works of Georg Lukács provided the theoretical basis for this endeavour. In this respect Mayer's understanding of literature, schooled by Lukács, coincided with the programmatic demands of cultural policy in the GDR.

This can be demonstrated by reference to his studies of Lessing, Goethe, Schiller, Heine, Büchner and Thomas Mann, to whom Mayer always returns, not to mention his work on French, English and Russian literature. In 1951 Mayer acknowledged the role of Johannes R. Becher, emphasising his

> große geschichtliche Leistung, [die] bekanntlich darin [bestand], die Kontinuität der deutschen Kulturentwicklung gefordert zu haben: in jenem entscheidenden Sinne allerdings, daß sorgfältig zwischen Echtem und Unechtem, zwischen Fortschritt und Reaktion geschieden werden sollte. Aber von einem Ende Deutschlands, einem 'Jahre Null' hatte er nichts wissen wollen.[16]

This attitude towards tradition was shared from the beginning by the great majority of GDR writers, including Hans Mayer. This sense of continuity was frequently denied in contemporary Western publications: the buzzwords 'Socialist Realism' and 'decadence' were dredged up to demonstrate the reality of stalinist cultural policy. The reception of the marxist realism debate and of exile literature did not start in the Federal Republic until the late 1960s. This means that contemporary West German critics of the GDR literary scene must have been completely baffled by the intellectual and historical background to the questions which were at issue there. Hans-Jürgen Schmitt identified a crucial question when, in 1973, he asked whether what might have been inherited from exile literature was not after all 'längst ein verpaßtes Erbe für die westdeutsche Literatur'.[17]

So the fact that Hans Mayer launched his career in literary criticism in the GDR was by no means a matter of chance; he found there, after all, a place where he could be effective and productive both as an exile and as a marxist. A few weeks after his arrival in Leipzig, at a conference of Germanists to which the Soviet military administration had invited all the Germanists in institutions of higher education in their zone, Mayer gave his first academic paper on questions of marxist literary criticism in Germany.[18] Nearly twenty years later several generations of West German students of *Germanistik* were to make up for lost time by devouring this text – *the* 'Mayer' – as the basis for a critical debate on the methodology of their subject.[19] At the Goethe bicentenary celebrations in Weimar in 1949 Mayer had given the principal address, entitled 'Spiegelungen Goethes in unserer Gegenwart'. Looking back, he remembered this as his 'erste große und ernstzunehmende Rede vor der Öffentlichkeit', as his 'Einübung in deutscher Literaturgeschichte'.[20] The previous year, while still in Frankfurt, Mayer had already edited a volume with a similar title, *Spiegelungen Goethes in unserer Zeit*, which contained, amongst others, articles by Walter Benjamin, Georg Lukács, Thomas Mann and Emil Staiger.

In view of such continuity, Western efforts (such as those of Peter Demetz in 1961) to discover an alleged 'Sklavensprache' in Hans Mayer, and to accuse the writer of leading a camouflaged existence in the GDR, subject to ideological pressure from the party line, are less than convincing.[21] Such assertions were by no means peculiar to Demetz, and may be summed up in the equation marxism equals following the party line equals stalinism. Yet there is room for a more nuanced historical evaluation of Mayer's position, and in this endeavour an examination of his uncollected essays and works can be extremely rewarding. Such an examination reveals that Mayer conformed to central marxist theoretical assumptions which informed the understanding of literature in the GDR. The views which Mayer propounded were not only part of the literary consensus in the GDR but were an attempt to shape that consensus, particularly where questions of literature's social function, its specific socio-historical purpose and the political standpoint of the author are concerned. Differences in the reception of his work by literary critics show how criteria for aesthetic judgements diverged in East and West, and that they were controversial even within the GDR.

Critical reactions to Mayer's book on Thomas Mann (1950), his second substantial work following the book on Büchner he produced while in exile, varied from harsh to muted. Mayer had placed himself between the two stools of Western and Eastern aesthetic criteria. Joseph Baur, of the West German conservative review paper *Welt und Wort*, objected to Mayer's 'soziologisch fundiertes orthodoxes System', hearing Lukács speak *ex cathedra*:

> Prof. Dr. Hans Mayer, Kapazität von Rang, unternahm es nun, den deutschen Dichter . . . literarhistorisch–materialistisch zu entkapitalisieren. In Thomas Mann sei eine humanistische Substanz wirksam, die . . . hinführe zum 'Proletariat' als dem einzigen Erbe der klassischen bürgerlichen Kultur'.[22]

Wolfgang Harich slated the book in *Die Weltbühne*, criticising its lack of 'Volksverbundenheit' and its profoundly non-marxist line. He further objected to Mayer's 'esoterische Andeutungen und Anspielungen für Eingeweihte', condemning them as an 'äußerste Rücksichtslosigkeit gegenüber den elementaren Bildungsbedürfnissen der weit überwiegenden Mehrzahl des Lesepublikums'.[23] These differences in the way Mayer was received make it clear that the 'Probleme einer materialistischen Ästhetik' in the GDR at this time were by no means solved; certainly not in the sense of the orthodox system which the West German reviewer assumed to exist. That reviewer's criteria also show that Mayer's methodological premises were not even a matter for discussion in one of the most influential review journals of the Federal Republic.

Precisely this dichotomy between Lukács's classicism and the contemporary socialist demand for 'Volksverbundenheit' in literature was to lead to disagreement in the debates later in the 1950s. Apart from widespread reading and discussion of Georg Lukács's works, which also set the standard in literary criticism, there were no teleological attempts in the GDR before 1956 to construct a materialist aesthetic in the light of changed socialist literary circumstances. Mayer's work in the early 1950s endeavoured to link the classical tradition with 'Volksverbundenheit'. On the occasion of the Festival of World Youth in Berlin in August 1951, the Deutsche Akademie der Künste distributed 40,000 copies of an issue of the journal *Sinn und Form* to the assembled young people. Hans Mayer took the opportunity to represent Heine's *Zeitgedichte* as a model for young people:

> Heines "Doktrin" ist ein Aufruf zum Kampf für diese künftige Welt! Und gerade der Dichter hat die große geschichtliche Aufgabe, nicht bloß Botschaften zu verkünden, sondern singend und kämpfend den Truppen der neuen Menschlichkeit voranzuziehen.[24]

And Mayer concludes with the emphatic words:

> wenn die Lehren von Marx und Engels durch Lenin und Stalin zur weltumspannenden Idee und zu einer Wirklichkeit gemacht wurden, die auf einem Sechstel der Erde bereits den Weg vom Sozialismus zum Kommunismus durchlief, so findet sich in dieser Bewegung auch der tiefste Gehalt von Heinrich Heines Dichtung und Denken für alle Zeiten bewahrt.[25]

In an issue of *Aufbau* of 1953 Dieter Noll referred to Mayer's book *Schiller und die Nation*, giving the writer credit for having recalled that Schiller has 'heute dem deutschen Volk im nationalen Befreiungskampf vieles zu geben'. Noll maintains that Mayer had discovered in Schiller's work 'Dokumente echten Nationalgefühls', including 'Gedanken und Äußerungen, die eine tiefe Verbundenheit mit dem Vaterland beweisen und alle reaktionären Entstellungen des Weltbürgerbegriffs zerschlagen'.[26]

In 1954 there was an even more emphatic critical reaction to the first volume of Mayer's *Meisterwerke deutscher Literaturkritik* and to the second volume of *Studien zur deutschen Literaturgeschichte*, which he edited together with Werner Krauss. The latter volume contained articles by Mayer on Johann Gottfried Schnabel, Gerhart Hauptmann, Hermann Hesse, Thomas Mann und Georg Büchner. Both works were considered to be exemplary in their methodology, as far as the academic discussion on tradition and future research in literary history were concerned.

It was in the essay 'Deutsche Literatur und Weltliteratur', which appeared in *Aufbau* in 1954, that Hans Mayer set out the most succinct and programmatic formulation of his approach to literature. Drawing on Lenin's famous notion of two cultures, 'zwei Nationen innerhalb einer Nation', Mayer expressly puts forward the thesis of two literatures, which 'notwendigerweise einer in Klassen gespaltenen Ordnung entsprechen müssen'.[27] This, according to Mayer, is clearly confirmed by literary developments in this century. The various lines of tradition that Mayer traces out in developing this thesis stand in almost polemical opposition to the controversial essay on contemporary literature he published two years later. Later he was attacked on precisely the grounds he had previously occupied.

In 1954 Mayer wrote:

> Es mag hier und jetzt nicht erörtert werden, ob die 'Zwanziger Jahre' wirklich noch einmal auf bürgerlicher Lebensgrundlage eine bedeutende Literatur hervorgebracht haben. Literaturhistoriker und Kritiker (Curtius und Rychner) . . . haben die Schriftsteller der zwanziger Jahre, jene also, die damals besonders wirksam waren (Gide, Proust, Valéry, Rilke, Hofmannsthal, Kafka, Hamsun, Eliot, Pirandello, Joyce) . . . als Ausdruck einer 'weltliterarischen Blüte' in unserem Jahrhundert bezeichnet. Man wird diese Bezeichnung sehr kritisch prüfen müssen; schwerwiegende Einwände liegen jedoch gegen jeden dieser Künstler und jedes seiner wichtigeren Werke auf der Hand.[28]

Under the new historical conditions Mayer can only conceive of the writer's task as a moral obligation:

> Wir stehen vor einer geschichtlichen Entscheidung und vor einer moralischen Entscheidung. Die geschichtliche Erfahrung besagt, daß nur auf der Grundlage eines Bekenntnisses zum gesellschaftlichen Neuen, nur in der Transzendierung der Bürgerwelt, lebensfähige Literatur, das heißt eine Literatur, die gelesen, geliebt und befolgt wird, möglich sein kann. Daß jeder Schriftsteller unserer Tage demgemäß wissen muß, von welchem Standpunkt aus er schreibt und zu schreiben gedenkt.[29]

Mayer's insistence on the social function of literature is directed against Western, essentially autonomous pluralism, and implies no rejection in principle of differences and individuality: 'Allein wir wollen sogleich sagen, daß innerhalb dieser Grundentscheidung Raum bleibt für unendlich viele Möglichkeiten und Individualformen des literarischen Schaffens.'[30]

His orientation towards Lukács and his preference for the 'great', definitive authors of classical and critical realism explains Mayer's comparative lack of interest in the development of contemporary socialist literature. Assertions that Mayer subjected himself to a kind of officially prescribed optimism and 'Volksverbundenheit' (Peter Demetz) are wide of the mark, in so far as Mayer largely kept out of the debates on literary policy of the day and avoided the discussions on contemporary socialist literature. Indeed, apart from his work on Brecht, he wrote almost no reviews of contemporary GDR literature. This point is central to an understanding of the conflicts with Leipzig Germanists which took place after the events of 1956 and 1957.

At the end of November 1956 Mayer wrote his much-quoted radio talk 'Zur Gegenwartslage unserer Literatur', calling for a fundamentally new orientation in literature. It was in this essay that he coined the phrase 'rotangestrichene Gartenlauben'. The strength of Mayer's attacks led to his talk being withdrawn from transmission, although it was published four days later in the Kulturbund paper, *Sonntag*. In the essay Mayer maintains 'daß es um unsere deutsche Gegenwartsliteratur nicht zum Besten steht'. Mayer points out, by way of example, that Hans Marchwitza's novel *Roheisen* had received a Nationalpreis, although the novel could hardly be termed artistically successful. 'Der Tisch unserer Literatur ist kärglich gedeckt. Wir durchleben magere Jahre', he goes on, including in his criticism the 'Bücherschrank des westdeutschen Herrn Neureich'; the literature of West Germany was, in Mayer's view, similarly meagre. The few exceptions he cites are those of Böll, Koeppen, Richter, Eich and Krolow, as well as the Swiss dramatists Frisch and Dürrenmatt. Mayer then compares contemporary literature unfavourably with that of the 1920s, years which he terms 'reicher und literarisch ergiebiger'. He criticises the easy route of turning, in a highly schematic way, every non-communist writer into something resembling a 'Sumpfblume im Morast einer sterbenden Bourgeoisie'. 'Man könnte neidisch werden', Mayer continues, 'vergleicht man die Fülle der damals neu auftauchenden Talente mit unserer gegenwärtigen Dürftigkeit.' Comparisons of the 1920s with recent non-German literature would yield a similarly gloomy picture, Mayer contends, for even outside Germany there is little evidence of 'literarische Opulenz'. Consequently, Mayer concludes, the question was one of 'eine literarische Weltproblematik'.

Mayer then recalls the Western assertion that 'die gegenwärtige Welt- und Menschenlage lasse sich überhaupt nicht mehr mit den bisherigen literarischen Mitteln und Gattungen wiedergeben'. He remarks that this fact had escaped a particularly large number of young GDR writers:

> Die meisten unserer Romanciers . . . hielten eigensinnig an der Romanform Balzacs oder Tolstois fest. Liest man ihre Bücher, so muß man den Eindruck haben, alle die Formprobleme des Romans, mit denen sich Thomas oder Heinrich Mann, Konstantin Fedin oder Aragon und Sartre, Musil oder Hemingway oder Döblin seit Jahren beschäftigt haben,

seien hier hochmütigerweise einfach nicht zur Kenntnis genommen worden.

Neither is lyric poetry spared Mayer's criticism: 'Ich will Hermlin und Peter Huchel, Fühmann und Georg Maurer ausdrücklich ausnehmen: aber neben ihnen wieviel gefällige Reimereien von Epigonen Paul Heyses oder Emanual Geibels, wieviel rotanges-trichene Gartenlauben!' Mayer saw the roots of this miserable state of affairs in the failure of writers to address themselves to works of contemporary literature, both bourgeois and non-bourgeois. He goes on to make the following plea:

> Will man immer noch so tun, als habe Franz Kafka nie gelebt, als sei der 'Ulysses' von James Joyce nie geschrieben worden, als sei das sogenannte 'epische Theater' bloß ein Hirngespinst des im übrigen recht achtbaren Bertolt Brecht? Wohlgemerkt: Es ist keine Rede davon, daß von mir nun eine Kafka-Renaissance oder gar eine Joyce-Imitation für unsere Literatur gefordert würde. Aber moderne Literatur ist nicht möglich ohne die Kenntnis der modernen Literatur ... Thomas Mann oder Brecht, unter den Lebenden vor allem Becher, waren ungemein interessiert an allem Neugeschaffenen. ... Will man also das literarische Klima bei uns ändern, so muß die Auseinandersetzung mit der modernen Kunst und Literatur in weitestem Umfang endlich einmal beginnen. Es muß aufhören, daß Kafka bei uns ein Geheimtip bleibt, und daß das Interesse für Faulkner oder Thornton Wilder mit illegalem Treiben gleichgesetzt wird.[31]

Mayer's challenge was taken up. In subsequent months *Sonntag* published a wealth of articles that examined Mayer's thesis. Most were critical, but a number were also supportive. These articles were accompanied by attacks, some vehement, in *Neues Deutsch-land*. In the period leading up to the SED's cultural conference in October 1957 the debate over Mayer's so-called 'Opulenztheorie' continuously and overwhelmingly dominated discussion. Even the speeches of Walter Ulbricht show evidence of indirect responses to the Leipzig academic.[32] West German Cold War publications covered the quarrel with Mayer over questions of 'sozialistische Gegenwartsliteratur' in enormous detail. West German authors could only dream of such treatment as far as their own delib-erations over aesthetic matters were concerned.[33] The words of Alexander Abusch in July 1957 show how seriously the conflict was taken in the GDR:

> Die Delegiertenversammlung unseres Schriftstellerverbandes im Februar stand ... nach einer vorangegangenen öffentlichen Diskussion von zwei

Monaten im Zeichen einer Auseinandersetzung mit Professor Hans Mayer; einer Auseinandersetzung, in der es um die prinzipiellsten Fragen der vierzigjährigen Entwicklung unserer sozialistischen Literatur ging and geht.[34]

Abusch's reference to forty years of socialist literature, which refers to the October revolution of 1917, indicates how the tradition of proletarian revolutionary, or Socialist Realist, literature, had (in the eyes of the SED) replaced the classical humanism which derived from the now discredited writings of Lukács. For this reason Abusch's attacks were directed against Mayer's notion of 'eine literarische Weltproblematik', because it was here that he united, without differentiation, bourgeois and socialist literature, denying the 'Klassencharakter' of literature, omitting any concept of 'Parteilichkeit', and relinquishing keystones of Socialist Realism. Indeed, Mayer was criticised on virtually the same grounds as Lukács had been.

If the literary developments leading up to the discussions on contemporary socialist literature in 1956 are ignored, the vehemence and the consequences of the Mayer debate can hardly be appreciated. Later accounts repeatedly give the impression that Mayer's criticism was a unique and individual strike against an otherwise homogenous front. Western accounts reduce the conflict to Hans Mayer's own person and to the question of whether Joyce and Kafka are intelligible for a GDR audience. What is more pivotal is the question of the time at which the conflict took place, and why Mayer's changed view of literature was clearly no longer acceptable at this time. The reduction of the argument to the question 'Joyce oder Marchwitza?' cannot, for example, explain Mayer's pre-eminent position within GDR German studies up to that point; in previous years he would hardly have come down in favour of Marchwitza either.

The discussions at the Fourth Writers' Congress in January 1956 are central to an understanding of this issue. This congress represented the start of a fundamental new orientation in literary approach, which was followed by numerous debates during the succeeding summer. Johannes R. Becher introduced the notion of 'Literaturgesellschaft' at this congress, and called on writers to take part in the creation of a new 'sozialistische Nationalliteratur'. This meant a programmatic break with the anti-fascist, democratic, re-education literature of the transition period, and, in contrast to the previous stress on pan-German concerns, a new emphasis on the independence of literary development in the GDR. It corresponded with the SED's resolution 'eine sozialistische Kultur zu entwickeln und sie dem ganzen Volke zu vermitteln'.[35] The documents relating to the Fourth Writers' Congress contain arguments similar to those later formulated by Hans Mayer, and also show evidence of critical attitudes towards a theoretical approach conditioned by Lukács. Contemporary literature came in for particularly sharp criticism in this respect.

In his congress report in *Sinn und Form* Georg Maurer emphasised the need to expand the Lukácsian canon and to subject publishing practice to critical revision. He suggested that there was much to catch up on:

> [Nachzuholen wäre] die Auseinandersetzung mit der gesamten Literatur des letzten halben Jahrhunderts, besonders mit dem deutschen Expressionismus, und die kritische Aneignung auch dieses bedeutenden Erbes. Nachzuholen wäre durch Verlage die Veröffentlichung zeitgenössischer humanistischer Werke, die bisher nicht erschienen, weil sie, wie Hermlin formulierte, 'nicht in allen Punkten den Moralbegriffen eines Lektors entsprechen ... In unserem Staat ... spielt die Literatur eine ernste, verbindliche Rolle. Viele Vorurteile gegen bedeutende Werke ergeben sich gerade aus diesem Ernstnehmen der Literatur, allerdings einem oftmals naiven, noch unentwickelten, allzu direkten Ernstnehmen'.[36]

Maurer quotes with approval Johannes R. Becher's attack on a tendency towards kitsch in GDR literature: '"Muffigkeit und Kitsch sind als solche erkannt, Gartenlaube und Plüsch führen kein behagliches, kritikloses Dasein mehr, des Spießers Wunderhorn krächzt schon auf letzten Löchern"'.[37] Hardly less acerbic criticism of the kitsch and dogmatism of contemporary literature had been dispensed by Anna Seghers in her explanation of why Western literature was superior to that of the GDR in many respects.[38]

The debates at the Writers' Congress were continued at the academic conference held in Berlin during May and June of 1956. On this occasion Mayer gave the keynote lecture, at Becher's request. Even at this stage an intense controversy arose between the proponents of 'aesthetic' criteria and those who supported the 'Primat des Inhalts' (Becher, Wolfgang Harich and Alfred Kurella). The views put forward by these three pointed up the dilemma which prevented the two sides from reaching agreement. By favouring content, they were simultaneously expecting too much and too little from literature. In terms of its essentialist and dogmatic schematism, the discussion was, in essence, falling behind even the debate on formalism. Nevertheless, Mayer noted in his conclusion what he regarded as the most positive result of the conference, namely 'daß auf dem Boden des Marxismus verschiedenartige Meinungen möglich seien'.[39] This conference had made one contradiction clear, within which Mayer was soon to be caught up. That contradiction consisted of cultural-political voluntarism, paired with a more or less essentialist understanding of literature, on the one hand, and on the other an inchoate materialist aesthetic and theory of literature, which could not do justice to the newly formulated demands of a 'sozialistische Literaturgesellschaft'.

At this point the rejection of Lukácsian notions of literature was justified solely in political terms; favouring the needs of the 'Volksmassen' and writers' experience of 'real life' left an aesthetic void. The evidence of this void explains why Mayer's criticism was irreconcilable with the prevailing view, since he was dealing essentially with strictly Lukácsian questions concerning the validity of a specific literary form which Lukács called 'Gestaltung'. In terms of literary policy this concept led, of course, to the 'Bitterfelder Weg', whose works obeyed the dialectic of form and content no less than many proponents of the 'Primat des Inhalts' could have foreseen. It would be wrong to become fixated on the personalised conflict over Hans Mayer, and so to regard the political and literary change of course of 1956 and 1957 solely as a caesura, or even a cul-de-sac, for in this case there are also continuities to be considered. The change in orientation meant a shift in the kinds of questions being asked, a shift towards a notion of literature which opened new pathways on the 'Bitterfelder Weg'. Younger authors who took advantage of the new directions included Christa Wolf, Brigitte Reimann and Heiner Müller, to name only some of the most prominent. Nobody disputes that the personal and factional costs of this change of course were very high.

In October 1957 Mayer took up an invitation from the Kulturbund Wuppertal to attend a conference on literary criticism. There he encountered for the first time Paul Celan, Ingeborg Bachmann, Hans Magnus Enzensberger and Walter Jens. Mayer was right when he later termed this first meeting 'folgenreich', for it marked not only his first contact with authors of the 'Gruppe 47', but also the beginning of his gradual shift towards 'dissidence', a process not without its ambiguities but one which was to distance him from literary debate in the GDR. The escalation of the 1956 conflict ended in an official academic break with Mayer and his mentor, Lukács. The crunch came when Hans-Günther Thalheim gave a lecture on the fortieth anniversary of the October revolution, delivered at the Institute of German Studies of the Humboldt University in Berlin. The title of the lecture was: 'Kritische Bemerkungen zu den Literaturauffassungen Georg Lukács und Hans Mayers. Zur Frage der Unterschätzung der Rolle der Volksmassen in der Literatur'.[40] Thalheim's polemical reckoning went so far as to interpret Mayer's concept of literature as a danger for the politics of world anti-imperialism. The characteristic Lukács style is unmistakably present in his speech:

> Die durch die idealistische 'Zeitgeist'-Soziologie bedingte Unterschätzung der schöpferischen Rolle der Volksmassen in der Literatur führt Hans Mayer zur Ablehnung einer noch vorwiegend zum Didaktischen neigenden sozialistischen Literatur und damit zur Leugnung des Entwicklungscharakters des sozialistischen Realismus, der gesetzmäßigen Entwicklung der sozialistischen Gegenwartsliteratur zu einer sozialistischen Klassik. Da aber für Mayer eine 'Blüte' der sozialistischen Gegenwartsliteratur nur möglich ist durch eine Orientierung der sozialistischen Schriftsteller auf die Spitzenleistungen eines angeblich Imperialismus und Sozialismus prägenden 'modernen Zeitgeistes', d.h. aber auf Werke spätburgerlicher Dekadenzliteratur, verläßt er, – wenn auch unbewußt – in dem Vortrag 'Zur Gegenwartsliteratur' – seine liberale antiimperialistische Ausgangsposition und leistet einer antisozialistischen, proimperialistischen Kritik und 'Aufweichung' des sozialistischen Realismus in Deutschland Vorschub, die letztlich den aggressiven Plänen der vom amerikanischen Monopolkapitalismus gelenkten Nordatlantikpakt-Organisation dient.[41]

Thalheim's supposed reckoning with Mayer's concept of literature does not in fact go beyond political condemnation, albeit a condemnation that includes the charge of acting as an enemy agent. There would be nothing more to add to this had Mayer packed his bags and, like others before him (such as Kantorowicz), turned the tables by returning vituperation from the platform of Western publications. But for almost six years he exposed himself to further 'Zerreißproben' and persisted in his marxist stance.

Any assessment of Mayer's conflict in the GDR that merely follows Cold War patterns by focusing on the term 'dissidence' fails to take account of the evident differences in the attitudes towards literature which were prevalent in the two German states at this time. Two reviews from 1958 make this antithesis eminently clear. In them the prominent writers Hans Mayer and Walter Jens, one of the leading literary critics of the Federal Republic, confront each other with their radically different notions of literature.

'Der interessanteste Literaturhistoriker deutscher Sprache ist ein Marxist', Walter Jens admits without envy in his positive review of Mayer's volume *Deutsche Literatur und Weltliteratur – Reden und Aufsätze* (1957).[42] But Mayer's functional understanding of literature arouses Jens's disapproval; the West German bemoans Mayer's neglect of quality as a criterion: 'Es ist sicher kein Zufall, daß der Autor viel von "Wirkung" und wenig von "Wertung" spricht.' Jens goes on to criticise in particular Mayer's disregard for lyric poetry:

> Freilich hat er es da besonders schwer, denn die Marxisten sind heute in der nicht gerade beneidenswerten Lage, ihre proletarische Wirklichkeit immer noch mit den formalen Mitteln des Spätbürgertums verherrlichen zu müssen. Um aber zwischen der Skylla 'bürgerlicher Realismus' und der Charybdis 'dekadenter Formalismus' entscheiden zu können, bedürfte es der Anerkennung einer konstanten, nicht gesellschaftlich gebundenen 'überhistorisch zu verstehenden ästhetischen Gesetzlichkeit'.[43]

Two months later Jens, in return, had to put up with rebukes from Mayer on the grounds of 'Methodensynkretismus' and 'soziale Einseitigkeit', when the East German academic reviewed his West German counterpart's book *statt einer literaturgeschichte*, which soon became a much-read work in the Federal Republic.[44]

In 1961 Hans Mayer was still making no secret of the fact that his political standpoints owed their allegiance to a particular system. During a debate between East and West German authors in Hamburg Mayer defended himself against attacks on those grounds. He was particularly spirited when such attacks came from Western colleagues who claimed to possess a notion of literature free of ideology, and who applied West German criteria to the assessment of GDR literature, unhesitatingly classifying it as 'free' or 'unfree'. Mayer repeatedly alerted his audience to the differences in the literary culture of the two states, defending himself in particular against the criticisms of his Western colleague Marcel Reich-Ranicki:

> Eines nützt der Diskussion nicht: Wenn wir die scharfen Gegensätzlichkeiten zweier deutscher Staaten, die beide eine ganz verschiedene Auffassung von der Konzeption der Literatur, der Funktion der Literatur haben, ignorieren und versuchen, uns etwa immer wieder das Gesellschaftsspiel zu machen, dem Apfelbaum vorzuwerfen, er sei kein

Birnbaum. Damit vertuschen wir, damit verkleistern wir das Problem. . . .
Die Frage ist: Wie äußert sich die Literatur, die Funktion der Schriftsteller
in zwei Staaten verschiedener gesellschaftlicher Grundlage? . . . Wir
haben ein neues Publikum, wir haben eine Funktion der Literatur. Unsere
Literatur hat selbstverständlich betont, daß, und zwar jeder unserer
Schriftsteller, wie mir scheint, mehr oder weniger eine Aufgabe hat, ein
bestimmtes Programm, eine bestimmte kulturpädagogische Funktion
zu vertreten.[45]

And in the spirit of his 1954 lecture on world literature, Mayer in
1961 made the following point about the individual writer in the
GDR:

Daß er hier eine durchaus kritische, divergierende Meinung haben kann,
ist selbstverständlich, und solange die vorhanden ist, wie für mich
etwa in meiner Tätigkeit als akademischer Lehrer auf dem Gebiete der
Germanistik, solange ist für mich die PEN-Charta in ihrem entschei-
denden Punkte erfüllt.[46]

Mayer remained true to his postulate of 1954 not only in spite of
but also because of his quarrels in GDR literary life. Admittedly,
he rather simplified that postulate by presenting it as reality. But
he is best judged by his own words: 'Eine Pluralität, die Möglichkeit
vieler ästhetischer Standpunkte und ihrer freien Entwicklung, die
ist durchaus gegeben.'[47]

In November 1961 Mayer took up an invitation from the Ministry
of Culture, delivering the main speech at Frankfurt an der Oder on
the 150th anniversary of Heinrich von Kleist's death. His speech
was entitled: 'Heinrich von Kleist: der geschichtliche Augenblick',
and made history as far as Kleist studies were concerned. His
lecture remains unassailed to this day. He makes a very serious
effort to clear up a number of 'Mißverständnisse',[48] and to deal with
Lukács's verdict against Kleist, which Anna Seghers had already
challenged in 1938. Mayer rehabilitates Kleist the 'outsider' as a
'geschichtliches Phänomen':

Ein bürgerlicher Künstler, dem sich der Abgrund geöffnet hat zwischen
bürgerlicher Weltanschauung und bourgeoiser Wirklichkeit. Die
tragische Größe Heinrich von Kleists besteht darin, daß er als einer
der ersten Künstler seiner Zeit den historischen Zwiespalt verstand,
der seit dem Thermidor in die Welt getreten war: zwischen Citoyen
und Bourgeois, Nationalität und Gesellschaftsstruktur. Er sah die
Zersetzung schon vor der Reife.[49]

Mayer reads Kleist as the great, though ambivalent, precursor of
Kafka, Brecht and Anna Seghers: 'eine Vorwegnahme in höchster

Ambivalenz: für die spätbürgerliche wie die nicht mehr bürgerliche Literatur unserer Tage'.[50]

As he recalls in his autobiography, Mayer received official confirmation that he had spoken well on this occasion: 'Meine alten Übeltaten von 1956 und 1957 waren durch Versöhnung offiziell getilgt.'[51] In 1962 the study of Kleist appeared in the West from the Neske-Verlag in Pfullingen. Mayer's Kleist lecture was at the same time the precursor of the arguments he advanced a year later, which were to set in train the review of research into Romanticism in the GDR.

In July 1962, together with Werner Krauss, he convened a conference at the University of Leipzig on 'Fragen der Romantikforschung'. In his introductory paper ('Zur heutigen Lage der Romantikforschung') he made a plea for a progressive new evaluation of the early Romantic period.[52] The congress report in *Weimarer Beiträge* commented extremely critically on Mayer's proposals.[53] Not for years were Mayer's views to become generally accepted by scholars of Romanticism both in the Federal Republic and in the GDR. Even in 1978 Mayer's work on Romanticism was entirely omitted from a volume on the subject produced by the Akademie der Künste.[54]

Mayer's personal decision to leave the GDR was not actuated solely by the critical discussion of his volume *Ansichten* (see above), a discussion initiated by the Party leadership in Leipzig. The final straw for him came slightly later, when the young student Volker Beyrich published an article attacking Mayer in the Leipzig *Universitätszeitung*.[55] The article bore the provocative title 'Eine Lehrmeinung zuviel'; Mayer reacted with what he termed 'tiefe Verstörung'.[56] With hindsight, Mayer regarded this turn of events as the public breaking of a pact, the pact being the fifteen years of his 'Wirken' in the GDR:

> ich war zu den 'Russen' gekommen . . . , um als Professor zu wirken und mitzuhelfen bei der Grundlegung einer veränderten Wissenschaft von der Gesellschaft und der Literatur [und hatte] mein Wirken als einen *Pakt* verstanden . . . mein Pakt wurde auch von der späteren DDR als ein gegenseitiger Vertrag verstanden . . . Nun war aber der Pakt gebrochen.[57]

During the spring and summer of 1963 the Western press kept a close eye on the conflicts building up around Hans Mayer, and some papers commented on his departure from the GDR with unambiguous clarity.[58] Under the headline 'Mayer-Flucht' a palpably satisfied *Der Spiegel* had this to say:

> Nach dem betagten Philosophen Ernst Bloch..., der 1961 im Westen blieb, und dem engagierten Literaten Alfred Kantorowicz..., der sich 1959 in die Bundesrepublick absetzte, hat die DDR mit Mayer ihre letzte geisteswissenschaftliche Attraktion verloren.[59]

Looking back, in 1987, Mayer had a thoroughly sober view of his new role in the Federal Republic:

> Was ich über Literatur in der Vergangenheit und Gegenwart dachte und im Druck veröffentlichte, war meine Sache. Das meinte den Verzicht auf obrigkeitliche Kontrolle, allein es bedeutete gleichzeitig die geheime obrigkeitliche *Nicht-Beachtung* all meines Tuns. Es war irrelevant für die Inhaber realer Macht... In der Bundesrepublik standen Literatur und Literaturwissenschaft seit der politischen Restauration der fünfziger Jahre zumeist in Verdacht, ein besseres *Hobby* darzustellen, das aller Notwendigkeit entbehrte.[60]

Christa Wolf was right; Hans Mayer had felt the full force of all the contradictions. Uwe Johnson congratulated him on his sixtieth birthday:

> Jetzt sind es Hotels und Kellner in Hannover, die wissen, was ihm nötig ist. Ich habe ihn begrüßt, als er kam, er war jetzt wieder für mich erreichbar, aber ich habe mich auch erinnert an den Schüler, den ich in Leipzig war, und mir die vorgestellt, die da seine jetzt nicht werden konnte, und ich dachte: Schade.[61]

It was to be almost twenty-five years before Hans Mayer was in a position to return to Leipzig, this time in response to an official invitation. At his former university he was overcome by what he termed 'lautloses Heulen'. This is how Hans Mayer described his emotions: 'Hier war ich gegangen, hatte ein Ziel, einen Weg. Später schrieb ich bessere Bücher. Hier aber, unweit von hier, hatte ich etwas bewirken können'.[62]

Clearly, the chapter of GDR literary history dealt with here was written almost exclusively by male authors, academics and cultural politicians. For that reason let us now remember the unnamed women, the female authors, the secretaries, academics and editorial assistants, the wives and the girlfriends, women who were no doubt involved in the debates but who were denied the right to air their views publicly by the institutional barriers of the literary establishments.

Notes

1 Hans Mayer, *Ein Deutscher auf Widerruf*, II, Frankfurt am Main, 1988, p. 94.

2 Christa Wolf, 'Zum 80. Geburtstag von Hans Mayer', *Ansprachen*, Darmstadt, 1988, p. 39.

3 *Ibid.*, p. 41.

4 *Ibid*, pp. 42–3.

5 *Ein Deutscher auf Widerruf*, I, p. 373.

6 Hans Mayer, 'Macht und Ohnmacht des Wortes', *Frankfurter Hefte*, 12, 1947, pp. 1179–81.

7 *Ein Deutscher auf Widerruf*, I, p. 404.

8 *Ein Deutscher auf Widerruf*, II, p. 94.

9 *Ibid.*, p. 270.

10 Wolfgang Emmerich, *Kleine Literaturgeschichte der DDR*, fifth edition, Frankfurt am Main, 1989, p. 56.

11 Ursula Wertheim, 'Die marxistische Rezeption des klassischen Erbes', *Beiträge zur marxistischen Literaturtheorie in der DDR*, ed. Werner Mittenzwei, Leipzig, 1969, p. 663.

12 Hans Mayer, *Gelebte Literatur*, Frankfurt am Main, 1987, p. 84.

13 *Ibid.*, p. 111.

14 *Ein Deutscher auf Widerruf*, II, p. 103.

15 Therese Hörningk, *Christa Wolf*, Göttingen, 1989, p. 20.

16 Hans Mayer, 'Johannes R. Bechers "Tagebuch 1950"', *Aufbau*, 9, 1951, pp. 826–7.

17 *Die Expressionismusdebatte: Materialien zu einer marxistischen Realismuskonzeption*, ed. Hans-Jürgen Schmitt, Frankfurt am Main, 1973, p. 8.

18 *Ein Deutscher auf Widerruf*, II, p. 98.

19 Hans Mayer, 'Literaturwissenschaft in Deutschland', *Fischer Lexikon Literatur*, II, Frankfurt am Main, 1965, pp. 317–33.

20 *Ein Deutscher auf Widerruf*, II, p. 33.

21 Peter Demetz, 'Geschichtsvision und Wissenschaft: über einige Arbeiten Hans Mayers', *Merkur*, 7, 1961, pp. 677–87, especially pp. 681–2.

22 *Welt und Wort*, 6, 1951, p. 33.

23 Wolfgang Harich, 'Hans Mayers Buch über Thomas Mann', *Die Weltbühne*, 26, 1950, pp. 801 and 802.

24 Hans Mayer, 'Anmerkung zu einem Gedicht von Heinrich Heine', *Sinn und Form*, 4, 1951, p. 180.

25 *Ibid.*, p. 184.

26 Dieter Noll, 'Schriften an die deutsche Nation', *Aufbau*, 10, 1953, p. 915.

27 Hans Mayer, 'Deutsche Literatur und Weltliteratur', *Aufbau*, 4, 1954, p. 311.

28 *Ibid.*, p. 313.

29 *Ibid.*, pp. 314–15.

30 *Ibid.*, p. 315.

31 *Sonntag*, 2 December 1956. See also *Über Hans Mayer*, ed. Inge Jens, Frankfurt am Main, 1977, pp. 65–74. All subsequent quotations are from this source.

32 See Walter Ulbricht, 'Zum Kampf zwischen dem Marxismus–Leninismus und den Ideologien der Bourgeoisie', *Neues Deutschland*, 5 February 1957.

33 See especially 'Parteikorsett für "DDR"-Literaturwissenschaft', *Ost-Probleme*, 9, 1 March 1957.

34 Alexander Abusch, 'Diskussionsrede auf der 32. Tagung des ZK der SED', *Zur sozialistischen Kulturrevolution: Dokumente*, II, Berlin, 1960.

35 Gudrun Klatt, 'Proletarisch–revolutionäres Erbe als Angebot: Vom Umgang mit Erfahrungen proletarisch-revolutionärer Kunst während der Übergangsperiode', in *Literarisches Leben in der DDR 1945 bis 1960*, edited by Ingeborg Münz-Koenen, Berlin, 1980, p. 258.

36 Georg Maurer, 'Nach dem IV. deutschen Schriftstellerkongreß', *Sinn und Form*, 1, 1956, p. 162.

37 *Ibid.*, p. 158.

38 See Anna Seghers, 'Die große Veränderung in unserer Literatur', in *Aufsätze, Ansprachen, Essays, 1954–1979*, Berlin and Weimar, 1984, pp. 80–116.

39 Georg Piltz, 'Die Fenster sind aufgestoßen', *Sonntag*, 17 June 1956, p. 12.

40 *Weimarer Beiträge*, 1958, pp. 138–71.

41 *Ibid.*, pp. 168–9.

42 Walter Jens, 'Ein kurzweiliger Gelehrter', *Die Zeit*, 12 September 1958.

43 *Ibid.*

44 Hans Mayer, 'Walter Jens, *statt einer literaturgeschichte*', *Deutsche Literaturzeitung*, Berlin, Göttingen, Heidelberg, Leipzig, München, 11, 1958, column 957.

45 *Schriftsteller: Ja-Sager oder Nein-Sager? Das Hamburger Streitgespräch deutscher Autoren aus Ost und West*, edited by Josef Müller-Marein and Theo Sommer, Hamburg, 1961, pp. 124 and 125.

46 *Ibid.*, pp. 125–6.

47 *Ibid.*, p. 110.

48 *Ein Deutscher auf Widerruf*, II, p. 243.

49 Hans Mayer, *Das unglückliche Bewußtsein: zur deutschen Literaturgeschichte von Lessing bis Heine*, Frankfurt am Main, 1986, p. 397.

50 *Ibid.*, p. 403.

51 *Ein Deutscher auf Widerruf*, II, p. 253.

52 Klaus Hammer, Henri Poschmann and Hans-Ulrich Schnuchel, 'Fragen der Romantikforschung', *Weimarer Beiträge*, 1, 1963, p. 176.

53 *Ibid.*, pp. 173–82.

54 *Arbeiten mit der Romantik heute*, edited by Heide Hess and Peter Liebers, Berlin, 1978.

55 *Universitätszeitung*, 22, 1963. See also: Werner Riedel, 'Eine Lehrmeinung zu wenig – eine Lehrmeinung mehr', *Colloquium*, 9/10, West Berlin, 1963, pp. 19–21.

56 *Ein Deutscher auf Widerruf*, II, p. 256.

57 *Ibid.*

58 See Lisa Dechene, 'Hans Mayers utopische Forderungen: ein fanatischer Kommunist im Widerstreit mit der SED', *SBZ-Archiv*, 11, 1963, pp. 165–7, and Heinz Klunker, 'Professor Mayers Bruch mit dem Regime', *Europäische Begegnung*, Cologne, 1963, pp. 605–6.

59 *Der Spiegel*, 37, 1963, pp. 24–6.

60 Hans Mayer, *Gelebte Literatur*, p. 96.

61 Uwe Johnson, 'Einer meiner Lehrer', in *Über Hans Mayer*, edited by Inge Jens, Frankfurt am Main, 1977, p. 82.

62 Hans Mayer, *Stadtansichten*, Frankfurt am Main, 1989, pp. 81 and 83–4.

Reifeprüfung 1961:
Uwe Johnson and the Cold War

Colin Riordan

In April 1953, as former Organisations-Leiter of his local Freie
Deutsche Jugend, Uwe Johnson was called upon to follow the FDJ
central council's lead by publicly condemning the religious youth
organisation Junge Gemeinde. The nineteen-year-old student's refusal to comply placed his continuing education in jeopardy, but
at the same time provided the material for his first, initially unpublished novel *Ingrid Babendererde: Reifeprüfung 1953* (Frankfurt
am Main, 1985). When the aspirant author submitted his novel to
the Aufbau-Verlag in 1956, he was himself unwittingly embarking
on a test of maturity. For Johnson's efforts to have his work published, and the nature of his themes, laid him open to manipulation and misinterpretation in ways which did not become fully
apparent until Hermann Kesten publicly slandered the author after
the closing of the Berlin border in 1961. In this essay I should like
to explore the ways in which Johnson's work was exploited for
political capital on either side of the border, and how far the
political Cold War was reflected in cultural antagonisms. This is of
particular interest in the case of an author who, having crossed
the border to settle in West Berlin in 1959, was frequently seen as
occupying a pan-German position, beyond the ideological divide.
With this in mind I want to consider how far political factors
determined the decision to reject Johnson's first novel, *Ingrid
Babendererde*, not only in the GDR but in the FRG, and whether
political considerations may have played a role in the acceptance
of his second novel, *Mutmaßungen über Jakob*, by the Suhrkamp
Verlag in 1959. Finally, an exploration of the Kesten affair of 1961
will help to shed light on the passion and prejudice which conditioned the relationship between writers of East and West during
these years.

In the *Frankfurter Vorlesungen* of 1979, subsequently published

as *Begleitumstände* (Frankfurt am Main, 1980), Uwe Johnson gave
a detailed account of his efforts to publish *Ingrid Babendererde* in
the GDR during the autumn of 1956. A brief outline of the novel's
external events will clarify the obstacles Johnson encountered when
he first submitted his manuscript for publication. *Ingrid Babendererde* tells the story of the last few days in school of a class
about to take the *Abitur* in April 1953, shortly after Stalin's death
and two months before the uprising. The *Reifeprüfung* becomes
political and moral, rather than strictly educational, however,
because the eponymous heroine comes into conflict with the
authorities in much the same way as Johnson did. She too is asked
to make an attack on the Junge Gemeinde, and, like Johnson,
refuses. Although, in contrast to the account Johnson gives of his
own speech, in which he describes attacking the smear campaign
itself and laying the blame at the government's door, Ingrid does
not refute the allegations against the Junge Gemeinde, she does
attack the kind of petty interference in the lives of individuals
which characterised socialism for pupils in the school. Although
her speech seems less politically controversial than the one which
Johnson says he actually made, she is shadowed by an agent of
the Staatssicherheitsdienst (SSD), and is left with no choice but to
leave for the West, along with her boyfriend Klaus. Johnson's fictional characters thus resort to a course of action on which Johnson
himself was reluctant to embark, remaining as he did in the GDR
until forced to leave by the impending publication of *Mutmaßungen
über Jakob* in 1959.[1]

Although *Ingrid Babendererde* was clearly politically dangerous
material, as even the brief outline of plot in the previous paragraph
indicates, Uwe Johnson made very serious efforts to get it published
in the GDR. He clearly regarded publication in the FRG as a last
resort. The novel existed in four versions, written between 1953
and 1956, and it was only the fourth version which Johnson actually
submitted for publication. In *Begleitumstände*, Johnson describes
the changes he made from version to version, and gives textual
examples. Johnson consistently argues that the changes were made
on aesthetic grounds. He decided to revise the first version after
reflecting that the author's youth emerged too distinctly in the
characters' naivety. The character of Erichson was therefore introduced as 'ein Zeuge' (*Begleitumstände*, p. 74), who was older
and more experienced than the main characters (indeed he is the
age Johnson was at the time of the revision). Erichson would be

able to bring his broader knowledge to bear on the political and constitutional problems with which the characters' minds and consciences were wrestling. In the third version, for reasons unspecified, Erichson actually tells the story. Parts of this version were preserved unchanged in the final manuscript; compare, for example, *Begleitumstände* pp. 81–2 with *Ingrid Babendererde* pp. 87–8. However, the resulting changes in narrative perspective introduced distortions which distracted from the story (see *Begleitumstände* p. 87), and Erichson was discarded as superfluous, resulting in the final version which is now available.

In 1985 this final version was published as *Ingrid Babendererde: Reifeprüfung 1953*, and since 1986 the original manuscripts of early drafts have been available for consultation in the Uwe Johnson Archive in Frankfurt am Main. This has made it possible to draw comparisons which are independent of Johnson's judgement in *Begleitumstände*.[2] Such comparisons reveal that although literary considerations may have prompted the changes, at the same time Johnson made political concessions in the form of self-censorship. The character of Erichson, for instance, is politically as well as intellectually more mature than the schoolchildren. His sceptical political stance emerges in a passage from the second version quoted by Johnson in *Begleitumstände* but omitted in the final manuscript. In that passage Erichson expresses his dissatisfaction with the prevalent brand of socialism. He chooses an overtly satirical means to make a direct attack on the government's campaign against the Junge Gemeinde, using a kindergarten as a metaphor for the GDR. 'Die Besten Kinder' (the Brechtian echoes are unmistakable) accuse 'die Bösen Kinder' of betrayal in terms which deride the GDR national anthem: 'Und unsere Sonnige Republik wollt ihr dem Schlechten Ausland ausliefern: so dass die Sonne nicht mehr schön wie nie über Deutschland scheint, über Deutschland scheint' (*Begleitumstände*, p. 77). He mocks restrictions on the freedom of expression:

> In der Tat geht es ja darum dass Religion ein bürgerliches Überbleibsel ist und eine andere Meinung. Es ist aber erstaunlich dass die Regierung diese andere Meinung nicht öffentlich verbieten mag; sie sagt doch: es gäbe nur eine richtige Meinung, und das sei die ihre. (*Begleitumstände*, p. 77)

Traces of this passage can be found in the published version on p. 145, but the context has disappeared, and the effect is less direct and more innocuous.[3] It is particularly noticeable that sentences containing the words 'Meinung' and 'andere Meinung' are removed.

The removal of such words characterises changes made to the pivotal episode of Ingrid's speech (compare *Begleitumstände* pp. 83–5 with *Ingrid Babendererde* pp. 174–5). Although both versions begin in the same way (with very minor variations), it soon becomes apparent that certain sentences have been substantially altered. The early version reads: 'Wir können ja wohl nicht alle Herrn Siebmanns Hosen tragen: und seine Meinung auch nicht' (*Begleitumstände*, p. 84). The published version has become: 'Wir können ja wohl nicht alle Herrn Siebmanns Anzug tragen, wir mögen uns auch nicht alle so benehmen wie er' (*Ingrid Babendererde*, p. 174). Another section previously ran: 'In dieser Zeit führen alle Wege zum Kommunismus: sagt Herr Siebmann. Das ist eben so seine Meinung, und er ist da sehr zuversichtlich' (*Begleitumstände*, p. 85). This was amended to: 'In dieser Zeit führen alle Wege zum Kommunismus: sagt Herr Direktor Siebmann, und wir haben das wohl begriffen' (*Ingrid Babendererde*, pp. 174–5). Even more striking is the ending of the speech. The ten lines from 'Herr Direktor Siebmann soll aber bedenken...' to 'mit verbotenen Hosen' (*Ingrid Babendererde* p. 175) are missing from the previous version, which contains a section approximately twice as long which is politically far more hard-hitting. First Ingrid comments sarcastically on Siebmann's remark 'Alle Wege führen zum Kommunismus', then she draws attention to the consequences of holding an opinion different to the officially sanctioned one:

> – Herr Siebmann hat vier aus unserer Klasse ins Zuchthaus gebracht im vorigen Jahr. Es ist wahr, dass die eine andere Meinung an die Schule geklebt haben, aber möchte Herr Siebmann für seine Meinung wohl auch fünfzehn Jahre im Zuchthaus sitzen?
> – Und dass wir alle so eine fürchterliche Angst haben. (*Begleitumstände*, p. 85)[4]

Severely critical passages such as this are by no means rarities in the early versions of *Ingrid Babendererde*. The original first manuscript in the Uwe Johnson Archive contains many other such instances of criticism which has been toned down or removed from the version presented for publication. A brief comparison of two chapters will illustrate this process. What was chapter 15 in the first manuscript has become chapter 20 in *Ingrid Babendererde*.

Both versions contain explanations of how Siebmann (the headmaster) had acquired his nickname 'Pius'. In *Ingrid Babendererde* we find:

> Niemand wusste warum Pius Pius hiess. Päpste haben so geheissen, und in der Tat stand Pius der Schule vor und ihrer Parteiorganisation mit solcher Autorität, aber es mochte nicht deswegen sein. 'Pius' ist lateinisch und bedeutet 'Der Fromme', und für die 12 A bedeutete dies im besonderen dass Pius auf eine fromme Art zu tun hatte mit der Sozialistischen Einheitspartei; indessen hatte er diesen Namen nicht von der 12 A. (*Ingrid Babendererde*, pp. 86–7)

In the first manuscript this passage had appeared as:

> Pius indessen – ja: 'Pius' ist lateinisch und bedeutet 'Der Fromme'. Für die 12 A bedeutete das im besonderen dass Pius auf eine fromme Art mit dem Sozialismus zu tun hatte, Pius glaubte an den Sozialismus. Das ist nicht einfach behauptend hingesagt; Pius hatte der 12 A mitgeteilt so sei es, und es sei gut so. Er war der Vorsitzende der Sozialistischen und Einheits-Partei (SED) an der Schule, und er stand ihr vor mit sozusagen päpstlicher Unfehlbarkeit die sich gut fügen mochte zu seinem Namen. (First manuscript of *Ingrid Babendererde*, p. 50)

The ironic tone of this passage, contained particularly in the words 'päpstliche Unfehlbarkeit', is missing from *Ingrid Babendererde*. Similarly, ironic references to 'Klassenkampf' and its supposed absence in a socialist state are altogether removed in the published version. Siebmann's defence of the government and attack on the Junge Gemeinde, which appears in chapter 20 of *Ingrid Babendererde*, was originally parodied as shrill, defensive and transparently bigoted. Indeed the whole of the chapter in the early version has quite a different slant. There is nothing conciliatory in it such as: 'Ach ja: Pius hatte irgendwo recht' (*Ingrid Babendererde*, p. 91). On the contrary, the chapter in the first manuscript is sharply critical throughout. Jürgen, for example, disapproves of people staying silent on the Junge Gemeinde issue, but hears Ingrid's voice in his mind reminding him of why: '– Ja weil sie ins Unglück kommen wenn sie aussprechen: hörte er Ingrids Stimme bekümmert zureden in ihm . . .' (First manuscript of *Ingrid Babendererde*, p. 55).

Johnson knew that he would be risking several years in prison himself if he presented such politically sensitive material for publication (see *Begleitumstände*, p. 74). So although the author stresses that the changes he made were for purely aesthetic reasons, he must also have known that to publish the manuscript in any of its earlier versions would have meant leaving for the West.

It seems, therefore, that Johnson's commitment to the GDR and to socialism, for all its faults in the contemporary manifestation, was great enough for him to censor his own work before even trying to have it published. Ironically, it may be that this very process left the novel between two stools.

For as it turned out, even the amended text was unpublishable for political reasons. The faint encouragement to dissidents which had been provided by Stalin's death was finally dashed by the invasion of Hungary in the autumn of 1956. Wolfgang Harich's arrest and the crackdown on dissident intellectuals in November 1956 put the matter beyond reasonable doubt. Even so, the Aufbau-Verlag did at first consider publishing the novel on condition that further changes were made. Johnson tried to comply, but realised that the kind of changes needed would alter the whole character of the work, and would amount to 'Streichungen in der Wirklichkeit' (*Begleitumstände*, p. 89). That literary quality was not the obstacle is clear from a letter Johnson quotes which he received from the editor of the weekly paper *Sonntag*:[5]

> Ich habe seit vielen Jahren kein Manuskript mit soviel Interesse gelesen, wie das Ihre. . . . Das Buch ist sauber, anständig, geistig klar und kompromisslos in der Lösung des aufgeworfenen Problems. . . . Sie werden jedoch verstehen, das wir im Augenblick keine Möglichkeit haben, Ihr Werk auch nur auszugsweise zu veröffentlichen.
> (*Begleitumstände*, p. 92)

Nevertheless, Johnson, encouraged by the anti-stalinist swing in Soviet policy and the 'Neuer Kurs' in the GDR, approached not only the Aufbau-Verlag (Brecht's publisher in the GDR), but also the Carl Hinstorff-Verlag, the Paul List Verlag, and the Mittel-deutscher Verlag, before finally turning to the Suhrkamp Verlag (Brecht's publisher in the West).

From *Begleitumstände* we know that Peter Suhrkamp was originally in favour of publishing the manuscript (see p. 96). Walter Maria Guggenheimer, who read it first, was likewise enthusiastic, as he recalled in the afterword to Johnson's *Karsch, und andere Prosa* (Frankfurt am Main, 1964). He called Johnson 'Ein Zwanzig-jähriger Klassiker' (*Karsch*, p. 87), having read the manuscript through in a single night. Given such powerful support, one can only concur with Heinz Ludwig Arnold's remark: 'umso verwunderlicher, daß dieser Roman damals nicht erscheinen konnte'.[6] In fact, the only opposition came from Siegfried Unseld, who argued vehe-mently against Guggenheimer's proposal that the manuscript should be accepted. Unseld's decision to publish *Ingrid Baben-dererde* in 1985, a year after Johnson's death, therefore placed him in rather an embarrassing position. Since the publisher's original opposition had, in the meantime, become a matter of public knowledge, he felt compelled to write an afterword to the edition of 1985, in which he tried to explain why he had objected to the book nearly thirty years previously, but felt it worth publishing posthumously. To his credit, Unseld frankly admits that his objections partly stemmed from both personal and political prejudice. He speculates that the enthusiasm of Guggenheimer and Suhrkamp may have predestined him to find fault with the novel, and concedes: 'sicher waren es außerliterarische Kriterien, die mir damals den Zugang zum Text versperrten' (*Ingrid Babendererde*, p. 258). He found the setting and the use of Mecklenburg dialect unfamiliar. He was irritated by the characters' immaturity and naivety. Unseld's political objections included a distaste for the FDJ's central role, with its 'parteiliche Atmosphäre, der ich hoffte, für immer entronnen zu sein' (p. 259).[7] He objected to 'die Voreingenommenheit der jungen Flüchtlinge, die mit ihren 18 Jahren nach West-Berlin übersiedelten, schon wissend, daß "sie umstiegen in jene Lebensweise, die sie ansehen für die falsche"' (p. 259). Finally, he balked at the stylised view of capitalism which seemed to Unseld to be drawn more from *Neues Deutschland* than from reality. Unseld could not have known that the disparaging references to the West were inserted only at the urging of GDR publishers.

Unseld admits in his account that he missed much of the irony in Johnson's treatment of life in the GDR. Of his objection to the FDJ's central role, he says: 'irrtümlicherweise wurde mir diese Darstellung nicht als Kritik des Autors deutlich' (p. 259). It would not be far-fetched to suggest that Unseld missed rather more of Johnson's irony than he was prepared to admit even nearly thirty years later. Part of the reason for that may have been that Johnson diluted the politically controversial material as far as he could without compromising his own beliefs; namely, to the point where it was clearly unacceptable to publishers in the GDR, but not severely critical enough for a Western reader such as Unseld. One might speculate that had Johnson submitted the first, more overly critical and satirical version to Suhrkamp, Unseld might have been better disposed towards it. The early version barely mentions the West, except ironically as 'das schlechte Ausland', and even hints at parallels between Hitler's régime and Ulbricht's GDR, by renaming the SSD the 'Geheime Staatspolizei'. Johnson's self-censorship may thus have left him with a novel which confirmed neither side's image of the other sufficiently to allow publication.

For the novel proposes a very distinct political position; one of anti-stalinist socialism that takes the constitution of the German Democratic Republic at face value.[8] There is no objection to the FDJ per se, for instance; the objection is to that organisation's unconstitutional attack on the Junge Gemeinde. Ingrid and Klaus leave the GDR not because they are disillusioned with socialism but because their consciences cannot allow them to sanction the prevailing breaches of socialist ideals. Ingrid does not voluntarily leave the FDJ; she is ejected. Furthermore, Ingrid has not taken advantage of an opportunity which has always been open to her; she could have gone to live with rich relations in Lübeck. Johnson himself remained in the GDR for as long as possible, and did not resign from the FDJ over the Junge Gemeinde affair. Although the SSD is mocked, in one of the most amusing scenes in Johnson's *oeuvre* (see pp. 210–11), the necessity for such an organisation is accepted, if grudgingly (see p. 107). To sum up, criticism of the GDR is even-handed, mostly consisting of gentle irony which points up the disparity between theory and practice. An FDJ functionary such as Jürgen Petersen is a distinctly positive character who defends GDR socialism thoughtfully, and has a very differentiated view of the Junge Gemeinde affair. Although he cannot see the sense of repressing the religious organisation, Jürgen can see that the state's intentions were good (see p. 91).[9] And many of class 12 A's criticisms are directed specifically against their own head-master: 'ihr einziger Vorwurf für die Demokratische Republik war manchmal doch der dass sie ihnen einen solchen Direktor habe vorsetzen mögen' (p. 163).

At the same time the characters in this novel go to the West only as a last resort. They clearly do not regard the West as a haven of freedom, nor do they consider themselves to be in shackles or under the heel of a communist dictatorship. The 'Magnet-theorie' of the 'Weststaatlösung' simply does not function in the world of *Ingrid Babendererde*. Ingrid, when asked about her visit to rich relatives in Lübeck, replies that 'sie seien schrecklich', and objects to the servile behaviour of their chauffeur (see p. 168). The scene of Klaus and Ingrid leaving Berlin for separate destinations in the Federal Republic is one of insecurity and sadness, stamped by a sense of loss (see pp. 201–2). This is not the spirit in which GDR citizens approached the West, according to contemporary popular opinion. Not only does the novel display a distinct commitment to socialism (perhaps too distinct for Western taste in 1957, the year in which Adenauer's CDU/CSU government gained an absolute majority), but it also displays an unmistakable scepticism with regard to the capitalist West.

Unseld maintains that Peter Suhrkamp rejected his 'politische Bedenken', and that Suhrkamp's reasons for not publishing after all remained his secret (see *Ingrid Babendererde*, p. 259). Yet the fact remains that in Suhrkamp's original communication with Johnson, Suhrkamp, without actually committing himself, had written: 'Es juckt mich, ein Buch daraus zu machen, und zwar sollte das Buch möglichst noch im Herbst herauskommen. Wir haben also gar nicht mehr viel Zeit zu verlieren' (*Begleitumstände*, p. 96). Something must have changed Suhrkamp's mind; it would not be implausible to suggest that Unseld (who repeated his objections as Suhrkamp left Frankfurt to meet Uwe Johnson in West Berlin) may have persuaded him that a Western audience would not take kindly to a novel like *Ingrid Babendererde* in the Federal Republic of early 1957, when Hungary was still fresh in the public mind. This is of course not to impute any notion of official, or even unofficial, censorship in this case. But not even Siegfried Unseld now argues that the non-appearance of *Ingrid Babendererde* was because of literary shortcomings; he could hardly have published it as anything other than a curiosity otherwise.[10] Perhaps Detlef Gojowy came nearest to the truth when he interpreted Unseld's unease as 'eine Berührungsangst vor östlichen Realitäten, die selbst vor allbekannten Sachverhalten und veröffentlichten Dokumenten zurückschreckt'.[11] So, I would suggest, *Ingrid Babendererde* was indeed the victim of a kind of literary Cold War, unwittingly aided by Johnson in his efforts to pitch his criticism at the right level. But it also throws up a further problem; why was *Mutmaßungen über Jakob* accepted by the Suhrkamp Verlag for publication without any hesitation?

There can be no doubt that *Mutmaßungen über Jakob* is a more mature work, and less rooted in small-town Mecklenburg provinciality than *Ingrid Babendererde*. But the novel's complexity, setting and use of dialect (as well as English and Russian) made it more inaccessible to Western readers than (as Unseld had argued) *Ingrid Babendererde* would have been. Commercially, then, *Ingrid Babendererde* might have been a better alternative. Perhaps

Unseld was anxious to atone for what he now perceived to have been a mistake; perhaps he felt that Suhrkamp, who had received the manuscript but died before reading it, would have wanted it published. Some clues to the matter may be found in the way in which Western reviewers approached *Mutmaßungen über Jakob*. Nearly all reviews of the novel were positive. Those which were not objected to the novel's avant-garde complexity. Given the fact that reviewers were confronted with a novel whose narrative structure is so intricate that even critics in the quality papers admitted to being little the wiser after the first reading, it is worth speculating on whether the positive reaction may have been political in origin, and whether such a reaction would have been forthcoming had *Ingrid Babendererde* been published in 1957.

Perhaps the most striking political distinction between *Ingrid Babendererde* and *Mutmaßungen über Jakob* is that the latter may be less easily interpreted as anti-West. One incident in the novel drew criticism of this kind; the occasion when Jakob finds himself fighting with West Germans in a bar. But Johnson was able to counter that this scene is part of Rohlfs's inner monologue; it is the image which comes into the SSD captain's mind as Gesine tells him of Jakob's visit to a bar in the West. The episode is thus evidence of Rohlfs's prejudiced view of life in the Federal Republic; Gesine actually describes Jakob getting on rather well with the people he meets in the bar. Moreover, such references to the West are rare in *Mutmaßungen über Jakob*; as an early reviewer put it: 'Die Wirklichkeit ostdeutschen Lebens ist immer wieder beklemmend nah – der Westen tritt dagegen zurück und bleibt unanschaulich'.[12] The use of the adverb 'beklemmend' to describe the immediacy of life in the GDR is striking. For although John Mander, reviewing the novel in *The Guardian*, was right to point out that the book is not anti-communist[13] (in the same way that *Ingrid Babendererde* is not anti-communist), *Mutmaßungen über Jakob* is much more susceptible of interpretation in that light than *Ingrid Babendererde* is, or would have been in the late 1950s. Although Jakob quite clearly chooses to return to the GDR, rather than remain in the FRG with Gesine, his death upon return was regarded by some as evidence either of some kind of moral retribution, or of retribution on the part of the SSD (though it is difficult to think of any motive for this), or as symbolic of the tragedy of a divided Germany. Two early reviewers, Günter Blöcker and Reinhard Baumgart, both insisted on seeing

Jakob as one who is at home in neither East nor West.[14] This is demonstrably untrue; Jakob's commitment to the GDR is beyond doubt. Yet *Mutmaßungen über Jakob* is so constructed that the characters' motives remain concealed, enabling this kind of comforting interpretation to be placed. Indeed the complex and subtle structure of *Mutmaßungen über Jakob* allowed reviewers considerable interpretative scope, something which would be less easy in the case of *Ingrid Babendererde*. Liberal critics were able to see Jakob as a tragic victim of the East–West divide, a figure transcending Cold War antagonisms. At the same time, the figure of Jonas Blach embodied the voice of reasoned dissent in the mould of the Harich group, while that of Rohlfs exposed the nefarious undercover activities of SSD agents. Unlike Klaus and Ingrid, who are forced into a course of action they would prefer to avoid, Gesine Cresspahl has made a clear and reasoned choice in favour of the West. Indeed, this most positive character in *Mutmaßungen über Jakob*, courted in various ways by Jakob, Blach, and Rohlfs, actually works for NATO.

For reviewers who missed or were prepared to ignore the subtleties of Johnson's first published novel, *Mutmaßungen über Jakob* was a means of airing anti-communist prejudice:

> Das Ganze bietet so das Bild eines Kolonialstils des Lebens und der Kunst. Unter einem fremden, aufgezwungenen Regime, das allmählich durch Gewöhnung angenommen wurde, entwickelt sich eine Freiheit aus zweiter Hand für die Gezähmten, die Unterworfenen, wie auch die Griechen sie unter den Römern besaßen. Da ist immer noch Literatur möglich, wie das Beispiel zeigt, aber doch nur eine von Gnaden des Herrenvolkes.[15]

Even more programmatic judgements may be found in West German provincial papers. One Krefeld lecturer compared the railway system in *Mutmaßungen über Jakob* with the programmed behaviour of people in the GDR. The local paper reports her lecture thus: 'Gleise, Signale, der ganze Betrieb der Eisenbahn, wie ihn der Bahninspektor Jacob [*sic*] sieht, sei gleichnishaft für die Menschen, deren Handeln und Denken auf Gleise gelenkt und signalisiert werde.'[16] In short, they very metatextuality of *Mutmaßungen über Jakob* made it a perfect candidate for publication in the prevailing atmosphere. Adverse public reaction similar to that of Unseld to *Ingrid Babendererde* was much less likely. Reviewers could interpret the novel in accordance with popular Western opinion, whether liberal and left of centre or conservative and right of centre. It is significant that although Johnson wrote *Mutmaßungen über Jakob* in the GDR, he wrote it with a Western audience in mind; the manuscript was not presented to GDR publishers until Johnson was living in West Berlin and *Mutmaßungen über Jakob* was already a success in the FRG. We know that Johnson was prepared to make certain compromises in tailoring *Ingrid Babendererde* for political conditions in the GDR; it may be less than a coincidence that *Mutmaßungen über Jakob* found such widespread approval amongst Western reviewers.

While politics may have played a much more extensive role in the publication histories of the first two novels Johnson wrote than has hitherto been supposed, the author initially kept his distance from explicit political statements. When Arnhelm Neusüss asked him if he was a marxist ('Herr Johnson, man munkelt, Sie seien Marxist'[17]), Johnson was (perhaps wisely) unwilling to allow himself to be politically labelled in this way. In late 1961, however, in the tense atmosphere which followed the building of the Berlin Wall, Johnson found himself caught up in Cold War antagonisms in a way which affected him until the end of his life. On 11 November 1961 the author Hermann Kesten was invited to give a talk entitled 'Die junge deutsche Literatur' at a symposium held in Milan, organised by Giangiacomo Feltrinelli to mark the publication of *Mutmaßungen über Jakob* in Italian. Kesten's remarks encompassed the building of the Wall and the comment that Bertolt Brecht was 'ein Diener der Diktatur'.[18] In reply Johnson contradicted Kesten on the building of the Wall, on Brecht and on other points. On 25 November Kesten published an article in Axel Springer's *Die Welt* which gave his account of the proceedings. The main points of his report are as follows.[19] Johnson, according to Kesten, 'sprach mit Verachtung von Moral. . . . Übrigens sei die Mauer quer durch Berlin (Ulbrichts Mauer) keineswegs unmoralisch (wie ich behauptet hatte!). Sie habe im Gegenteil ihre positiven Seiten. . . . [Die DDR] mußte die Mauer bauen, und das sei gut, vernünftig und sittlich'. With regard to Brecht: 'Kurz, Johnson machte aus Brecht einen hilflosen Feigling, einen amoralischen Erfolgsjäger, zum ergebenen Opfer [*sic*] und Werkzeug eines Ulbricht.' Kesten described Johnson's alleged view of capitalism: 'Darauf verurteilte Johnson den Kapitalismus und die westlichen Länder samt der Bundesrepublik, im Gegensatz zu der sittlichen Deutschen Demokratischen Republik.' He ended his diatribe with the sentence: 'Sind das die Produkte der Erziehung im Diktaturstaat Ulbrichts?' The passionate bitterness of Kesten's feelings towards Johnson are revealed in the attack he made on Johnson's literary worth:

> Indem er ein Potpourri aller Stilexperimente zusammenkocht, von Faulkner und Brecht bis Döblin und Robbe-Grillet und Strittmatter und J. R. Becher, ward er ein hilfloser Supermanierist und bemüht sich mit Erfolg, die deutsche Sprache so weit zu 'verfremden', daß man immer wieder glaubt, eine Rohübersetzung aus dem Kaschubischen zu lesen oder Parteibroschüren aus der DDR.

This is worth quoting in full if only to show the transformation which must have taken place in Kesten once he had unmasked Johnson as a communist; Kesten had, after all, agreed to take part in a celebration of the young author's first novel translated into Italian.

In fact, Kesten had grotesquely misrepresented what Johnson had said in Milan. Johnson was fortunate to be in possession of a tape-recording which documented his actual remarks. Kesten declined an invitation to attend the press conference in Suhrkamp's publishing house on 5 December at which the tape-recording was to be played, noting that 'Es ist bekannt, daß man ein Tonband beliebig manipulieren kann'.[20] Johnson was able to show that Kesten's version was unrecognisable as anything Johnson had said in Milan. He countered all accusations point by point. Just by way of example, these are some of Johnson's actual remarks with reference to the Wall:

> Diese Mauer ist nur ein Ereignis, ein wirkliches Ereignis, das die Menschenrechte verletzt, wie sie in einer westlichen Konvention festgelegt sind, die von dem Ostblock nicht anerkannt wird.... Die ostdeutschen Kommunisten haben, als sie diese Mauer zogen, nicht die Absicht gehabt, unmoralisch zu handeln, sondern sie befanden sich in der Notwehr.

Johnson was shocked by the affair, not only by the vehemence and distortions of Kesten's attack but also by the improper behaviour of the West German press: 'Ich bin außerordentlich enttäuscht, daß es in der Bundesrepublik Presseorgane gibt, die Beihilfe zum Rufmord leisten.' If this remark is to be taken at face value, then one can hardly fail to be surprised at Johnson's naivety. If nothing else, it shows the author's distress at feeling the effects of Cold War rhetoric on his own person.

The matter by no means ended with Johnson's denial of Kesten's charges, for the affair was raised in parliament by Heinrich von

Brentano, former foreign minister and the man who had compared Brecht's later poetry with that of Horst Wessel.[21] Brentano had read Kesten's allegations and demanded that the Villa Massimo stipendium (awarded to Johnson in 1959), should be withdrawn: 'Wir haben die Gewissensfreiheit in Deutschland, das ist selbstverständlich, und Herr Uwe Johnson kann in Deutschland sagen, was er will. Aber er hat keinen Anspruch darauf, von dieser Bundesrepublik als Stipendiat und Sprecher in das Ausland geschickt zu werden.'[22] On being told of the untruth of Kesten's allegations, Brentano refused to back down, merely altering his argument to assert that Johnson had 'eine ganz negative Einstellung zur Bundesrepublik'. The whole affair dragged on for months, making Johnson the target for widespread anti-communist invective. Even in 1962 he became subject to a savage attack from ex-Nazi Kurt Ziesel, who justified Kesten's remarks by saying that Johnson's words had merely been 'in deutliches Deutsch übersetzt', and explained Johnson's positive reception in the FRG as follows:

> Wer sich wie Johnson literarisch auf die Ebene unverständlichen Kunstgewerbes begibt und jede verbindliche Verurteilung des Kommunismus ablehnt, wer die Teilung Deutschlands und die verbrecherische Herrschaft des Bolschewismus zu gepflegten Gegensätzen im Geiste 'sublimiert' und moralische Überlegungen dann ausklammert, wenn es die prokommunistischen Neigungen unseres literarischen Clans stört, vor dem liegt die gesamte bundesdeutsche Intelligentia enschließlich der ihr hörigen politischen Prominenz bewundernd auf den Knien.[23]

It would be wrong to imagine that passages such as this were too extreme to have any effect. The popular conception of Johnson as a 'getarnter Kommunist' (as Wolfdietrich Schnurre called him)[24] led to demands for his books to be boycotted (which indeed they were, by many booksellers), and to efforts to have his readings stopped at provincial halls round the country. Indeed, the organisers of one such reading from *Das dritte Buch über Achim* were compelled to publish a comprehensive rebuttal of Ziesel's allegations in the local paper in order to justify not cancelling the occasion. In their rebuttal they also felt it necessary to distance themselves from Johnson's signing of the 'Gruppe 47' manifesto, which action they termed 'politisch unklug'.[25] By 1962, then, public perception of Johnson in some circles had transformed him from champion of freedom to traitorous communist.

There are a number of ironies associated with the Kesten affair. It is ironic that Ziesel, a writer who had published widely in the

Third Reich and had been a member of the NSDAP, found common cause with Hermann Kesten, a Jew forced into exile in 1933. The two men (naturally enough) held opposing views on how authors who had published in Germany between 1933 and 1945 should be treated. Yet the Johnson issue placed them in the same camp. Ironically again, Johnson's original disagreement with Kesten in Milan had been (in part) over the latter's assertion that 13 August 1961 marked a caesura in German literature. Johnson found out to his cost that the closing of the border had indeed proved a watershed, as public attitudes towards him changed in the wake of the row with Kesten. Although events proved Kesten right on that point, one cannot help feeling that his was a self-fulfilling prophecy, since it was in part the activities of vehement anti-communists such as Kesten himself which helped polarise public opinion of the West German literary scene.

Johnson was genuinely surprised and shocked by the treatment he received as Cold War cultural antagonisms flared up into the journalistic equivalent of a hot war, and he himself became the favourite scapegoat of right-wingers such as Ziesel. The devastating effects which the Kesten–Brentano affair had on Johnson are both documented and evidenced by the long section devoted to the matter in *Begleitumstände*, which retraces the events in enormous detail (see pp. 206–41). The author's sense of bitterness and injury had not abated by 1979 when he resigned from the Deutsche Akademie der Sprache und Dichtung (Darmstadt), that institution having refused to withdraw what Johnson regarded as misleading references to the Kesten affair (see *Begleitumstände*, pp. 237–8). Perhaps the most telling evidence of Johnson's feeling of persecution appears in the epithet the writer applies to his attacker in *Begleitumstände*: 'Senator McKesten' (*Begleitumstände*, p. 231).

Johnson thus found that official and public perception of him mutated in a bewildering fashion between the years 1956 and 1961. Regarded as a barely tolerable dissident in the GDR (he found himself without a job, having to rely on friends for help), he was viewed with a mixture of friendliness and suspicion on attempting to have his first novel published in the FRG. The suspicion abated somewhat after the appearance of *Mutmaßungen über Jakob*, partly because the novel was frequently viewed as a condemnation of the GDR.[26] At this point he found himself patronised as a product of communism who had seen the light; an early reviewer had this encouragement for the newly-arrived Johnson: 'Aber die epische

Begabung ist groß. Sie wird sich entfalten, wenn der junge Autor, jetzt in Berlin lebend, den Trunk der Freiheit in sich verarbeitet hat.'[27] The draught of freedom became a bitter one for Johnson, who by 1961 realised to what extent his literary activity had made him into a political pawn, despite strenuous efforts to avoid precisely that fate.[28] Perhaps it was naive of Johnson to expect not to become embroiled in the prejudices which surrounded the two Germanies at that time. His reaction was to withdraw from public life as far as possible, eventually seeking sanctuary in England. Uwe Johnson possessed an extraordinary capacity to preserve his literary equanimity and political convictions; the same plea for democratic socialism evident in *Ingrid Babendererde* can still easily be detected in *Jahrestage 4*, written thirty years later. But neither of the two Germanies between 1956 and 1961 was the right place to make that plea; Johnson paid the price.

Notes

1 In *Begleitumstände* Johnson says that he had originally intended to remain in the GDR and publish *Mutmaßungen über Jakob* under an assumed name until it was pointed out to him the the SSD would not take long to uncover his deception (see p. 152).

2 Although a thoroughgoing comparison of the various manuscripts would reveal much about Johnson's early development as a writer, such a study would breach the confines of the present essay. I intend to focus on those points which reveal that political considerations may have dictated changes.

3 This 'Märchen' may have been replaced by Klaus Niebuhr's 'Ins Unreine' (pp. 178–80), which is more subtle and less overtly critical.

4 A variation on this incident was to be described at length in Johnson's *Jahrestage 4* (see pp. 1713–21).

5 It seems that the manuscript was passed to the paper by Wolfgang Harich, who was chief reader at the Aufbau-Verlag, and also wrote for *Sonntag* (see *Begleitumstände*, p. 90).

6 Heinz Ludwig Arnold, in the *Süddeutscher Rundfunk*, 19 June 1985.

7 Unseld does not mention the criticism which Johnson must himself have found objectionable; that the descriptions of nature in *Ingrid Babendererde* are reminiscent of 'Blut und Boden' literature (see *Begleitumstände*, p. 97).

8 This is a political stance which Johnson held, with minor adjustments, from the early 1950s onwards, and is one which Gesine Cresspahl holds. It is a definable position of democratic socialism, and certainly not 'neither left nor right', as Kurt Fickert proposes in a study published in 1987 (*Neither Left nor Right: the Politics of Individualism in Uwe Johnson's Work*, New York, 1987).

9 This passage from *Ingrid Babendererde*, p. 91, was unchanged from the previous version, representing as it does a redressing of the political balance in favour of government policy (compare *Begleitumstände*, pp. 82–3).

10 Although reviewers were divided over the novel's quality in 1985, there were few who felt that its literary shortcomings were such to disqualify it from publication.

11 Detlef Gojowy, '*Uwe Johnson*: Ingrid Babendererde. Reifeprüfung 1953', *osteuropa-archiv*, May 1987, pp. 407–8 (p. 408).

12 Theodor Wieser, ' "Mutmaßungen über Jakob": Roman von Uwe Johnson', *Neue Züricher Zeitung*, 9 December 1959, p. 6.

13 John Mander, 'A view through the Gate', *The Guardian*, 25 May 1960, p. 4.

14 Both the reviews in question have been reprinted as Günter Blöcker, 'Roman der beiden Deutschland', and Reinhard Baumgart, 'Hoffnungsvoll und hoffnungslos: utopisch', in *Über Uwe Johnson*, edited by Reinhard Baumgart, Frankfurt am Main, 1970, pp. 10–13 and pp. 15–20.

15 Wolfgang Grözinger, 'Zeichen an der Wand', *Hochland*, 52, December 1959, pp. 177–9, quoted in *Über Uwe Johnson*, p. 14.

16 'Der Bahnbetrieb ist ein Gleichnis', *Westdeutsche Zeitung*, 21 February 1962. Comparisons between the private car as representative of individual freedom and railways as a means of collective marshalling were not uncommon; see Jürgen Link and Siegfried Reinecke, ' "Autofahren ist wie das Leben": Metamorphosen des Autosymbols in der deutschen Literatur', in *Technik der Literatur*, edited by Harro Segeberg, Frankfurt am Main, 1987, pp. 436–82 (especially pp. 445–6).

17 Arnhelm Neusüss, 'Uber die Schwierigkeiten beim Schreiben der Wahrheit: Gespräch mit Uwe Johnson', *Konkret*, 1, 1962, pp. 18–19 (p. 18).

18 Kesten's remarks on Brecht were relayed by (amongst others), Giangiacomo Feltrinelli, 'Kesten wurde ausgepfiffen', *Abendzeitung (München)*, 1 December 1961, p. 9.

19 All quotations from Kesten's article refer to 'Mutmaßungen über Johnson: Höchst Seltsames über die Berliner Mauer', *Die Welt*, 25 November 1961, p. 1. (This article first appeared in a local paper; *Abendzeitung (München)*, 21 November 1961, p. 7.)

20 This and subsequent quotations from the press conference are drawn from ' "Mir ist gelegen an Fairneß . . ." Erklärung von Uwe Johnson auf der Pressekonferenz des Suhrkamp-Verlages am 5. Dezember 1961', *Deutsche Zeitung und Wirtschaftszeitung*, 7 December 1961, p. 14.

21 Johnson had referred to this in his novel *Das dritte Buch über Achim*, which had just appeared: '– Das ist ja klar: sagte Achim: Daß eure nicht schreiben wie der . . . , der zum Gesicht des Staates vor der Welt einen Irgend bestellte, der nämlich den Bertolt Brecht verglichen hat mit einem Zuhälter und Schläger?' (*Das dritte Buch über Achim*, Frankfurt am Main, 1973 (first published 1961), pp. 279–80).

22 This and the subsequent quotation from Brentano appear in Walter Busse, 'Haltet aus!', *Der Spiegel*, 20 December 1961, p. 22.

23 Kurt Ziesel, *Die Literaturfabrik: eine polemische Auseinandersetzung mit dem Literaturbetrieb im Deutschland von heute*, Vienna and Cologne, 1962, p. 48 and pp. 50–1.

24 According to a report by Ingrid Seidenfaden, *Deutsche Zeitung*, 3–4 February 1962, Schnurre's actual words at a lecture in Munich were: 'Ich nenne Uwe Johnson inhuman und einen schlecht getarnten Kommunisten.'

25 Josef Nordlohne, 'Nochmals: "Uwe Johnson in Vechta"', *Oldenburgische Volkszeitung*, 27 November 1962, p. 4.

26 This is not to say that all reservations were abandoned; as Helmut Jaesrich put it: 'man kann es den Leuten nicht übelnehmen, wenn sie ihn [Johnson] sogar ein klein wenig suspekt finden' ('Quer über die Gleise', *Der Monat*, December 1959, pp. 71–4, quoted in *Über Uwe Johnson*, p. 9).

27 Hansludwig Geiger, 'Zwischen den Fronten', *Evangelischer Literaturbeobachter*, 36, 1959, p. 714.

28 Johnson always refused, for example, to term his change of residence from East to West 'Flucht', preferring the politically neutral term 'Umzug'.

'Und wenn man sich überlegt, daß damals sogar Leute wie Adorno daran teilgenommen haben . . .': Alfred Andersch and the Cold War

Rhys W. Williams

In a particularly informative interview with Hans Magnus Enzensberger, broadcast in October 1974,[1] Alfred Andersch was quick
to leap to the defence of his literary generation. He insists that,
while the Cold War was at its coldest in the early years of the
Adenauer period and while institutions like the Kongreß für die
Freiheit der Kultur were established, with CIA backing, to win the
propaganda war against communism, the younger generation of
post-war writers, of which Andersch saw himself as representative, opposed the restoration politics of the CDU government. From
his tone it seems clear that Andersch, who was an admirer of
Theodor Adorno in that period, became aware only later of the
way in which, wittingly or unwittingly, writers and intellectuals
had been drawn into the cultural politics of the Cold War. The
context of his remarks is significant: he is concerned to defend the
writers of the early 1950s against the charge of a younger, and
more radical, generation that they sought refuge in literature and
were unequal to the task of opposing the direction which the new
Federal Republic was taking. For Andersch, the generation of 1968
is mistaken: 'die Schriftsteller . . . haben dieses justemilieu [*sic*] der
deutschen Restauration gestört, den "Kalten Krieg" haben die
damals jüngeren deutschen Schriftsteller auch nicht mitgemacht'.[2]
Enzensberger's scepticism is directed as much against the methods of writers of the 1950s as against the fact of their opposition,
but his remarks pose a particular set of problems for Andersch
criticism. Did Andersch in fact oppose the restoration politics of
the Adenauer period, and if so, how effectively? Was this opposition reflected in his essays, his publishing and editorial activities
and his work in broadcasting? Can his claim to have been free

from involvement in the Cold War be sustained? Is it possible to discern Cold War attitudes in his creative writing?

When Andersch returned to Germany in 1945 on his release from an American prisoner-of-war camp, he had impeccable political credentials. Before 1933 he had been Communist Youth Organiser for Southern Bavaria and had taken his first tentative steps in political journalism in the columns of *Die Neue Zeitung*, the organ of the RGO, the Revolutionäre Gewerkschaftsopposition, a communist splinter group of the Allgemeine Gewerkschaftsbund. In his autobiographical fragment 'Der Seesack' (1977) Andersch refers to a report which he wrote on a textile workers' strike in Augsburg.[3] The strike began on 3 June 1931 and was defeated by 9 June. Although none of the articles in the newspaper is signed, the article which appeared on 6 June 1931 entitled 'Genug des Hungerns – ein Ende dem Lohnraub' bears some of the hallmarks of Andersch's later style.[4] Interestingly, the issues of *Die Neue Zeitung* which deal with the textile workers' strike also contain the serialisation of Willi Bredel's novel *Maschinenfabrik N & K*. If this was the company which Andersch kept in 1931 (when he was only seventeen), it can perhaps be explained by his family background. The polarisation of political life which marked the end of the Weimar Republic was mirrored in a striking way within the Andersch household. His father, Alfred Andersch senior, had been a founding member of the Thule-Gesellschaft, an extreme right-wing, anti-Semitic group in Munich, founded in early 1918 by Baron Rudolf von Sebottendorf. The Thule-Gesellschaft encouraged the foundation of the Deutsche Arbeiterpartei (DAP) in 1919, under the leadership of Anton Drexler. Adolf Hitler was member 555 of that party, and embarked, through its connections, on his political career. We learn, from *Die Kirschen der Freiheit*, that Andersch's father took part in the Hitler putsch of November 1923. Andersch's direct involvement with the Communist Party lasted a relatively short time. After Hitler's seizure of power and the burning of the Reichstag, Andersch, like most communist functionaries, was arrested and sent to Dachau. He emerged after six weeks, thanks to his mother's effective intervention on his behalf; she secured his release by pointing to the not insignificant contribution which Andersch's late father had made to the rise of National Socialism. Andersch himself was briefly re-arrested in the autumn of 1933, and reacted, perhaps not unnaturally, in view of the threat of a return to Dachau, by breaking with his Communist Party affiliations.

On his own admission, he abandoned the realm of politics for that of art and literature. Whether, as some biographers insist, Andersch was under Gestapo surveillance until 1944 is doubtful. His release in 1933 was probably conditional both upon good behaviour and upon the promise to provide information on his communist acquaintances. It is this likelihood which lends poignancy to Andersch's return, in his post-war writing, to the theme of betrayal under threat.

Certainly, Andersch retreated from politics in the years after 1933, and began a literary career. Inspired by a visit to Italy, he wrote several poems in neo-Romantic vein, which he submitted to the criticism of his literary mentor, the writer Günther Herzfeld-Wüsthoff. In 1937 he married and moved to Hamburg, where he began work on a series of prose sketches. The earliest is dated 18 November 1939, the latest 30 August 1943. Evoking the landscape and moods of the North Sea coast, these 'Stimmungsbilder' have a static and painterly quality. In February 1942 he submitted a longer prose piece, *Skizze zu einem jungen Mann*, to the literary section of the *Frankfurter Zeitung*, just about the time when he was released from military service after the invasion of France and after he had served as part of the occupying force. Early in 1943, Andersch applied for membership of the Reichsschrifttumskammer and was able, in his questionnaire, to deny his membership of the Communist Party, even before 1933. Clearly, after a decade of enforced accommodation to National Socialism, Andersch had long been considered of no threat to the régime. In October 1943 Andersch was called up once more, and by April 1944 he was in Denmark; it was here that he received a letter from the Suhrkamp Verlag, declining his projected volume *Erinnerte Gestalten*. One of the three stories in that volume was, however, published in April 1944 in the *Kölnische Zeitung*. Although after the war, for understandable reasons, Andersch was to be silent about his literary activities before 1945, he had published both in the communist press before 1933 and under National Socialism. He was, if only just, a writer of 'innere Emigration'.

Andersch's experiences as a POW in the United States were to have a decisive influence on his later position. After a period in Fort Ruston in Louisiana, Andersch was transferred, in April 1945, to Fort Kearney, Rhode Island, where he joined the editorial team of *Der Ruf*, a fortnightly periodical which, from 1 March 1945, was distributed to all other POW camps in the United States. Andersch contributed regularly to the periodical from April until August, when he left the editorial team to attend the re-education courses in nearby Fort Getty.[5] The articles which Andersch contributed fall into three categories. First, his attempts at creative writing: 'Abschied von Rom' was part of a bigger project on which he had been working since his arrival in the USA, a work which has since been published as 'Amerikaner – Erster Eindruck' (1982). This short piece, together with 'Fräulein Christine', 'Frühlingslandschaften' and 'Tagebuchblatt aus der Eifel', reflects the profoundly auto-biographical concerns of Andersch's subsequent writing, but also echoes his early literary efforts under National Socialism, with evocative landscapes from which human concerns are banished. A second group are reviews and reports dealing with American literature and music, in keeping with one of the primary functions of the periodical, namely to inform its readers about American values. A third group is of more direct relevance here: Andersch addresses the question of future political and cultural life in Germany, advocating 'Selbsterziehung zur Mässigung, kritischem Denken [sic], sorgfältiger Überlegung'.[6] Speaking for a 'young generation', which he identifies firmly with those who have experienced the War and faced death, Andersch eschews a narrowly political message: 'Denn nicht darauf kommt es an, dass die Jugend nun irgend ein gewerkschaftliches, parteipolitisches oder konfessionelles Programm annimmt, sondern dass all ihre Begeisterung dem Dienst am Menschen, seiner Freiheit und Würde gilt'.[7] Here we may observe at a very early stage the rejection of ideology, the suspicion of party politics, which was a legacy of National Socialism and which, in the years after 1945, characterised the political stance of the Munich *Ruf*. In August 1945, Andersch was accepted for the re-education courses held at Fort Getty; the selection criteria were strict: of the first 18,000 POWs whose applications were vetted, only 816 were deemed acceptable.[8] In 1947 Andersch was to recall his experiences of 'Umerziehung in der Retorte' with nostalgia: for a man whose formal education had ceased at fifteen, Andersch was clearly enthusiastic about his contacts with American academics: Professor Howard Mumford Jones of Harvard lectured on American literature, Professor Henry Ehrmann (New York) and Professor Arnold Wolfers (Yale) on history, and Professor Thomas Vernor Smith (Chicago) on politics. The presupposition was that the group of German prisoners would form an élite and would be responsible for helping to shape the future of Germany on their early return. The values which Andersch acquired, the principles of liberalism, national self-determination and freedom of expression, were part of the baggage which he brought back with him to Germany in the autumn of 1945.

'Getty oder die Umerziehung in der Retorte' is a valuable essay because it conveys at once both Andersch's idealistic Americanism and his disillusionment with the realities of the American administration in Germany. By 1947, he can argue that the élite of Fort Getty 'gehören nun zum Vortrupp des Volksteils, welcher der gespenstischen Restauration dieses Zerrbilds einer Demokratie mit immer stärkerer Ablehnung zusieht'.[9] Having joined the staff of *Die Neue Zeitung*, Andersch wrote also for *Rat und Tat*, a paper for German POWs which was produced, from November 1945, as a Sunday edition of *Die Neue Zeitung*. In an essay entitled 'Die Menschen denken verschieden' in January 1946, Andersch reports on an imaginary conversation between two German prisoners and adds:

> wenn man bedenkt, daß in Deutschland gar keine Demokratie besteht ..., sondern eine Militärdiktatur. Allerdings eine Militärdiktatur mit 'Naturgesetzen'. Mit dem Gesetz der Meinungsfreiheit zum Beispiel. Und mit dem anderen Gesetz, daß sie einmal von einem freien demokratischen Deutschland abgelöst werden will'.[10]

Here we find the certain assurance that Germany will one day be a free and democratic country, much tempered by the realisation that for now Germany is, in however benevolent a form, a military dictatorship. Yet Andersch's attitude revealed no particular anti-Soviet bias: in April, writing under the name Hellmuth Andersch, he could survey the publishing enterprises of all four zones and single out the Aufbau-Verlag in the Soviet zone as 'am aktivsten im Kampf gegen das Erbe des Nationalsozialismus'.[11] With the foundation of the German version of *Der Ruf*, which first appeared on 15 August 1946, Andersch was able to develop his ideas on the future of Germany. His inaugural editorial, characteristically entitled 'Das junge Europa formt sein Gesicht' propounds a synthesis of socialism and humanism and echoes his views from the earlier American article in his definition of humanism as 'die Anerkennung der Würde und Freiheit des Menschen'.[12] For all his enthusiasm for socialism, Andersch insists that the younger generation in Europe would be prepared to abandon the socialist camp if it perceived socialism as jeopardising human freedom in favour of orthodox marxist determinism. Produced under American licence, *Der Ruf* is sympathetic to the ideals of American liberalism, but insists on the German right to self-determination, a claim which was, sooner rather than later, to bring the editors into conflict with an increasingly anti-communist American line. By 15 September 1946, Andersch can assert once more that Germany is not yet a democracy and that, if the Americans are to remain true in practice to their democratic ideals, the 'Freiheit und Gleichberechtigung Deutschlands'[13] must be instituted. In another column of the same issue, Andersch can attack the decision of the censor to ban Chaplin's *The Great Dictator* for German audiences: 'die Tragikomödie der 're-education' geht also weiter'.[14] In November 1946 Andersch's editorial refers to the provisional character of the situation in Germany and highlights 'die Sehnsucht der Deutschen nach der Vereinigung'.[15] Through re-unification, he argues, Germany would become a neutral zone, outside the East–West conflict, a country in which a new synthesis might be attempted between the values of East and West. Too close a dependence on the occupying powers in either East or West will produce, he warns, the inevitable division of Germany. Lest his argument appear too critical of American strategy, Andersch tempers his arguments with a report, within the same edition of the periodical, of a conference of European intellectuals, held in Geneva. He concludes his account by attacking the decision of Ilya Ehrenburg not to appear, and criticising Lukács's contribution for subordinating the individual to the collective.[16] In December 1946 the editorial again warns that German nationalism is being fuelled by the failure of the occupying powers to find a solution to the German Question.[17] By 15 March 1946 in a long article entitled 'Die sozialistische Situation', Andersch, beneath a provocative epigraph from Marx, reports on socialism in Western Europe: the new socialist ideal of Western Europe involves a repudiation of totalitarian structures, an emphasis on individual freedom. The present situation in the Soviet Union is 'das stärkste Hindernis für eine sozialistische Entwicklung Europas'.[18] But despite these negative comments on the Soviet Union, Andersch's unambiguous commitment to socialism in Western Europe was bound, in a climate of international tension, to arouse American suspicions. It is not difficult to see why the removal of Andersch and Hans Werner Richter as editors of *Der Ruf* in April 1947 should have been the price demanded by the Americans for the continuance of the licence. Lest it be thought that Andersch singled out the Americans for criticism, it should be noted that he was equally opposed to developments in both the French and British zones. His travel report 'Wintersende in einer frierenden Stadt' castigates the British military government for its failure to implement the nationalisation of key industries, despite the support of the majority SPD in Hamburg.[19]

After leaving the editorship of *Der Ruf*, Andersch did not, as has been frequently asserted, abandon his commitment to political journalism and join his fellow authors in the abortive periodical *Der Skorpion*.[20] He undoubtedly felt the tension between his literary and journalistic activities, but he continued to write for a variety of periodicals, notably *Frankfurter Hefte*, *Ende und Anfang*, *Horizont*, *Volk und Zeit* and *Neues Europa*. His three contributions under the title 'Linkes Tagebuch' in *Neues Europa* reveal his changing political attitudes. The currency reform has made the existence of the huge variety of periodicals problematic, and Andersch confesses 'abgrundtiefe Skepsis gegenüber der Wirksamkeit von Leitartikeln, Analysen',[21] but is still willing to reflect, in imaginary dialogues, on the political scene. With one of his interlocutors he agrees 'daß die SED als mögliche Heimat ausschied',[22] even though he is disillusioned with the SPD. Nor does Adenauer's policy fill him with enthusiasm, even if he is prepared to concede that the 'Weststaat-Idee' is perfectly feasible. The second of Andersch's contributions focuses on Berlin: 'Im Berliner Ostsektor ein Omnibus, verkleidet mit einem Transparent, auf dem zu lesen stand: "Hinaus mit den Amerikanern aus Berlin, diesen Kriegsbrandstiftern und Spaltern der deutschen Einheit!". Als ich das sah, wurde mir speiübel.'[23] This observation is a prelude to an attack on the SED and an appeal to readers to support the people of West Berlin against the blockade. The third article contains an imaginary conversation between Andersch and an academic who has been offered a chair at a university in the Soviet zone. While the Soviet zone has everything that socialists in the West are fighting for (educational reforms, agricultural reforms, nationalisation of key industries), the academic is unwilling to accept the political system in the Soviet zone, with its party functionaries and its repressive measures. These three articles offer a revealing picture of Andersch's political views in 1948. Andersch rejects 'den sturen Schumacher-Kurs',[24] the refusal of the SPD in the Western zones to negotiate directly with the SED, but he is clearly appalled by the political realities of the Soviet zone, vehemently opposed to the SED, and critical of the Western powers for resisting nationalisation plans in the Western zones. The term 'heimatlose Linke', symptomatically, echoes throughout all three articles. By 1948 Andersch has rejected the communism of his youth (exemplified for him now by the SED); he attacks the restoration politics of the CDU, with its attendant dangers of supplying a new respectability for National Socialists, and he has become disillusioned with the values of the Americans, having seen the 'New Deal' politics of Roosevelt give way to a Truman doctrine of containment. He retreats into a purely intellectual commitment to vaguely left-wing views, finding its expression, characteristically, in the perspective of the diarist, the outsider.

The close connection between politics and literature emerges in Andersch's fascinating essay *Deutsche Literatur in der Entscheidung*, which was read to the second meeting of the 'Gruppe 47' and remains one of the few theoretical texts which the group, with its dislike of ideology, ever countenanced. Indeed, Andersch's later disillusionment with the 'Gruppe 47' may be explained, to some extent, by its eclecticism and reluctance to adopt a clear programmatic line. Andersch's essay is remarkable for three reasons: first, it is a brave statement from someone whose literary and intellectual status were by no means firmly established; secondly, it is a document which translates into literary judgements precisely the political dilemma which Andersch was voicing elsewhere; and thirdly, it provides a framework for the rehabilitation of much of the writing of the Third Reich, for the acceptance of some of the writing of exile, and for the assimilation of both these traditions into a new style of post-war writing. In short, Andersch provides here the justification for a specifically West German literary tradition, one which he was to foster with extraordinary success in his editorial and broadcasting activities over the next decade. Both the 'Gruppe 47' and Andersch's various editorial and broadcasting ventures helped to define West German literature; their activities were not congruent, but they clearly overlapped.

Andersch purports to offer in his essay an analysis of the literary situation in 1948. If something rather different emerges, it is as much because of what Andersch leaves out as because of what he includes. He opens his essay by insisting that he, as a 'Publizist', is more interested in contemporary trends than an academic critic would be, more concerned with sociological and political factors than is currently fashionable. This method is, he concedes, dangerous, particularly in view of 'die tiefe Verwandlungsfähigkeit des Menschen im Allgemeinen, des künstlerischen Menschen im Besonderen'.[25] The possibilities of casting off a past life of 'mauvaise foi', of undergoing a Sartrean conversion, or exercising a new Sartrean choice, form a framework for the whole essay, as its title illustrates. It is not difficult to perceive the attractions of such a view for German writers of Andersch's generation in 1948. If the compromises of literary life under National Socialism may be defined as 'mauvaise foi', then they may be cast off by making a new existential choice. Considering what we now know of the extent of Andersch's literary activities in the Third Reich, activities of which few would have been aware in 1948, Andersch's essay acquires new autobiographical urgency. Given his own position, it is particularly poignant that he should assert: 'Jede Untersuchung des Zustandes der deutschen Literatur, ... muß daher von einer sorgfältigen Betrachtung des wahren Verhaltens des deutschen Geistes in den Jahren der Diktatur ausgehen' (*AAL*, p. 113).

Although he is aware that the term 'innere Emigration' covers a multitude of different reactions to the régime, Andersch agrees not merely to use the term, he also raises it to a central position, typifying all the literature which was produced within Germany after 1933. His argument is curious: since all explicitly Nazi writing is not worthy of the name literature, it may be conveniently forgotten. It follows that all literature produced in Nazi Germany was written in opposition to the régime. 'Eine Zeugung des Dichterischen aus dem Geist des Nationalsozialismus gab es nicht' (*AAL*, p. 114). The sleight of hand enables Andersch to argue that any analysis of literature produced in Germany between 1933 and 1945 is an analysis of the literature of 'innere Emigration'. Some rather dubious figures may thus be saved: Hans Grimm, Erwin Guido Kolbenheyer, Wilhelm Schäfer, Emil Strauß. These figures, for Andersch, displayed 'eine Art subjektiver Ehrlichkeit' (*AAL*, p. 116) and could thus be regarded as opponents of the régime. In order to illustrate the tragedy of this group, Andersch helps his argument along by devoting some attention to the least problematic figure, Ernst Wiechert. A second, older, generation is described as belonging to a tradition of 'bürgerliche Klassik': Gerhart Hauptmann, R. A. Schröder, Hans Carossa, Ricarda Huch, Gertrud von Le Fort. Apart from Carossa, who attempted 'aus sehr noblen Gründen' (*AAL*, p. 117) to compromise, all the others are described as opponents of the régime, driven by their humanistic values into isolation. A third and final group of writers who remained within Germany are subsumed under the category 'Widerstand und Kalligraphie', a group containing figures like Stefan Andres, Horst Lange, Hans Leip, Martin Raschke and Eugen Gottlob Winkler. This group maintained their independence from the Reichsschrifttums-kammer through the form of their work. Andersch concludes his section on those who remained with a study of Ernst Jünger, whose 'conversion' is adduced as proof that genuine artistic achievement was identical with opposition to National Socialism. Andersch's admiration for Jünger is based on a reading of Jünger's symbolic style as the only effective weapon against totalitarian control.

Turning to the literature of opposition, Andersch begins by insisting that resistance was infinitely more difficult in Germany than France, not least because nationalism preserved French writers from collaboration with the Nazis but encouraged German opponents of Hitler to mute their criticism. One cannot help feeling that Andersch is indulging in quite understandable self-exoneration, both for himself and his generation. His attitude to the literature of exile is ambivalent: he admires those who went into exile, but insists that they can influence the future literature of Germany only if they return. Here Andersch enters a debate in which the central issue was the question of Thomas Mann's return to Germany, an issue which, incidentally, dominated the question of writing in exile at the Berlin Writers' Conference in October 1947. For Andersch, whose admiration for Mann is attested not only by his imitation of Mann's work during the 1930s but also by his sympathetic essays in the post-war period, Mann's work represents 'die Zugehörigkeit Deutschlands zur atlantischen Kultur' (*AAL*, p. 124) which he defines, significantly, as openness, willingness to change, commitment to humanitarian values. When he turns to 'realistische Tendenzkunst', the writing of those who bitterly opposed National Socialism, like Heinrich Mann, Werfel, Arnold Zweig and Döblin, Andersch is critical. These writers forfeit his approbation in that their realism is tainted by didacticism, by 'propagandistische Vorzeichen' (*AAL*, p. 125). Similarly, a group entitled 'Satiriker' (Tucholsky, Polgar, Ossietzky, Walter Mehring, Kästner) are too much satirists, for him, and not sufficiently true artists. Nor is he convinced by 'die proletarischen Schriftsteller' (Oskar Maria Graf, Willi Bredel, Anna Seghers, Theodor Plivier).

What inhibits their work, for him, is 'ihre allzustarke Binding an eine erklärende Dogmatik der gesellschaftlichen Vorgänge, ihr Glaube an eine wissenschaftliche Methodik' (*AAL*, p. 127). If Ernst Jünger encapsulated the writers of 'innere Emigration', it is Brecht who embodies the strengths (and weaknesses) of the writers of opposition. For Andersch, Brecht's anti-German sentiments, however understandable, diminish his achievement, and Brecht's return to Germany will alone convince Andersch of his value to the new generation of German writers.

Considering, in a final section, the future of German literature, Andersch singles out some new trends: Langgässer's *Das unauslöschliche Siegel*, the work of Schnurre, Kolbenhoff, Borchert, Weyrauch and Eich. Foreign influences are commended: Henry Miller, Camus, Silone and Koestler. Andersch commends two figures here (Koestler and Silone) whose much publicised repudiation of communism made them significant figures in the history of the Cold War in Europe. The essay closes with some bitter comments on the 'colonial' status of German literature under occupation: the role of the left-wing intellectual in Germany is, Andersch contends, doubly difficult: he must defend democracy both against those who give democracy a bad name by their current imposition of undemocratic practices in Germany, and against those who become so disillusioned by the contrast between democratic theory and practice that they revert to their old fascist ways. Andersch's ideal is a 'Synthese von Freiheit und sozialer Gerechtigkeit', a programme which is, in a context of the incipient Cold War, bound to bring him into conflict with both Americans and the Soviet Union. Andersch's 'war on two fronts' involves self-criticism, a fearless examination of the values implicit in one's own position. In a footnote he praises the resolution taken at the First German Writers' Conference, held in Berlin in October 1947, calling on German intellectuals to distance themselves from the propaganda campaigns of both East and West. It is the examination of the past and present which, Andersch believes, will enable German intellectuals to cast off the errors of the past in an act of existential choice.

Andersch's *Deutsche Literatur in der Entscheidung* aroused controversy in literary circles. When the last section of the essay was reproduced in the periodical *Horizont*, the editor, Günther Birkenfeld, drew a clear contrast between Andersch's views and those of Alfred Döblin, whose pamphlet *Die literarische Situation* (1947) had presaged a Catholic renewal in German literature, 'eine neue Epoche der Metaphysik'. Birkenfeld reproduced Andersch's final section and offered a reply: 'An die "temporären" Nihilisten'.[26] Nihilism, it will be remembered, was the charge which had been levelled against Andersch and Hans Werner Richter in *Der Ruf* and in the ill-fated *Skorpion* enterprise. Birkenfeld sympathises with Andersch as a representative of a 'Heimkehrer' generation, but dismisses the charge that Germany is languishing under colonial conditions. Birkenfeld, who was to become a major figure in the Cold War in Berlin, irritates Andersch by his use of the term 'nihilistic' to describe the literature of the 'young generation', as whose spokesman Andersch sees himself. In a tetchy reply Andersch defends the literature of realism, which is 'die Grundlinie, der rote Faden, der mein Pamphlet durchzieht'.[27] He also had to contend with opposition from the Soviet zone: Johannes R. Becher wrote to him on 5 May 1948 to protest that Andersch had located his literary antecedents in the expressionist period and had neglected the decisive influence on him of his period in emigration. Becher defends his changing style by arguing that the accessibility of his work to those who do not customarily read poetry is a major determinant of his new approach. Perhaps these two responses may serve to illustrate how Andersch's views had placed him in a curious no man's land between the ideological fronts that were being drawn up in 1947. Certainly, his pamphlet, when it was first read to the 'Gruppe 47' at its second meeting in Ulm, was well received by the authors present, who regarded it as a statement representative of their position. Why that should have been is interesting: Andersch has managed in his essay to rehabilitate nearly all the writing which went on in Germany in the Third Reich, to blur the distinction between those writers of an older generation who continued to write in Germany and a younger generation whose voice was first heard after 1945, to define this new possibility as anti-communist, or at least anti-stalinist, yet as a possibility equally opposed to American control, and to argue for a realism which is ill-defined enough to permit a plurality of styles. With his subsequent radio and editorial activities Andersch was to continue to pursue these ends and in so doing to make a major contribution to the establishment of a specifically West German literature.

The Cold War was merely beginning when Andersch first developed his ideas on the future of German literature in 1947. Although he then took up a position between the fronts, as it were, he was also to qualify his views with the intensification of East–West tension. He is, to his credit, aware of the problem: he cannot criticise communism without appearing to side with the Cold Warriors, but cannot, by the same token, praise communism without appearing to be a fellow-traveller. Nowhere is the dilemma more apparent than in his essay 'Thomas Mann als Politiker', which was written in 1950 but not published until 1955. He praises Mann for refusing to accept the Cold War axiom, 'die Gleichsetzung der Stalinistischen Diktatur mit den faschistischen Systemen, insbesondere mit der Hitler-Herrschaft' (*BK*, p. 22). Andersch's spirited defence of Thomas Mann is conditioned no doubt by the irritation which Mann caused in 1949 by attending the Goethe celebrations in both parts of Germany. Nevertheless, Andersch stresses Mann's commitment to the West, yet his simultaneous refusal to choose either German state as his home. Given the East–West tensions Mann is forced, in Andersch's terms, to occupy 'den Stand zwischen den Linien, den Posten im Niemandsland' (*BK*, p. 26). Concluding his essay with unstinted praise for Mann's dream of 'die Synthese von Freiheit und Sozialismus' (*BK*, p. 27), Andersch appears to be identifying himself fully with Mann's position, sharing his isolation. Mann's warm reaction to Andersch's essay, when it eventually appeared, suggests that Andersch had successfully diagnosed Mann's dilemma.[28]

Only a year later, however, Andersch became more critical of developments in the East. His essay 'Jugend am Schmelzpott einer Kultur' (1951) attempts a survey of intellectual developments in Europe to the extent in which they impinge on German youth (by which he clearly means West German youth). In Western Europe he laments that left-wing intellectuals are neglected in favour of their conservative counterparts: he laments that 'der integrale Marxismus Emmanuel Mouniers'[29] is unknown in Germany, though concedes that French literature is otherwise well known, if partially understood. Interestingly, he remarks particularly on German ignorance of surrealism. Clearly, his own views involve a kind of mixture of literary modernism with Euro-communist sympathies. German literature, he insists, has become a matter of literary academies, while a truly German academy is a pipe dream: 'Diese würde eine Einigung zwischen Bert Brecht, Thomas Mann, Carl Schmitt, Gottfried Benn und Ernst Jünger voraussetzen – eine absurde Vorstellung!'[30] Here Andersch lists disparate figures who are treated extensively and with obvious approval in his own literary essays. It is as if he were conceding that figures from his own literary canon belong to a unified German scheme of things which the politics of the Cold War have rendered an impossibility. Noting that Johannes R. Becher has been elected to the Presidency of the German PEN club, he wonders whether 'die ihm angeschlossenen Mitglieder aus der Ostzone nun auch noch die "Formalismus"-Richtlinien der 5. Tagung des Zentralkomitees der SED schlucken'.[31] He concludes his survey of German culture with the argument that the true socialist experiments are going on in the West, and that German culture is still woefully ignorant of them. The task of Western intellectuals is 'zu wissen, daß Deutschland zum Westen gehört, zu verstehen, daß sich im Westen gegenwärtig eine Revolution vollzieht, welche die russische weit übergreift, weil sie sich von der Ideologie gelöst hat'.[32] Growing cynicism about developments in the GDR is matched by equal cynicism about the lack of interest in West Germany in specifically Western socialist experiments.

Perhaps the most significant statement about the GDR is contained in Andersch's sympathetic review of the periodical *Sinn und Form*. In the essay 'Marxisten in der Igelstellung' Andersch praises the journal precisely because it has the format and standing of *Die Neue Rundschau* in the West. It is 'gleich einer Insel . . . in der Flut ostzonaler "Kultur"-Veröffentlichungen'.[33] The periodical proves, for Andersch, that it is impossible to equate the totalitarianism of National Socialism with that of the GDR, a common enough response in the West at the time. For Andersch, it is the quest for literary quality which has pushed the periodical to the margins of the stalinist state. But the dangers of totalitarian pressure are not minimised. Andersch argues that in the GDR, as in Nazi Germany, literature may all too easily become 'Kalligraphie', a style of aesthetic escapism. Here we see Andersch beginning to fall victim, despite himself, to the Cold War identification of the GDR with the Third Reich. His praise for *Sinn und Form* is predicated on the assumption that what is of high literary quality must of necessity find itself in opposition to the régime, a direct echo of his reflections on literature in Nazi Germany in *Deutsche Literatur in der Entscheidung*. This Cold War analogy reappears explicitly in Andersch's essay 'Luise Rinser vorübergehend wichtig', in which he fulminates against Johannes R. Becher and *Sonntag*, the organ of the Kulturbund zur demokratischen Erneuerung Deutschlands. After comparing the language and attitudes of *Sonntag* with the SS newspaper *Das Schwarze Corps*, Andersch moves to an outspoken attack on the GDR, inspired by his discovery that *Sonntag* had attacked a mail order company for advertising Western books:

> Sie werden kommen und uns Friedens-Resolutionen vorlegen. Wir werden sie nicht unterzeichnen. Aber wir werden die Werke von Anna Seghers, Stefan [sic] Hermlin und Heinrich Mann bei uns ausbringen, lesen und diskutieren, und wir werden Bert Brecht unsere Bühnen offenhalten. Wie es bei uns der gute Brauch einer noch so relativen Freiheit will. Mögen dann Pen-Club-und Akademie-Präsidenten mit ihnen über Frieden und deutsche Einheit viele Worte machen, – wir werden sie nur fragen, warum wir die Bücher des Ostens bekommen, sie aber die Literatur des Westens noch in den Antiquariaten heimsuchen.[34]

By 1951, it is clear that Andersch is himself falling victim to the prevailing Cold War rhetoric. His radio feature of that year, 'Menschen im Niemandsland' offers an illuminating insight into his development. Conceived as a kind of scrapbook for 1951, it was broadcast by the Norddeutscher Rundfunk in June 1952. Isolating apparently disconnected incidents and events of 1951, the feature attempts, by skilful juxtaposition and association, to create an image of a world trapped between the superpowers. Moving briskly from atom bomb testing in Nevada, via a discussion between Einstein and a brain cell researcher on the socio-political responsibility of the scientist, to the Korean War, Andersch seeks to locate the problems which the world faces in East–West tension. His two British soldiers in Korea are aware that they are fighting a localised conflict as a means of preventing a global one, yet they are trapped between this insight and the realisation that they are fighting against an enemy against whom they bear no ill will. Interspersed with this political argument are extracts from the diaries of André Gide, whose death occurred in 1951. Other tensions in the world are illustrated by the exile of the Dalai Lama from Tibet, the nationalisation of the Persian oil fields and the departure of the British workers, tensions in Egypt, with the threat to nationalise the Suez Canal, and an incident on the Czech border, when a passenger train is shunted across the West German border and a number of passengers opt to remain in the West. Both the kaleidoscopic structure and the presentation of individuals as the victims of broader political decisions over which they have little control are intended to give credence to the title 'Menschen im Niemandsland' as a representation of the human predicament in 1951. But one is left with the overwhelming impression that

Andersch is employing the images to express his own sense of political isolation within the Cold War. When the Czech Watzek opts for freedom in the West (and the Gide quotation: 'Ich baue nur noch auf Deserteure'[35] is appended to the incident), we need to recall that Andersch's own mother's maiden name was Watzek, and that he was himself to appropriate the Gide quotation as an epigraph for *Die Kirschen der Freiheit* in 1952. Desertion, for Andersch, is clearly not merely a physical escape; it implies the necessity to free oneself from all ideological systems. If Andersch's public views at this time were becoming more strident and cynical, towards both East and West, his private views were even less restrained. Writing to his mother on 12 May 1951 about his brother Martin's involvement in 'Ost–West-Gespräche', he dismisses the talks as an 'SED-Propagandakiste', adding: 'Das sind die größten Feinde der Kunst, die es je gegeben hat, schlimmer als die Nazis.'[36]

Try as he would, Andersch found it virtually impossible to maintain his precarious balancing act. In the early 1950s his attitudes hardened. Ever more critical of the GDR, he was forced to demonstrate his even-handedness by even more vehement outbursts against the conservative 'Restoration' in West Germany. In a sense Andersch's views on communism in the course of the 1950s are unexceptional. He echoes the Cold War attitudes which were part of public life, yet paradoxically lays claim to a cynical or resigned detachment by dint of his equal disapproval of so much of Western politics. His letters to Arno Schmidt in the 1950s reveal him as an outspoken critic of restoration values in West Germany, though Schmidt was even more uncompromising and Andersch may well have been encouraging him in his splendidly vituperative outbursts. He delights in Schmidt's diatribes against Germany and appears to share his plans for emigration to Ireland, for, as Schmidt puts it: 'Bei solcher Lage der Dinge ist I. [Ireland] tatsächlich für uns das einzige "freie" Land in Europa; denn frei kann ich nur den nennen, der weder dem Westen noch dem Osten angeschlossen ist.'[37] While this argument was calculated to appeal to Andersch, he was planning his own emigration to Switzerland, but could not mention it to Schmidt, who harboured highly colourful, and much publicised, anti-Swiss sentiments.

Although this essay is not primarily concerned with Andersch's literary production, a brief glance at his major works and his editorial roles up to 1961 shed light on the dilemma which I have outlined. *Die Kirschen der Freiheit* (1952) devotes itself, at least as far as the outward action is concerned, to a desertion (Andersch's own) from the German to the American lines in Italy. But much of the work is devoted to an ideological desertion, Andersch's abandonment of the Communist Party after his experiences in Dachau in 1933. If the scene of his physical desertion takes place 'between the fronts' in the 'Wüste', then Andersch's ideological and political stance, involving a desertion from both sides (the restoration values of Germany and a communist alternative) leads him likewise into extreme isolation. Two further elements are overlaid on Andersch's account of his desertion: an existentialist framework derived from his post-war reading of Sartre, and the justification of a modernist aesthetic. The identification of desertion with modern art is characteristic of Andersch's aesthetic position in the early 1950s: just like the deserting Andersch, 'Picasso und Apollinaire ließen sich . . . in die Freiheit fallen' (*KdF*, p. 127). It seems clear that modernism in art is the object of suspicion on both sides of the ideological divide and corresponds, therefore, with the position of man 'in no man's land'.

It is this association of a political dilemma with an artistic style which explains why Andersch should, in the 1950s, have championed modernism with such enthusiasm. In 1949 he edited a series entitled 'Europäische Avantgarde', with texts by Camus, Sartre, Simone de Beauvoir and Malraux. Later, when he moved to Radio Frankfurt (which became the Hessischer Rundfunk) he edited a series which included texts by Böll, Arno Schmidt, Weyrauch, Hildesheimer and Bachmann. In 1955 Andersch became editor of the 'Abendstudio' of the Süddeutscher Rundfunk in Stuttgart, and simultaneously editor of the periodical *Texte und Zeichen*, which epitomised the avant-garde, oppositional literature of the Adenauer era. But the opposition to restoration conservatism was only one facet of what Andersch helped to create. Based on his assumption that avant-garde art embodied a rejection of both the National Socialist legacy and the doctrinaire cultural policies of the GDR, Andersch, perhaps unwittingly, created a cultural climate which was specifically West German. Critical, but not dangerously so, of Cold War attitudes in the West, but dismissive of much that was produced in the GDR, Andersch, in his non-aligned yet western-orientated canon, created the liberal, modernist, eclectic taste of the Federal Republic. In his radio programmes Andersch introduced to West Germans Ionesco and Beckett, Faulkner and Wilder, while in *Texte und Zeichen* he published, in some cases for the first time in Germany, works by Beckett, Borges, Char, Dylan Thomas, Neruda, Vittorini, Pavese and Barthes. Andersch virtually ignored what was going on in the GDR; *Texte und Zeichen* did include a brief survey of work published in the GDR and reprinted a short story by Karl Mundstock, but these were its only genuflexions towards East Germany. While East Germany was fostering a tradition of Socialist Realism, Andersch was shaping a Western alternative. This alternative was modernist, yet pluralistic and undogmatic. It was broad enough to contain the conservative writers of both exile and 'innere Emigration' (Thomas Mann, but also Ernst Jünger and Gottfried Benn) and the more obviously experimental writers (Heißenbüttel, Bense, Arno Schmidt). It effectively blurred the distinction between those who had remained in Germany, those who had emigrated and returned to the West, and those who were beginning a literary career within the 'Gruppe 47'. It created a kind of Western 'Erbe', excluding only those who were receiving official sanction in the GDR. It might be construed as mischievous to call it a NATO theory of literature, but, for all its opposition to Adenauer's 'Weststaatlösung', it supplied a kind of literary counterpart to just such a 'Weststaatlösung', looking for its models to France, the United States and Italy, and largely ignoring events behind the Iron Curtain.

Just how Western-orientated Andersch's activities were may be seen by his own recollections of his editorial activities. In a fictionalised account of his days with Radio Frankfurt, which appeared in 1969 under the title 'Der Redakteur 1952', Andersch describes how Franz Kien (a thinly-veiled cipher for Andersch himself) conducted his editorial activity. He saw himself confronted with 'Bücher und Manuskripte aus Westdeutschland, England, den USA, Frankreich und Italien',[38] a clear enough statement of the Western orientation. Four years later, under the more ironic title 'Ein intellektuelles Ghetto', Andersch paid tribute to the 'Abendstudio', the cultural programme of the Hessischer Rundfunk, twenty-five years after its inauguration. By now he was willing to assess its role more objectively. He recalls the departure of Hans Mayer: 'Ich begriff damals nicht, daß das Ausscheiden Hans Mayers aus dem Frankfurter Sender signalisierte, was schon begonnnen hatte, obwohl Konrad Adenauer noch gar nicht Bundeskanzler war: der kalte Krieg'. Looking back, Andersch is all too aware of the shortcomings of the programme: 'Am ehesten kommt man noch zu einem positiven Urteil über das ABENDSTUDIO, wenn man konstatiert, was es ausließ. Beispielsweise hat es den kalten Krieg völlig ignoriert.'[39]

The fact that Andersch was perhaps more conditioned by the Cold War in the 1950s than he would at the time have been prepared to admit is also reflected in his creative work. *Sansibar oder der letzte Grund* (1957) has two plots, an inner and an outer one, which run curiously counter to one another and may only be reconciled in the light of Andersch's political views in the 1950s. The outward action involves escape from Nazi Germany in 1937, but the inner action, located within the central character, Gregor, focuses on his disillusionment with the Communist Party. While the work may be read as a historical reconstruction of a flight from Nazi Germany, it is noticeable that the historical concreteness is missing. The Nazis are simply 'die Anderen', a threatening authoritarian power. It was perfectly possible for Andersch's readers to view the story as a depiction of flight from East Germany, for it cannot be accidental that Andersch chose as his setting what was by 1957 the East German port of Rerik. For many readers the red towers of Rerik must have had a less ambiguous and more topical meaning than Andersch perhaps intended. While his group of escapees flee from Nazi totalitarianism, Gregor flees, at least intellectually, from communist totalitarianism. One may speculate that the popularity of the text derived in some measure from its curious ambiguity: it could be read in two ways. Ostensibly, it dealt with a historical situation in 1937, but for contemporary readers after the Hungarian uprising, it could readily acquire a further resonance.

If this interpretation of *Sansibar* appears fanciful, it is worth reflecting on Andersch's state of mind in 1956. In an essay of that year entitled 'Der Rauch von Budapest' (published in the volume *Die Blindheit des Kunstwerks* in 1965, but omitted from the later Diogenes edition), Andersch makes his clearest public statement about the GDR. For him, the smoke of Budapest is the same smoke as that of Auschwitz; both are the consequence of totalitarian terror. He distinguishes two brands of communism: a true and a false variety. 'Der wahre Kommunismus ist nichts anderes als der linke Flügel der Demokratie',[40] but the communism of the Soviet Union, and by extension of its loyal ally the GDR, is 'ein weißer Terror, ein Terror der falschen, der faschistischen Kommunisten'.[41] East German intellectuals should, Andersch asserts, be invited to distance themselves from Ulbricht's policies: 'Die Linie Ulbrichts ist die Linie der künstlerischen Reaktion und des geistigen Todes'.[42] Even here, it should be noted, Andersch appears to be mainly concerned about the aesthetic and intellectual implications of GDR cultural policy; political factors seemed to hold less interest for him. The year 1956 saw, in the Federal Republic, the banning of the Communist Party. Looking back, shortly before his death, Andersch noted, to his own obvious astonishment, 'KP-VERBOT 1956. Warum es nicht wahrgenommen?'[43]

Andersch's literary and creative interest moves in the course of the 1950s increasingly towards a purely Western theory of socialism, and as such into increasing isolation from practical politics. Events in the GDR appear not to interest him overmuch; his literary and cultural interests are confined to Western varieties of socialist experiment. *Die Rote* may serve as an example. It is located in Italy, where Euro-communism seems yet a possibility. But its central male character, Fabio Crepaz, is a disillusioned communist, one of a long line of such characters in Andersch's writing. Germany is represented by two equally unattractive aspects: the background of Nazi terror represented by Kramer on the one hand and the materialistic obsessions of the 'Wirtschaftswunder', epitomised by Herbert and Joachim on the other. If West Germany offers no hope of fulfilment for Franziska, the heroine, she may at least gain some sense of belonging with Fabio's family in Mestre. Even the much attenuated form of Italian communism is no answer; Fabio is a disillusioned *ex*-communist and, perhaps more significantly, a musician. Once again it is art (literature, music and painting) which alone is associated with the kind of 'socialism with a human face' which Andersch seeks vainly in the political structures of the time. But even with this implicit rejection of communism, Andersch's book touched nerves made raw by the politics of the Cold War. Some critics were drawn to read into the title an ambiguity which hardly seems justified, turning the 'Red-Head' into a 'Red Woman'. In an atmosphere of ideological hysteria, the depiction of a woman falling in love with an ex-communist violinist was more than some critics could bear. Paradoxically, its context makes *Die Rote* into both less and more of a political book than it appears today. Less political, in that the novel is located in the thin strip of no man's land between the fronts of Euro-communism and conservative restoration, a no man's land which is, moreover, associated more with art than politics; more political, in that German critics were not slow to read into the novel an ostentatious rejection of the Federal

Republic in favour of an albeit vague socialist alternative. Clearly, there is much more to the novel besides its politics, but the exercise of teasing out these political implications has the virtue of pinpointing the dilemma which Andersch faced. In a fascinating radio programme on the subject of conversion, which took place in January 1958, Andersch's reaction is to lament that there is nothing that one may convert to:

> Die überlieferten Gegensatzpaare der politischen und künstlerischen Auseinandersetzung sind aus den Scharnieren geraten – der Bürger ist zum Manager, der Kommunist ist zum Spießer, zum Patrioten und zum staatserhaltenden Element geworden. Alle Modellvorstellungen einer versinkenden Epoche schön ausgeflügelt zwischen rechts und links, rot und schwarz, revolutionär und reaktionär, all das scheint haltlos ineinanderzustürzen.[44]

The building of the Wall in 1961 was to initiate a major shift in Andersch's thinking. Only after 1961 was the subject of the GDR to stimulate him to creative work. In 1962 he wrote *Ein Liebhaber des Halbschattens*, the first work to raise the German–German theme, while the novel *Efraim* (1967) is a Berlin book *par excellence*. Andersch was to undergo a gradual process of re-education over the last two decades of his life, and by the early 1970s he had discovered that the literature of the Soviet Union was not all crude Socialist Realism of the 'boy meets tractor' variety. As a postscript to this study of Andersch's development through the Cold War, it is illuminating to cite his Open Letter to Konstantin Simonow of 1975. Here Andersch confesses his complete ignorance of Soviet literature and admits that he is more of a 'Westler' than he had realised. A 'Westler' he defines as a Western intellectual who 'übernimmt . . . , kritiklos, die Nachricht, bei der Literatur der Sowjetunion handele es sich um eine staatlich gelenkte Propaganda–Unternehmung, um belletristische Interpretationen von Parteiaufträgen' (*ÖB*, p. 199). He recalls his own experience in the post-war period:

> *Was* haben wir nachgeholt? Merkwürdigerweise nicht zuallererst die Bücher der deutschen Emigranten, die in New York, Mexiko und Moskau entstanden waren, die kamen erst später, und manche von ihnen, besonders diejenigen des linken Flügels der deutschen Emigration, sind bis heute noch von uns kaum wahrgenommen worden. Worauf wir uns stürzten, waren Amerikaner, Engländer, Franzosen, Italiener. Hemingway, Faulkner und Vittorini. Eliot, Gide und Sartre. Unsere spezielle Aufmerksamkeit widmeten wir der Literatur der Avantgarde: Kafka, Proust, Joyce und der neuen Lyrik jeglicher Observanz. . . .

Russisches fand nicht statt. Von 1945 bis 1958 tauchte weder ein einzelner sowjetischer Autor noch die moderne Literatur der Sowjetunion als Ganzes am Horizont unseres Denkens auf.... In den sechzehn Nummern dieser Zeitschrift *Texte und Zeichen* ist nicht ein einziger Beitrag eines sowjetischen Autors, keine einzige Rezension eines sowjetischen Buches erschienen. ... Ich war ein 'Westler', geradezu das Schulbeispiel eines 'Westlers'! (*ÖB*, pp. 199–201)

With characteristic frankness Andersch confesses his shortcomings, admitting that he was more determined by the atmosphere of the Cold War than he knew. In his defence one could note that his catalogue of the literature which he did indeed promote reads deceptively like a literary history of the Federal Republic. Although, at the time, Andersch shaped a notion of culture which felt itself to be in opposition to the restoration values of the Adenauer period, it was in many ways an expression of precisely those values.

Notes

1 'Gespräche mit Alfred Andersch: Hans Magnus Enzensberger, "Die Literatur nach dem Tod der Literatur" ', *Über Alfred Andersch*, edited by Gerd Haffmans, second edition Zurich, 1980, pp. 200–21.

2 *Über Alfred Andersch*, p. 204.

3 *Literaturmagazin 7; Nachkriegsliteratur*, edited by Nicolas Born and Jürgen Manthey, Hamburg, 1977, pp. 116–33.

4 See Margaret Littler, *The Politics of Perception: a Study in the Works of Alfred Andersch*, unpublished Ph.D. thesis (University of Manchester, 1989); see also Bernhard Jendricke, *Alfred Andersch mit Selbstzeugnissen und Bilddokumenten*, Reinbek bei Hamburg, 1988, p. 25.

5 Since a number of the articles and reviews which Andersch published in *Der Ruf* appeared under pseudonyms and since existing bibliographies list only some items, I append a list of articles which I have identified. Clues to Andersch's authorship are found in his literary papers in the Deutsches Literaturarchiv in Marbach am Neckar: (pseud. Franz Achleitner), 'Münchner Frühlingshut', *Der Ruf*, 1 May 1945; 'Abschied von Rom', *Der Ruf*, 15 May 1945; 'Die neuen Dichter Amerikas', *Der Ruf*, 15 June 1945; (pseud. Anton Windisch), 'Fräulein Christine', *Der Ruf*, 15 June 1945; (anon.), 'Frühlingslandschaften: Dänemark 1944. Louisiana 1945', *Der Ruf*, 15 June 1945; (FA = Fred Andersch), 'Ein Mahner', *Der Ruf*, 15 June 1945; (FA), 'Thomas Mann', *Der Ruf*, 1 July 1945; (pseud. Thomas Gradinger), 'Tagebuchblatt aus der Eifel', *Der Ruf*, 1 July 1945; (anon.), 'Deutsche Kunst in Amerika', *Der Ruf*, 1 July 1945; (pseud. Fritz Wangel), 'Symphonie-Orchester in Amerika', *Der Ruf*, 1 July 1945; (anon.), 'Deutsche Jugend wohin?', *Der Ruf*, 15 July 1945; (anon.), 'Deutscher Geist: in der Sicht Thomas Manns', *Der Ruf*, 15 July 1945; (FA), 'Black Boy', *Der Ruf*, 15 July 1945; (pseud. Thomas Gradinger), 'Pueblos und Puritaner', *Der Ruf*, 1 August 1945; (FA), 'Zeitungen lesen', *Der Ruf*, 15 August 1945; (FA), 'Amerikanische Profile: Robert Frost', *Der Ruf*, 15 August 1945; (pseud. Thomas Gradinger), 'Unsere Mädchen', *Der Ruf*, 15 August 1945.

6 'Deutsche Jugend wohin?', *Der Ruf*, 15 July 1945.

7 *Ibid.*

8 This information is contained in Jérome Vaillant, *Der Ruf: Unabhängige Blätter der jungen Generation (1945–1949): eine Zeitschrift zwischen Illusion und Anpassung*, Munich, New York and Paris, 1978, pp. 44–7.

9 *Frankfurter Hefte*, 2, 1947, p. 1093.

10 (Anon.), 'Die Menschen denken verschieden', *Rat und Tat*, 8, January 1946.

11 'Verlagsaufbau trotz größter Schwierigkeiten', *Rat und Tat*, 27, 5 April 1946.

12 *Der Ruf*, 1, 15 August 1946.

13 'Der grüne Tisch', *Der Ruf*, 3, 15 September 1946.

14 'Chaplin und die Geistesfreiheit', *Der Ruf*, 3, 15 September 1946.

15 'Die Zonen und der Weltfriede', *Der Ruf*, 6, 1 November 1946.

16 'Eine Konferenz des jungen Europa', *Der Ruf*, 6, 1 November 1946.

17 'Grundlagen einer deutschen Opposition', *Der Ruf*, 8, 1 December 1946.

18 'Die sozialistische Situation: Versuch einer synthetischen Kritik', *Der Ruf*, 15, 15 March 1947.

19 'Wintersende in einer frierenden Stadt', *Der Ruf*, 16, 1 April 1947.

20 See Helmut Peitsch and Hartmut Reith, 'Keine "innere Emigration" in die "Gefilde" der Literatur: Die literarisch–politische Publizistik der Gruppe 47 zwischen 1947 und 1949', in *Nachkriegsliteratur II: Autoren, Sprache, Tradition*, edited by Jost Hermand, Helmut Peitsch and Klaus R. Scherpe, Berlin, 1983, pp. 129–62.

21 'Linkes Tagebuch I', *Neues Europa*, 3/16, 1948, p. 9.

22 *Ibid.*

23 'Linkes Tagebuch II', *Neues Europa*, 3/17, 1948, p. 8.

24 'Linkes Tagebuch I', *Neues Europa*, 3/16, 1948, p. 10.

25 *Alfred Andersch Lesebuch*, edited by Gerd Haffmans, Zurich, 1979, p. 111. Unless otherwise indicated, subsequent quotations are taken from the Diogenes Studienausgabe and page references are given after quotations in the text. The following abbreviations are used: *Das Alfred Andersch Lesebuch* = AAL; *Die Kirschen der Freiheit* = KdF; *Die Blindheit des Kunstwerks* = BK; *Öffentlicher Brief an einen sowjetischen Schriftsteller, das Überholte betreffend* = ÖB.

26 *Horizont*, 3/7, 1948, p. 4.

27 *Horizont*, 3/13, 1948, 13, p. 9.

28 Thomas Mann's response is reproduced in *Über Alfred Andersch*, edited by Gerd Haffmans, second edition, Zurich, 1980, pp. 9–10.

29 'Jugend am Schmelzpott einer Kultur', *Aussprache*, 3, 1951, p. 8.

30 'Jugend am Schmelzpott', p. 9.

31 'Jugend am Schmelzpott', p. 10.

32 'Jugend am Schmelzpott', p. 13.

33 *Frankfurter Hefte*, 6, 1951, p. 208.

34 *Frankfurter Hefte*, 6, 1951, p. 349.

35 This is contained in André Gide's diary entry for 11 May 1941.

36 '. . . *einmal wirklich leben': ein Tagebuch in Briefen an Hedwig Andersch 1943 bis 1975*, edited by Winfried Stephan, Zurich, 1986, p. 66.

37 Arno Schmidt, *Der Briefwechsel mit Alfred Andersch*, edited by Bernd Rauschenbach, Zurich, 1985, p. 107; the letter is dated 23 December 1956.

38 *Merkur*, 27, 1969, pp. 159–60.

39 'Ein intellektuelles Ghetto: Erinnerung am 25. Jahrestag seiner Gründung', *Frankfurter Rundschau*, 1 December 1973.

40 *Die Blindheit des Kunstwerks und andere Aufsätze*, Frankfurt am Main, 1965, p. 20.

41 *Die Blindheit*, p. 19.

42 *Die Blindheit*, p. 19.

43 Alfred Andersch and Konstantin Simonow, *Es gibt kein fremdes Leid*, edited by Friedrich Hitzer, Munich, 1981, p. 90.

44 ' "Literatur und Konversion": Gespräch zwischen Hans-Egon Holthusen, Georg Böse, Martin Walser und Alfred Andersch', pp. 26–7. This programme was first broadcast on 10 January 1958. I am grateful to the Süddeutscher Rundfunk for permission to quote from the typescript.

Index